5/13

OUTSIDER II

OUTSIDER II

always almost: never quite

~~~

AN AUTOBIOGRAPHY

Brian Sewell

QUARTET

First published in 2012 by
Quartet Books Limited
A member of the Namara Group
27 Goodge Street, London WIT 2LD

A catalogue record for this book
is available from the British Library

ISBN 978 0 7043 7291 7

Typeset by Antony Gray
Printed and bound in Great Britain by
T J International Ltd, Padstow, Cornwall

One friend more than any other has, in caring for my dogs, enabled me to write this book. 'I hate dogs,' he has said a thousand times when removing the evidence of loose bowels and revolting stomachs (as must all who share their lives with animals), and yet he has affectionately and diligently fed, watered and walked them, and on their deaths has felt as much distress as I and in tears seen them to their graves.

Acknowledgements

Such a book as this must begin, as a rule it seems, with acknowledgements for help and information. I have only one to make – to my mother, whose keeping of diaries was indefatigable until, during the later Eighties, dementia eroded both her sharp mind and what was engaging in her personality; then her records declined into notes of the cost of milk delivered to the house and the frequency of burglar alarms that disrupted sleep. These diaries I had not read until, occasionally uncertain of a date in my own, less scrupulously kept, I turned to them and found, not only the information I sought, but her comments on my life. I had no idea of the extent to which she had invaded my privacy, had timed the coming and going of men casually encountered as bedmates for an hour and had commented, always adversely, on the motives of others who lasted a little longer and might, briefly, qualify as lovers; her vilification of others still, who graduated to staunch friend from random fuck, was the pure bile of jealousy. Of one she was particularly envious, seeing him as a constant and lasting threat to her supremacy in my affections. She was mistaken; a man's love for a lover, male or female, does not impinge on or clash with his love for his mother – only the mother herself can affect that unique emotional bond, and mine, consumed with irrelevant hatred, poisoned ours, destroyed it. I am, nevertheless, deeply grateful to her for her diaries.

I am also grateful for my own, but wish that I had been more persistent with them, for often their keeping fell away for months, the thought of writing in my hours of leisure, when writing is my work, almost repellant. On the other hand, my journals of journeys are sedulous in their detail, recording not only what I saw and did, but even my dreams and the wanderings of my mind – how odd, during a sleepless night in Istanbul, to ponder the implications of an inscription on a drawing by Dürer in the British Museum – occasionally enlivened by elementary drawings and the groundplans of fallen buildings – but then all these were written for the benefit of the books that were to follow (always almost, never quite). Knowing now that they will not, that they belong to an activity and period of my life to which there can be no return, I shall read them once more, reduce them to a set of notes that to another traveller might be useful on, for example, the early churches of Cappadocia and Turkish Armenia, and destroy the private jottings. All the diaries too, my mother's as well as my own, will be consigned to a bonfire (to keep for an unknown posterity too many papers is an insidious vanity).

Contents

OUTSIDER II

CHAPTER I

Introduction

I have three times in a long life experienced some significant understanding of myself – epiphany, in its modern and shallow sense of any sudden realisation, now the fashionable term for such enlightenment – at twelve, twenty-one and in my eightieth summer.

At twelve, in the deep midwinter of 1943–44, the earth of the school's playing fields so frozen that the fierce rough and tumble of rugby football was quite out of the question, we were sent on a cross-country run of three miles or so, an endurance test for scrawny little boys ill-nourished on the meagre food rations that reached London at the height of the Second World War. I had no experience of long-distance running; mine was the quick sprint baulked by a tackle, rarely more than twenty yards, perhaps embellished by a swerve or two, breathless only when thumped to the ground by an opponent, the stitch, that deep disabling pain in the side induced by long continuous exercise, no part of it. Running across country, however, was – at least in part – precisely that long continuous exercise, the pace and stride regular, sometimes for hundreds of yards, the stitch and the nausea that accompanied it, the enemy lurking within my body, with only a hedge or ditch or gate to break the rhythm with a leap. On that first freezing day I ran – and ran. I leaped all obstacles. I discovered that the further I ran and leaped, the easier it became, and was aware of something beyond the physical experience – elation. This was something I could do alone; it was not a team sport, I had no other players to take into account, and whether I won or lost was entirely my own responsibility. I won that first race, and won it by such a margin that I was accused by the referee – who happened to be Mr Keevil, the art master – of cheating, and was sent off to run half the course again. That small injustice left no mark, but the sense of elation did and cross-country running became a secret pastime – secret because not shared – and still, so many years later, it haunts my unconscious and surfaces in dreams.

At twenty-one, in September 1952, I reported to Aldershot for my two years of National Service in the army – and my solitary running stood me in good stead. There, over rough heathland tracks, we ran in heavy army boots for seven miles, sometimes as an exercise, sometimes as a punishment. For me it was an escape from military drudgery, a time – the only time – when as a squaddy I could be alone, my body doing its pleasurable duty on the run but my brain let loose to contemplate the conflict between imposed (even unthinking) obedience to Queen and country and my chosen and educated obedience to a Christian and Catholic faith, the obligation to respect the Seven Virtues and to be generous with the Seven Works of Mercy. The issue of such obedience arose when we were trained to fire rifles and, screaming abuse, plunge bayonets into the bellies of the sacking and straw lay models that represented the enemy. I might, I thought, in the event choose not to fire a lethal shot, not to inflict a mortal wound with the stab of a bayonet that no soft tissue could resist (we were advised to strike low, avoiding the ribs from between which the bayonet might be difficult to withdraw, the image painted for us of a soldier dying at the end of a rifle violently shaken to, as it were, get him off the hook, quite vile), but being trained to do so was not only not the deed itself, but not the time to make a moral point to an uncomprehending sergeant. The real argument must wait until and if I found myself on active service in Korea, Malaya or any other theatre of war (as was quite possible) in which a young National Serviceman might be compelled to use his weapons in order to preserve himself or his companions. There, of course, lay the rub: why should I have the moral luxury of saving my soul if, in saving it, the young soldier to the left or right of me were to lose his life

Introduction

through my action or inaction? This epiphany was slow to mature but in the end was sudden; almost disconcertingly I learned that I had changed, that I had developed in my brain a place of ice-cold reason remote from religious belief, moral philosophy and an educated sense of right and wrong, and knew that, were it necessary, I would kill. Again I felt elation; I felt, indeed, that in commanding circumstances there was nothing that I would not do – and God, not I, must take responsibility for sorting out the moral mess.

In 2010, early in my eightieth summer, I completed an account of my early life, thinking (mistakenly) that I might celebrate its publication in July 2011 on my eightieth birthday. Very long, insofar as any autobiography can, it began at the beginning of my life and concluded on 9 February 1967 when, at thirty-five, I was halfway through my biblical allowance of three score years and ten. For two decades friends – one in particular – had urged me to write it, pleading that what I knew of the art world, its workings and its characters, should be recorded; but I wanted to deal with other aspects of my life as well and thought an autobiography at sixty premature and, since I hoped for more years of sound mind and physical activity, was not yet ready to reveal what I believe to be essential in such books – the truth, the whole truth and, if not quite nothing but the truth, unfettered honesty. I did not at that stage, writing journalism as well as art criticism, want to discuss my homosexuality, for queers are rare among the desks of Fleet Street and editors were (and still are) all too ready to exploit the old-fashioned sensation attached to any revelation that a man is sexually attracted to his kind. I did not, at that stage, want to discuss my illegitimacy, for my father had a legitimate son whose life might have been rocked by the sudden appearance of a half-brother. I did not want to discuss my childhood, fatherless, in the sole care of a gifted and intelligent mother still very much alive, and with the remnants of her beauty, who had brought me up in the Thirties, deeply impoverished at a time when illegitimacy was a terrible stigma for both the parent and the child.

These were, however, the facts and factors that formed my character as an Outsider, homosexuality a driving force that could be, and was, resisted, only for me to recognise, almost too late, how much damage that resistance had done, and the illegitimate birth that had to be kept secret, that made me dissemble throughout my schooldays and, particularly, my years in the army and at Christie's. There, where my final interview in 1958 was with Sir Alec Martin, a vile, arrogant and ignorant old martinet who had obscured his working-class origins and converted his cockney speech into a post-Edwardian affectation, his first words were more accurate and wounding than he knew – 'Well, we know you've no social connections, but . . . ' But I was a good enough art historian and judge of quality to catalogue paintings sent to the firm for sale and he was prepared to employ me.

I stayed with Christie's for nine years until, weary of the blindness and obstruction of my departmental head, the Honourable Patrick Lindsay, I asked for a department of my own, Prints and Drawings by Old Masters. I had created it and built substantial turnover. It was a category of which Patrick knew nothing; he knew very little of anything to do with art, had no eye for it and was much given to declaring that this picture must be catalogued as by Reynolds and that by Gainsborough for no better reason than that he had told the owners so; where drawings were concerned he had neither knowledge nor experience, nor even an instinctive eye for quality. Christie's was a partnership and to be the director of a department meant becoming a partner, involving some re-apportioning of shares (somehow to be paid for by the new partner) and the unanimous agreement of all on the existing board. Patrick argued against my appointment and in such terms that made the prospect of any long-term career at Christie's suddenly insufferable; I had two friends on the board of directors, one of them David Carritt, a now forgotten wayward genius in the tradition of Bernard Berenson, and it was he who immediately told me of Patrick's response to the proposal – 'We've got one homosexual on the board (David); we don't need another . . . ' I resigned.

In spite of Patrick, leaving Christie's was painful. The longest episode of my life – longer than school, the army or the Courtauld Institute, it had been a period of continual growth in knowledge and experience, of constant opportunity to explore great museums and collections and the dark places of the art market, though I felt that I had given the firm as much as it had given me. And I was leaving it, not because I had exhausted its resources, nor because it had exhausted mine, nor for any professional advancement elsewhere, but because I was damned for being queer.

Writing my scrupulously honest account of childhood, boyhood and early maturity often felt like self-administered psychoanalysis – deeply painful and disturbing – and, re-reading the typescript before it was sent to a publisher, I experienced my third epiphany, dispassionately examining myself and seeing, for the first time and with absolute clarity (though far too late to profit from the revelation) what had been amiss with my life and career, what had been my own fault and folly, and what had been brought about by circumstance. I saw too that I had achieved my objective with it, not just as a record of my experience in the art market and the handing-on of things known but not published, some dating back to the early decades of the twentieth century, but that I had dealt frankly with the business of being both a bastard and a bugger and how this came about. This last had not been easy: that I cast aside so many decades of deceit that became dissembling and dissembling that relaxed into an attitude of 'I don't care what they think as long as I don't have to talk about it' at last became a purpose – the good it might do, the reassurance it might offer to the many who, particularly in early adult life, suffer extraordinary anguish from being cut away from unknown parents, one or both, and those who, in these still quite unenlightened times, are for their homo-sexuality made to feel Outsiders.

CHAPTER 2

Scratching a Living

I had made no preparation for leaving Christie's; I had told very few outside the firm of my intention; I had made no overtures and had no inkling of another job; I had not done what most leavers did – taken a copy of the catalogue subscription list, an invaluable record of names, addresses, telephone numbers and interest all over Britain, America and Europe. A cleverer man than I would have prepared his ground and not left the firm so precipitately. I had no money, having recently bought a large, ugly and near derelict house in Barnes, inconveniently south of the narrowest and most fragile bridge over the Thames, had been defrauded by an incompetent builder who had set fire to it, and was burdened with mortgage repayments that must monthly be settled.

This was midwinter, the first months of 1967, and for the moment there was no means of heating the icily cold house. Wires dangled from square gaps in the plaster where sockets and switches should have been, and radiators lay propped against the walls, not yet connected to pipes that in the boiler room below were not connected to a boiler for which I had paid, but which had not been delivered by the dismissed builder. I could cook and boil water with which to shave, but bathing was the shivering business of showering in water cold enough to freeze – as it did, in a pipe embedded in a wall on the first floor which, when it thawed, brought down the plaster in that room and the ceilings of the floor below. To such an ice-well no sane man would bring a lover and the only comfort was my dog, Susie – or, more properly, Susannah, named so after a beautiful girl I knew, whose carelessly elegant body language the pup's so much resembled. Claudio – who today would have been my civil partner, but then had to be explained as 'my Sicilian cousin, two or three times removed' – was in Sicily, doing his Christmas and New Year duties by his family.

Claudio, who could so easily have been one of a thousand casual lovers, one-night stands or urgently furtive sexual encounters in Hyde Park, had replaced all these. It had been a slow business – seven years in all. At first he was just another boy who might last a day or two – and to the promiscuous me that was initially enough – but, eight years my junior, he was physically puppyish and intellectually little brotherish, and his haphazard English amused me, forcing both of us into an absurd polyglot vocabulary that sometimes, too often in quite unsuitable circumstances, overflowed, with helpless giggling the consequence. Amusement developed into the sort of affection one might have for another man's dog, and eventually one's own, and for a while he and Susie were neck and neck. Steadily he reduced my promiscuity to the point at which he could begin to demand my constancy: 'I will kill you if . . . ' were the first words of many such demands that ended 'with a stiletto, just behind the ear, a wound so small that no one will know why you are dead.'

He was not small, dark, hairy and tough – as one might suppose a Sicilian to be – but tall and languid, his hair blond and floppily straight and his eyes large and dark, with something about him that was Florentine and Quattrocento. His skin was flawless and pale biscuit in colour, hardly darkening in summer, and golden body hair grew only in his armpits and in as neatly defined a patch as is to be found in the groin of a classical nude. I grew to be faithful to him when he was in England – as he was for months on end – but when his employers, the Italian state tourist board, sent him to Italy in the summers, that was a loyalty too demanding for me to maintain, and I lapsed into the opportunities for promiscuity so abundant on the towpath by the Thames between Hammersmith Bridge and the boat sheds at Putney. There the thrill lay not only in the hunt but in the menace of darkness, for it was lit only by the moon and, until one's night vision kicked in, one could see nothing and perception was left to other senses – it is odd how much hearing is heightened in such circumstances; there was also the danger of the sudden presence of the river police patrolling in a boat with the engine shut down and all lights off, the fierce beam of its searchlight suddenly cutting through the night. Far from running, the safest thing to do then was to lie flat and still in what small cover there might be, with one's face turned away from the beam. Often there was no time to disengage and we lay like a brace of spoons waiting for boredom to move the boat on. There was never much conversation, but occasionally my trophy was an oarsman who preferred to be taken home; to my amusement, these were always sheepishly passive, uncooperative in any foreplay, just wanting to be fucked – something to do with the repetitive action of rowing, I suppose.

My relationship with Claudio, a thing by this time of adoring tenderness, had not the slightest connection with the animal business of the towpath and he was never aware of that coarsely physical side of my nature. His long summer absences heightened my need for him to satisfy its other side, the side that feasts on looking, hearing, touching with the fingertips his silken skin, entering his body the most discreet and unselfish climax to these preliminaries. Always a bond of autumn, winter and spring, even this hibernal period had to be broken in its depth by Claudio's return to his parents in Taormina as one year turned into another, but this time, with the house in cold chaos and my career at Christie's shattered, his absence was particularly telling. He always resisted the pressure to stay in Sicily, determined to spend his life with me – and indeed he did return to London late in February 1967, but twelve months later he did not. Instead, there was a letter. He was his father's only son, it said, the last of a Norman line reaching back a thousand years unbroken, the Corvaya name unchanged, and as the only heir to the defunct marquisate he must, his father had argued, marry and beget a son. He did neither. He could not confess that he was queer and, in growing misery, he stayed in touch, but we grew apart and, when his father died, it was too late. He sold what property there was, bought a very good cast of Rodin's *Thinker*, moved to an apartment in Madrid and revived the title for use there. From time to time, at whim, he came to see me, always with a butch guttersnipe in tow, the last of them under the delusion that he was required to fuck everyone in sight, until a decade or so ago, Umberto Marturana, his boyhood friend in Taormina, came instead, to tell me that Claudio had been murdered, his skull cracked (by the Rodin, I wondered?) and his apartment stripped. Rent boys were suspected, but none was ever charged.

*   *   *

In Claudio's absence I was hamstrung. Without the daily discipline of going to work at Christie's, I felt lost, and there was little I could do about the house until I had money enough to pay another builder. We had talked of dealing in antiques, and that we could manage, for in 1967 one could easily begin trading with as little as £100, buying from one shop and selling to another for immediate small profits; Claudio had the cheek for this as well as an instinctive eye for quality, a sound visual memory and – as it seemed all Italians in London had – contacts with the 'mafiosi' who played so significant a part in the London auction rooms. Without him, however, I could do nothing to turn our thinking aloud into a plan; I brooded, and the more I did so, the less I wanted to be another unctuous dealer in Church Street, Kensington, or bluff in Long Melford, pretending that my battered household furniture was genuinely Georgian. By the time Claudio returned, I was exploring other avenues.

What could I do? What did I want to do? I went to see my vet. It was, I thought, an opportunity to change my life, to escape the tyranny of paintings right and wrong, to abandon the art market, its thrills, disappointments and moral dilemmas, and instead do something that seemed right and good. Russell Williams – Rusty to his friends – vet and oarsman, thought not, but in the spirit of 'Don't take my word for it' sent me to consult an eminence in the Royal Veterinary College. 'You have no biology, no physics, no chemistry, no maths, no evidence of ability in any scientific discipline and within six months you will be thirty-six. Even with all the preparation that you need and supposing that you sail through all exams, you will be forty-three before you qualify and more probably forty-five if we make allowance for failures on the way, for your mind is not as receptive now as at normal student age. Then you will need money to set up or join a practice, and within twenty years or so you will retire. It makes no sense. Stick to what you know.'

This inspired the thought that I might return to my studies again, aiming at a Ph.D., Rubens still my first choice, selling the house to fund it. I turned to Anthony Blunt for advice. 'What will you do with it if you complete it?' he asked. When I suggested that I might teach, might even apply for a post in the Courtauld Institute, he laughed. 'You'll be forty, with luck, competing with people not much more than half your age for a job at the bottom of the heap. Don't. You've left it too late.' A note in my mother's diary records that the following Sunday I descended on her house at Castle Hedingham and burnt all my notes and essays from school and the Courtauld and then threw my army uniforms onto the pyre; it ends with: 'He certainly is not well. Coffee poisoning?'

In spite of Anthony's discouragement and this futile gesture of wiping out my past, I applied for a post as tutor in art history in an art school – now long gone – conveniently nearby in Hammersmith, just across the fragile bridge; a Ph.D. was not among the requirements. As evidence of experience I could offer only a handful of lectures at university level long ago and the weekly lessons I had for some five years been giving in Brixton Prison. From this I knew that I could control a class of adults, catch and keep their interest, could teach, indeed, for demand for my classes grew until they were so large that they could only be accommodated in the prison chapel. I had learned that even the least educated prisoners, provided that I treated them as my equal, did not patronise them and encouraged them to interrupt with questions, could be taught something of that most improbable of academic disciplines, the history of art and the how and why of looking at pictures. How much of a *tabula rasa* some of my prisoners were was perhaps made clear when one asked outright if I was queer. I countered the question with 'Why do you ask?' – and to this the answer was, 'Well, Sir, you've shown us nothing but naked men this evening.' A glance at my list of slides was enough to remind me that flagellations, crucifixions and entombments had figured largely in my argument. For a week or so I believed that among my pupils were prisoners who had so little education that they knew nothing of the life of Christ (true even of Courtauld students now) and had never seen such images, but I was later to wonder if the true purpose of the question was to discover where my sexual sympathies lay, for some prisoners took advantage of the darkness. To my 'What on earth . . . ?' enquiry when I first thought a scuffle of some kind was happening (no guards were ever present), the response of one of the older men – 'I don't think you ought to look, Sir' – encouraged me to do just that. It was an episode of sodomy. I am sure that there were others, less excitedly conducted.

At the Hammersmith art school I was one of only two applicants for this piffling part-time job, the other was Theo Melville, a rather younger ex-Courtauld student. The interview was before a band of worthies on the further side of a long table and it seemed to have gone well, their interest in my Brixton prisoners paramount, but when the Chairman asked if there were any more questions, a man at the end of the table, balding and in a formal black jacket with a hint of gold chain about his belly, carefully put his fingertips together and said in a high-pitched churchwarden tone, 'Tell me, Mr Sewell, what is the common factor of excellence shared by Leonardo da Vinci and Picasso?' To this I heard myself respond – too quickly and with no gentling embroidery – 'There isn't one.' I had the impression that he had perhaps spent hours formulating this exquisite question and my response, honest but too immediate, was taken for a dismissive, even humiliating, rebuke – I should have hedged it about with nonsense so as not to make him look the fool he surely was. The board gave the job to Theo.

I was left with no alternative but to use my knowledge of the art market and its workings, but without funds. It was at this point that Eliot Hodgkin, fine collector and painter of delicate and quirky still lives, offered to lend me, for two years and without interest, £2,000 – rather more than my final year's salary at Christie's. As I had known him for only four years, this was an astonishing gesture. In the summer of 1962 I had seen in the window of Mallet's, Bond Street dealers in fine furniture and giltwood thrones, a strange little painting of dry stalks, dead leaves and bursting seed pods, as magical as though Salvador Dali had revised one of Ehret's botanical studies, retaining an eighteenth-century draughtsman's accuracy of observation but adding an hallucinatory excitement that extended the image far beyond mere realism. *Mrs Riley's Milkweed* was by Eliot and was to be had for sixty guineas – and to put that sum into perspective, my salary then, at a thousand a year, was enough to rent a basement flat in Kensington and run a dashing open Daimler. Mallet's could tell me nothing of Hodgkin, nor of Mrs Riley, nor even of milkweed or the painting's provenance, but I did not care. I bought the painting, and I have it still.

That desiccated sow-thistle, that bursting brimstone-wort, proved an *open sesame*. I had had it for a year or so when, one high summer evening, Carlos van Hasselt, then newly late of the Fitzwilliam and just appointed to the Netherlands Institute in Paris, came to dinner, saw the milkweed, and asked if Eliot was a friend. I was in awe of Carlos, master of seven languages and deep-dyed art historian, who knew, as equal, famous men whose names I knew only from the spines of books, and whose expertise in my chosen field of old master drawings far exceeded anything that I might learn in a lifetime; that he knew Eliot told me at once that the man who had painted *Mrs Riley's Milkweed* was no nonentity, no country cottage bumpkin with a delicate touch. With a telephone call and a taxi I found myself whisked into the presence of a painter whose Chelsea flat was a treasury of marvellous paintings by Corot and Delacroix, and of drawings by the ilk of Ingres, Degas, Fragonard and Liotard that made me ill with envy. There was not the slightest hint of grandeur about these small masterpieces – they were a cherished part of Eliot's domestic scene, part of his daily life and nourishment, reticent and intimate in scale, some standing in their own right as finished works of art, others perfect art historical documents that added to our perceptions of some greater work elsewhere, and that were in turn informed by awareness of those works. My fumbling and confused instincts as a magpie acquirer of scraps immediately recognised that this collection was the work of a clear eye and disciplined passion.

Not a Hodgkin painting was to be seen in this brilliant company, for Eliot was a man of modesty and claimed no place with older masters, but at last he was persuaded to open the doors of the cupboard that was his studio and show me the tiny pictures of fruit, flowers, eggs and feathers that he painted with such delight and diligence. Enchanted by two paintings of kohlrabis, purplish pink and acid green, gentled by a ground of greyish marble, I bought both. He chuckled, and told me that I had, in fact, bought one picture – he had painted five kohlrabis in a row, and when no one bought the long narrow frieze he had sawn it in two. In time I added parsnips, turnips, lemons and a lime, the lichened tombs of churchyards and a view in Switzerland; by a stroke of luck I found large early oil paintings that Eliot thought lost, one of which, a gaudy thing of a Christmas tree, he wished had stayed so. He thought me mad to buy so many, but they gave me a direct and simple pleasure that has never diminished.

He was a kind man. When he found me in despair amid the depredations of a dishonest builder in a house that had cost me every penny I possessed, he sent me his builder and a carpenter, who worked until the house was habitable, and whose bills he paid; he took only the repayment of the money, and would accept neither interest nor gift.

Five years later, when moving into my next (and almost final) house and I had carelessly left the side door open, he went into my dining room, put two roses into a celadon vase, broke away petals so that they fell at its foot, and put among them a curl of paper with his signature, exactly as though he had painted a characteristic still life for me. It is the only work by Eliot that I have owned but not been able to keep. Another I particularly regret not buying: it is the detailed study of the internal wall of a terrace house in Chelsea, revealed in 1976 by the demolition of its neighbour, a pattern of vile distempers made lovely by the artist's eye; sunlight fell on the wall only in the morning, giving the colours a peculiar intensity, and Eliot for a week or so rose early, slid between panels of corrugated iron that he had unbolted, painted amid the rubble of the site and left before the first builders arrived for work. He would not sell me the picture for he thought it suitable for the Royal Academy the following summer. He sent it, priced at £300, and it was rejected. Still he would not sell it – 'No. I shall send it in again.' And so he did, a year later, with the price raised to £500, and it was accepted and sold at the private view.

Eliot had a certain pride in his work, but no vanity. The small still lives by which he is best known were, for the most part, painted in tempera with meticulous care, minute attention to detail and a high state of finish, but such fine work was eventually responsible for the decline of his sight and his decision in the autumn of 1982 that he would paint no more. The saddest work that I have ever done was arranging the dispersal of his studio and the sale of all his preparatory studies for the elegant murals to which he turned his hand in the 1930s; it was characteristic of Eliot that he should make so clear-cut a decision and rid himself of the clutter of a life that he felt was past. The sale took place at Christie's in January 1983; his remaining tempera paints and brushes he sent to David Tindle, whom he did not know but whom he thought a good painter, and settled down to die. In spite of failing sight and the depredations of an ataxia that increasingly disordered his body, this he managed with good spiritual grace on 30 May 1987. Neil MacGregor, then newly Director of the National Gallery, read the lesson at the memorial service of our shrewd, generous, mischievous and Christian friend, and most of his collection was bequeathed for the benefit of charity.

With Eliot's £2,000 I trawled the many private dealers in old master drawings working from homes in Kensington, Hampstead, St John's Wood and even Golders Green, many of them of German and Austrian origin. These, fleeing penniless from the Nazis in the later 1930s would, had British universities as many faculties of the history of art as now, have found academic posts, but even the then unique Courtauld Institute was not much more than a finishing school and had nothing to offer them. Some had worked in major museums and universities, others had been independent scholars at a time when to be a scholar for the sake of scholarship was still possible on small means, and that there was a widening market in old master drawings was largely their responsibility. They were part of an extraordinary cultural influx from central Europe that during World War II began to have an influence here in all the arts, burgeoning with the BBC's wonderful Third Programme soon after the war, and that changed for ever our performance and understanding of all genres of classical music and the visual arts. The book recording their transformation of British culture and connoisseurship has never been written and now never will be, for it is too late – they are all long dead and my generation, the astonished witnesses first to benefit from their influence, is already following them.

With the help of these small dealers I was able within three months to mount an exhibition of drawings at the Alpine Gallery in South Audley Street (part of the Alpine Club, since removed to Wimbledon), long the traditional exhibition site for art dealers without premises. It was the suggestion of Peter Claas who, I now suspect, had already reserved the later weeks of May but had too little stock to fill the gallery. It was to be of fifty drawings each and some of mine I had to borrow from other dealers taking only a tiny commission if they sold, but, as Peter argued, with advertisements in art magazines and catalogues to distribute to his clients, it was an effective way of informing the Old Master Drawings world that I was no longer at Christie's but functioning as a dealer – and indeed, Peter's clients immediately became mine.

I learned a great deal from him, much of which I did not like. The most wretched of scraps can be made to seem important with a decorative mount and a good and obviously expensive frame; a client thus seduced, even a close friend in Peter's tight-knit homosexual circle, must be confirmed in his choice with weasel words – and one must always put the greatest effort into selling the drawing in which there is the highest profit, never revealing any uncertainty about an important-seeming attribution plucked, if not from the air, from a reproduction in a book with which it shares only the faintest resemblance. Friendly museum curators were to tell me that I had done myself no good with this transitory alliance, yet I was grateful for it, for if nothing else, it was an indication that I might be able to repay Eliot without difficulty. Besides, in many other ways Peter had become an engaging friend, outrageously and unashamedly queer, yet happy to flirt with my mother to the point where he could claim that they were engaged, and some of his friends thought him serious. My mother, however, though briefly amused to be his prop at the opera and other public places (her diary entry for 8 June 1967 records that it was Peter's sixtieth birthday, that she went to his cocktail party and then on to have dinner with the Swedish ambassador), wearied of the game and eventually refused to play it; I suspect that she was unsympathetic to his sexual preference for swarthy working men in their forties, slightly gone to seed.

It was this preference that drew him to retire to Malta when the lease on his elegant flat in Upper Brook Street had to be renewed. As no house on the island was quite what he wanted, he determined to build his fantasy, but bedding his builders led to inflated bills, his refusal to pay them and their blocking access to the site with a barrier topped with the legend 'Peter Claas – go back into the cunt of your mother' printed on a placard. He had no choice but to abandon Malta and, moving to Rome, was content there for some years until the persistent ailments of the old consumed his small income and compelled his return to London and the benefits of the NHS; his days ended in a dreary room in Ennismore Gardens – always the address of those who have abandoned hope. He left me a matched pair of drawings in red chalk, their subjects preposterously posed male nudes, their fussily decorated mounts elaborated with cartouches that, with characteristic enterprise, attribute them to Lagrenée.

Such drawings are known as Academies, the life classes of students in the eighteenth century perhaps their most common origin; many are fine drawings with some reasonable hope of attribution at least to the circle of an identifiable master, but more are bought for their mildly erotic nature – though this is always more the perception of the buyer than the intention of the artist. Among Peter's friends there was a steady market for such images and if they were too vague or too much covered at the crutch he was given to improving them with the help of a restorer employed to remove drapery and discover a full set of genitals. Size and angle therefore rarely disappointed and no one seemed to notice that the chalk (the most common medium for such studies), particularly when red, was often an imperfect match. One client who insisted on inspecting Peter's Academies but never bought one, eventually wrote a cheque for a nude who had been circumcised – most improbable in the eighteenth century (though Louis XVI was trimmed for ejaculatory reasons) but shrewd lateral thinking on Peter's part.

The exhibition had been a modest success but I needed sources of drawings other than my fellow dealers and the major auction rooms if I was ever to build the essential of every art dealer, a stock of material new to the market. I took to trawling the minor auction rooms in London, Bonham's in Montpelier Street, Bonham's in Chelsea (a most depressing dump), Phillips, Harrods, Knight Frank and Rutley, and others in the business of rapid clearance and never mind the unwitting mistakes of negligence. In these, prints and drawings, if not framed, were sold in unsorted and uncounted parcels, often almost too heavy to carry, just as they had been at Christie's before I insisted on being diligent there; these were sold for virtually nothing. This trawl was a deadly discipline, but if it was to be worth doing it must be done with scrupulous regularity and friends had to be made among the porters willing to bid in my absence (for my presence would betray my interest) and guard my purchases from predators. Among the worthless prints and amateur watercolours an etching by Picasso, two by Canaletto, a dozen by Charles Meryon (a great but forgotten etcher, colour-blind and, eventually, insane) and another dozen by Edmund Blampied (the Whistler of Jersey) were among my early rewards. Much later, to my surprise, I was outbid in a really dismal sale at Bonham's, for two huge folios of drawings, photographs and documents by and connected with Thomas Sidney Cooper, a long-lived painter of cows and sheep in pastures near his native Canterbury; nicknamed 'Cow Cooper' he spanned the nineteenth century. I was not interested in the handful of finished watercolours, nor in the sheets of sketches of figures and horses, in some cases several on a single sheet, every motif carefully initialled T.S.C., all in a remarkable dark brown ink, all with some resemblance to sketches by Géricault, though this did not occur to me at the time. I had pushed the price further than I wished to pay because I was intrigued by the photo-graphs and related drawings, for these demonstrated a working process that it had never occurred to me that Cooper might have used. The photographs, all of his own paintings, were large, in sepia, and on very thin paper; many were whole, and to these were glued motifs cut from other paintings, then re-photographed as finished works. In these, and in pencil drawings on tracing paper, there was clear evidence that Cow Cooper used photography to plot the compositions of paintings in which the groups of animals in one landscape had simply been transferred and reproduced from others. There is, as far as I know, no record of his employing assistants, but in 1865 he established a school of art in Canterbury, where students, many of them women, followed the customary academic training of drawing plaster casts of antique sculptures; among these there were perhaps some willing to assist him with his landscapes while he secretly cheated with the cows and sheep. His output was prodigious.

The sale took place in the morning. Early in the afternoon I telephoned the young dealer who had staggered away with this heavy and unwieldy burden, to offer to buy the photographs and tracings. 'I've burned them,' he said. 'Already?' said I. 'Yes' came the answer and he cut the line. It was not long before the small drawings in that intense brown ink appeared on the London market, in the gallery of a small but reputable dealer who was something of a friend. With the initials T.S.C. removed he had bought them as by Géricault. I told him what I knew and left the rest to his conscience. I have since seen them in the most distinguished collections, public and private, in Europe and America. No one should buy drawings attributed to Géricault without a recorded provenance dating to before 1970.

Together with the photographic material destroyed were certificates of Cooper's attendance, as a student, at academies in Brussels and Antwerp; he is otherwise recorded only as a teacher there in the early 1820s. Thus that young dealer not only foisted false Géricaults onto the market, but corrupted what we know of Cooper.

A coup that gave my finances a tremendous boost and opened a new market for me was the discovery and purchase of a pair of bound volumes of late eighteenth-century Swiss landscape prints, in colour, in pristine condition within the battered bindings. Of these I knew, thanks to the catholicity of my interests as a student and my great good fortune in having been instructed in the byways of the print market by old Harold Knight after his retirement from Colnaghi's, the last English connoisseur in the field; but I also knew that though fashionable among print collectors early in the twentieth century, particularly among Alpinists (a sometime Chairman of Christie's, Robert Wylie Lloyd, had on his death at ninety in 1958, bequeathed a huge collection of them to the British Museum), they were in 1967 utterly forgotten and neglected in Britain. To find a buyer for them I must go to Switzerland.

And so I did, to Jürg Stuker, a dealer and auctioneer in Berne, who pressed into my hand the largest banknotes I had ever seen, in the highest denominations, making the largest sum of money I have ever physically held. Jürg, slightly preposterous, queer, given to wearing the jewelled and enamelled royal orders of Bessarabia, Roumelia and Pless that he collected for pleasure, their origin largely the satrapies of the Balkans and the minor principalities of central Europe, living in a castle, holding court, became something of a friend. I dare say he cheated me – it is what art dealers do when on their honour to pay a fair price – but I did well enough from our dealings and for years he provided an immediate buyer, not only for Swiss prints, but for the Swiss paintings that also occasionally appeared, as unremarked, on the parochial-minded London market. Plump, perspiring and unprepossessingly dapper, Jürg broke in terminal grief on the death – through the dread combination of BMW and tree – of his blond and beautiful lover, a perfect Aryan.

That friendly and hospitable dealers did indeed cheat, I was to have proof soon enough. One from New York, Helene Seiferheld, 'borrowed' one of the best of my finds – a large and dramatic on-the-spot study of the Colosseum by Vanvitelli – to show, on commission, to a client, and we agreed a price from which she was to take her cut. Over the next year or so I asked many times if her client was interested, her answer always that these things take time.

When, eventually, I asked for the return of the drawing, she said that it was with the Metropolitan Museum for consideration; this did not greatly please me, for I considered the Museum my own client, indeed every dealer's client. Then came news that the purchase was agreed, but that payment was delayed until the next financial year. When her cheque at last arrived it was with an apologetic 'let me make it up to you' invitation to stay in her gallery – an apartment in a brownstone house just off Third Avenue – when next I was in New York. This, some months later, I accepted, only to find among the journals left lying about with careless elegance to impress her clients, an old annual report from the Metropolitan recording the purchase of the Vanvitelli and the sum paid for it. The Museum had been her immediate client and had at once bought and paid for it; thus she had had the use of my money for two full years, and though she had doubled the agreed price, had still taken her cut from the figure that I had asked. I wrote a note of thanks for her brief hospitality, stapled it to the open page of the report, and early the following morning transferred to a small and cheap hotel in Columbus Avenue so riddled with cockroaches that they fell from the ceiling onto my nakedness in the rusty bath, but it was run by a friendly family from Prague with European ways.

That I had carefully laid down the terms under which the Vanvitelli was to be sold – the price to be asked, the percentage of the dealer's cut, and the offer only to be made to a private client unknown to me – was because I had earlier been on too vague a footing with Agnew's when effecting a substantial transaction for their benefit; most dealers offered a ten per cent commission for the successful introduction of a client, the deal unspoken but settled with a cheque in the post. John Wyndham, Lord Egremont, Conservative politician under Macmillan, Trustee of the Wallace Collection and, above all things, hereditary custodian of Petworth (which he too enthusiastically described as 'the finest house in Europe'), asked me to inspect a portrait of a boy, attributed to

Bronzino, that he had seen in Agnew's, the firm so long established in Bond Street that it had become the *pars pro toto* of the art trade. Geoffrey Agnew, the booming, bullying monster then in charge, showed me the painting; it was neither better nor worse than a number of similar paintings attributed to Bronzino, but lacked, I thought, the spark that distinguishes the portraits of boys of the Medici family in the Ashmolean and the Uffizi. To Lord Egremont I was frank; I told him that the portrait was of the period and place, and in good condition, but that the attribution to Bronzino would never be without questioners; as for the price, this was by no means a bargain. He seemed to be in thrall to the painting and, not as worried as he should have been by my lack of enthusiasm, told me what he was prepared to pay for it, modestly below the asking price. Geoffrey leaped at the offer and the deal was done. For me, however, there was no cheque from Agnew's and, bumping into Geoffrey some long weeks later, I asked him when I might expect it – to be met with the pretence of surprise, followed by blunt refusal: a lofty man, he put his arm round my shoulders, told me that I should have assumed nothing but made my expectations clear when we were bargaining. The books, he said, were now closed and could not be reopened. I was furious that he had cheated me so, but loathed him more for the avuncular intimacy of his gesture and his patronising implication that I might benefit from such a useful experience.

There was straighter dealing at the very bottom of the trade. Ernest Pepper in Newcastle, for example, who maintained what can only be described as a bulk supply business with art dealers in Scandinavia, needing more bulk than could be found locally, asked my help. It was easily given, though hard physical work: I sat through truly awful sales at Bonham's every Thursday, buying for very small sums paintings of landscapes, still lives and, particularly, children, twenty or so from every sale; these, on alternate Saturdays, I drove to Newcastle and sold to Pepper, returning to London the same night. The regular profit this provided was ploughed back into more and more drawings, but it was not a trade I much enjoyed.

*   *   *

Much of my last full year at Christie's had been devoted to an inventory of the old master drawings at Chatsworth – one of the world's greatest collections – and those who have since leafed through them must have seen among many scholarly notes and suggested changes of attribution some with my initials and those of David Carritt too. Noël Annesley, then my assistant, soon to be my successor (though neither knew this at the time) and, eventually, a high panjandrum in the firm, was with us. Together we greatly amused the Duchess, Debo, who was, as it were, in charge of us – never was there a merrier summer or serious work so pleasurable. When I left Christie's she asked me to undertake a similar inventory of the neglected old master prints at Chatsworth, but a couple of weeks of preliminary sorting in August (when the art market is pretty well dead) convinced me that to do this properly would entail months of concentrated work with much travelling to compare the most rare examples with those in other major print collections. It is not good enough, for example, simply to record the presence of landscape prints in colour by Hercules Segers, an early contemporary of Rembrandt (who owned eight of his paintings), for each of these very rare things is in some way unique and the apparatus of print scholarship requires precise observation of every technical difference – of the one hundred and eighty-three currently known impressions from the fifty-four currently known plates, no two are identical. In my then circumstances I could do no more than sort, identify and list the most important prints and, with lasting regret, bow out.

There was, however, one lateral benefit – the development of my friendship with Tom Wragg, curator of all the Chatsworth collections, whom I had known since 1958 when Christie's offered twenty-four paintings from the house, including two by La Hyre and Le Sueur that in the light of my contribution to the Royal Academy's exhibition earlier that year (The Age of Louis XIV) had been of particular interest to me. He was the most approachable of men, with a local touch to his speech, entirely without vanity in appearance, dress or manner, yet gravely respected by the lofty Londoners with whom he had so often to deal, and the guru of the north in that it was to him the art dealers of Derbyshire and thereabouts turned when they acquired something out of the ordinary; if he did not know the answers, he brought these things to Christie's when next on a jaunt to London. This little bit of business he transferred to me and it became an occasional source of decent drawings and paintings entirely new to the London market. Should I have had qualms of conscience in this diversion? I gave exactly the advice that I would have given had I still been with Christie's, offering to deliver the goods there, or, if the inevitable delay in selling at auction (often of months) was not acceptable, offering to buy outright; I doubt if Christie's lost a penny, for those in urgent need of a sale would certainly have sold elsewhere.

My only other crossover from Christie's was Captain Arthur Simmons, a florid thick-skinned man who tanned his face with almond oil until it looked like pork crackling, with whom I had often had to contend at Christie's. He drove Rolls-Royces because he dealt in them, but they also opened doors for him – literally – the front doors of decent houses whose owners, short of cash, were to be persuaded into swapping pictures for a splendid car. What was it about an old but well presented Rolls, the cellulose paint gleaming, the enormous headlamps blinding in their shining chrome, the classic architecture of the radiator proclaiming imperial status, that released the Toad in sane and gentle men? The Devil failed to tempt St Anthony with naked women, but Arthur Simmons would have succeeded with a Rolls. He drove to the door in a machine worth a thousand pounds, and drove away in a taxi with a painting worth ten times that sum, in a carved giltwood frame worth another thousand. Would it, I wondered, have worked with an Alvis or Lagonda? Probably not.

Making more money from the swaps than ever from straight purchases, he began to advertise for pictures in the personal columns of *The Times*, and once, when overwhelmed with offers, paid me to accompany him on a long trawl to Gloucestershire and back, eliminating paintings that were of no serious value; for those that were, he would return later with a suitable motor (men like Simmons always spoke, not of cars but 'motors'). By the end of the first day I loathed the man, so sharp had been his dealing and so loud his behaviour in the pub in which we spent the night, so loud his shouting for a better Burgundy, so loud his ghastly tweeds, and even doubted the genuineness of his captaincy. Our last stop on the second day was at the house of a woman with one quite decent painting, whose instinct, clearly, was to have nothing to do with him. He bullied and cajoled to a point that sickened me and weakened her resolve; in capitals I wrote in my notebook 'Don't sell. Throw us out,' and held it so that she could read it over his shoulder. And throw us out, she did. Simmons, for all the distinction endowed by his captaincy and splendid cars, was nothing but a 'knocker', an ignorant cheat of whom few house-holders could be rid without parting from their silver teapots for a sixpence.

That I became known in the London trade as a dealer who never deals pleased me well enough; of course I dealt – how else was I to earn my living? – and I bought from and occasionally sold to dealers, but I chose never to work with them, never to enter into agreements not to bid against them, never to join the ring or any form of syndicate. In this I was greatly helped by the independence of most dealers in the field of old master drawings, their preference, like mine, to work alone, and by collectors to whom, at Christie's, I had given sound advice from time to time. These, finding me no longer there, sought me out, and though some were not queer, it was evident that most were and that some

sort of queer support mechanism had come into play. I sensed
something fraternal that had little to do with collecting drawings
but in which homosexuality was the shibboleth. In some cases
there was a cosiness for which I did not much care, as though
simply to be queer made me a member of some sort of brotherhood or sect. With others there was no obvious hint of knowing
or sharing, only a relaxation of formality. Herbert List, for example,
Jugendbewegung photographer of beautiful boys in the 1930s and
the Joachim Lenz of Stephen Spender's autobiographical novel,
The Temple, knocked on my door within days of my leaving
Christie's; he talked about the range of drawings he had bought
ever since his student days at Heidelberg, looked askance at the
scatterbrained things I had, and told me how his taste had slowly
narrowed to concentrate only on Italian examples. Over the few
years until his death in 1975 he was a faithful client, always drinking
coffee (on which he was an expert – it had been his family's
business) while he made up his mind, picking my brains about
drawings seen elsewhere, never gossiping about his earlier life and
his work with the camera, yet seeming at ease as though nothing
between us need be revealed or concealed. On his very last visit,
however, something was concealed; he seemed disquieted and
oddly shabby too, shrunken within his old raincoat; he found a
drawing that he wanted, but his mind seemed on some more
distant matter when he scurried off with it. No one told me when
he died.*

Ulrich von Artus was not queer. Thirty years too late he was
the perfect German boy for Herbert List, blonde of hair, biscuit of
skin, lithe and athletic, but not queer. An apprentice at Christie's

---

* I later learned that Herbert had, in 1972, sold his Italian drawings en
  bloc to Adolf Ratjen (1910–1989), a collector who, generously, did not
  take possession until after his death and whose payment allowed Herbert
  to continue to buy at the highest level in an increasingly rare and
  expensive market. The Ratjen Collection is now in the National Gallery,
  Washington.

for some months in the summer of 1966, he was the son of Friedrich von Artus, an art auctioneer in Frankfurt. We became friends; he lodged in my house, got drunk (he was addicted to Pils and Fernet Branca) and set fire to his bed, destroying my best blanket, an expensive thing of camel hair embellished with (and in this there was a Wagnerian irony) a broad band of Swastika decoration at each end. I last saw him in the winter of 1970 when, as captain of the Frankfurt Rugby Club, he telephoned to say that he was short of a hooker for an important match on Saturday and would I play for him. At thirty-nine and not having played for well over a decade, I was a fool to agree, but it proved a rip-roaring match and I enjoyed every moment of it. Ending the day in a Spanish restaurant, consuming gargantuan quantities of paella and rioja, every member of the team performed that ancient act of manliness and unity, the corporate vomit, when, from the overheated bodega, we stepped into the cold night air. I have not since been drunk. Within months Ulrich was dead, seized by some galloping cancer.

What Friedrich von Artus wanted of me in 1967 was advice that prevented him from letting slip a masterpiece. The art market in Germany had still not recovered from the tragedies of World War II. Before that war there had been many eminent and reliable art dealers in almost every city, most of them Jewish; these and their Jewish clients were largely victims of Nazi anti-semitism in the Thirties, and the German art they did so much to foster – Expressionism and Neue Sachlichkeit – was damned, destroyed and sold abroad in Switzerland by Hitler's henchmen. These dealers lost their stocks and the collectors their collections through forced sales and expropriation. Well into another century this is still an emotional and inflammatory matter, now often one of very high value too, but in the 1930s the effects of the Great Depression had all but destroyed the art market in Europe, and in London old Oliver Brown, who ran the Leicester Galleries (just off Leicester Square), had throughout the decade a variant of *Van Gogh's Chair*

(Tate)* without his pipe, on consignment from a client at only £800, yet it remained unsold (and is now untraced and *hors de catalogue*); Brown also had almost forty landscapes by Kokoschka for which there were no takers at £200 apiece, and as many paintings by Max Liebermann in which no client showed interest at any price. Auction records demonstrate that the demand for Old Masters was just as weak – a double page in one Christie catalogue of 1933 lists only four paintings, of long provenance, two by Poussin, two by Claude, for which the total sum paid was less than 1,000 guineas. Sir Denis Mahon's collection of great paintings by Guercino, Reni and other seventeenth-century masters was founded on that sort of sum. These facts should perhaps be borne in mind when paintings, said to have been the subject of forced sale under the Nazis, are claimed by the descendants of former owners who, had they brought their paintings to England and sold them, would have got as little as they did from the Nazis.

Such claims were tentative in the 1960s and still uncommon, but von Artus was anxious not to be drawn into disputes that were profoundly uncomfortable for innocent parties; nevertheless he involved me in two other matters that were far from innocent, the second closely connected to Nazi expropriation. The first was the valuation of a collection outside Munich of paintings attributed to Titian, Velazquez, Veronese, Rubens, Rembrandt and others of first rank. I was to fly to Munich, take a taxi to the Drei Könige Hotel and breakfast there with someone who would drive to the Schloss in which the pictures were; my contact was persuasive – it is the only time that I have breakfasted on the brains of a lamb. The drive was aggressive and confusing, as though I was not to know precisely where I was taken (as I did not), and the Schloss more a rich man's villa of the late nineteenth century than some turretted castle of the

---

* The Tate's acquisition was through the Courtauld Fund in 1924, direct from Van Gogh's family via the Leicester Galleries as agent; Oliver Brown maintained his tie with the family at least until 1938.

Wittelsbachs. I was introduced to some eight or ten elderly men the cut of whose hair and evidence of old wounds reminded me at once of drawings by Georg Grosz of army officers after the Great War. That is what I think they were – though after World War II – and I feared that they might be Nazis rather than Junkers grown old. They explained that the paintings were an old family collection concealed during the war, not for sale, but to be valued as security for a loan. I had encountered this before, at Christie's, but it was usually the lending bank that commissioned the valuation to protect its interests. So far I had not seen a single picture, nothing in the spacious entrance hall, nothing in the room in which we were; when I asked to see them we moved to another room, once a ballroom, perhaps, where some seventy paintings by old masters stood on the floor, leaning against the panelling. The light was appalling and time and again I had to carry pictures to the windows to make any sense of them – and they made very clear sense indeed.

This was not an ancient family collection. This was a hotch-potch very recently acquired. If some were familiar it was because I had myself catalogued them at Christie's, and on the backs of all were the characteristic inventory numbers, dates of sale and lot numbers of Christie's, Sotheby's and Bonham's. Not one canvas was by the painter to whom it was attributed on the list given me, and I knew at once that I was being drawn into a fraud. I sensed too the unwisdom of blurting out the truth. Instead, I laboured over the list noting on it the information I had gleaned and estimating the real value in code, adding extra noughts for the benefit of the man at my shoulder who, thinking that I understood no German and having asked if they were pounds or Deutschmarks, told his fellow conspirators that I was putting satisfactory five-figure valuations on the wretched things. They pressed me for a gross figure – I refused, arguing that I had much research to do before that would be possible, shook hands with all the old rogues and was driven back to the Drei Könige for an early supper before catching my plane. With ghoulish humour the driver ordered brains again, insisting that I had so much enjoyed them for breakfast that he must repeat the treat. I told von Artus of the fraud and that I would send him neither the valuation nor the bill for my flight and services; unlike Geoffrey Agnew, he was apologetic and did not tell me that I would profit from the experience.

The more disturbing matter was Friedrich's introduction of Baruch, the only name by which anyone knew this shabby figure in the art market. 'Hier ist Baruch' was his greeting on the telephone, 'Hier ist Baruch' his salutation on the doorstep. He spoke only German, he sought only inexpensive paintings and he paid in cash; he divulged no means of making contact, gave no warning of impending presence and disappeared as swiftly as a wary cat. We met in Frankfurt, but once he had my address I could never shake him off and, to my distaste, our association lasted for some years until its fruitlessness exhausted him. Of him I learned two intriguing things, the first of which he evidently regretted; it was that though a Jew he had survived in Germany not only throughout the Thirties but through the war itself, surviving because he revealed the whereabouts of works of art that might otherwise have remained unknown to the Nazis, Jew betraying Jew. Not a dealer, and certainly not a scholar, I suspect that he had been an insurance broker or something of the kind with access to inventories. After the war his knowledge could, perhaps, have been invaluable in the recovery of works of art, and in a sense it was, for he chose to work for Ante Topic Mimara, who became a millionaire art collector and close confidant of General Tito, President of Yugoslavia. Quite when these two rogues came together we shall never know, but my hunch is that it was before or early in the war, rather than in the pan-European chaos after it, and that Mimara's few good paintings (not one of which has any known provenance) were acquired as a consequence of Baruch's betrayals.

Few, anywhere, knew anything of Topic Mimara, though he claimed to have begun collecting when a child and to have bought his first important antiquity in his very early twenties, until 1963, when Thomas Hoving, then curator of the Cloisters in New York, a department of the Metropolitan Museum, and later Director of the museum itself, brought Mimara out of the shadows by purchasing from him *The Bury St Edmunds Cross*, a medieval masterpiece that had no recent provenance. Rumour and insinuation multiplied, boosted by Mimara's boast that he had been the art adviser and friend of Hermann Goering, the rapacious Nazi leader whose collection of paintings and objects he had helped to form before and during the war. Of this there is no proof, though Mimara was in Berlin at the outbreak of war and spent most of it in Lörrach in Oberrhein, a few kilometres from Basel where Swiss safety lay if suddenly he needed it; it may have been mistaken vanity – my own belief is that in claiming this he adopted what had been Baruch's role as servant of Alfred Rosenberg, Goering's chief instrument in the sequestration of works of art from Jewish collectors. In the confusions of 1946 Mimara was appointed to the Yugoslav Military Mission in Berlin to supervise matters of cultural restitution, was given a diplomatic passport that enabled him to travel anywhere he wished in the vast range of ravished Europe, and was subsequently accused of transferring to Yugoslavia works that had been pillaged from Italy, France, Czechoslovakia and other central European countries. By the mid 1950s he had accumulated a huge collection for himself, of which he presented a substantial part to the then Socialist Republic of Croatia in October 1973, and had promoted himself to an ancient title of the Austro-Hungarian Empire.

When, early in 1983, I learned that in September Mimara's gift was at last to be accessible to the public and that a catalogue had been published boasting paintings by Raphael, Michelangelo, Parmigianino, Castagno, Caravaggio, Giorgione, Titian, El Greco, Velazquez, Rembrandt, Rubens, Van Gogh and most of the Impressionists, I went to see the collection. Housed in the Villa Zagorje, some distance from the centre of the Croatian capital, it proved to be, not the boasted Louvre of Zagreb, but an embarrassing assembly of travesties and misattributions, though the outright fakes were outnumbered by canvases to which preposterous signatures had been applied and by portraits and other subjects that had been heavily reworked. In anticipation I had mistakenly paid Mimara the compliment of supposing that among his pictures might be found the missing *Portrait of a Young Man* by Raphael, a masterpiece removed in the last months of the war from the Czartoryski Museum in Cracow for the benefit of Hans Frank, Gauleiter of Poland, never again seen, but of which there had been faint whispers from behind the Iron Curtain. It was not, of course, in Mimara's collection, in which not one painting in the selection on view suggested that he possessed a jot or tittle of the informed scholarship or instinctive eye of the true connoisseur, and everything conformed with what I knew of Baruch's purchases through von Artus. My notes on Mimara's paintings are despairing – 'Entirely repainted . . . fake . . . feeble imitation . . . very damaged . . . crude copy . . . ruined fragment . . . laughable . . . feeble . . . grotesque . . . ' The collection is now housed in the largest and most palatial eponymous museum premises in Zagreb, inviting ridicule. When, in 2009, in an essay on 'The Museums of Zagreb' (see Jadranka Beresford-Peirse, ed., *Croatia: Aspects of Art* . . . pp. 194–207), I first let slip some of this material, I caused outrage and was briefly *persona non grata* in Croatia.

*   *   *

The British art market today is very different from the art market of the later 1960s. At the top of the tree were the Bond Street Boys who thought they knew everything but, in fact, knew very little (except for Colnaghi's, and even that firm was soon to be stripped of its worthy reputation). To these the history of art and its associated connoisseurship was a mysterious academic discipline beyond their comprehension, attribution was a matter of the wild surmise and quality was measured in terms of distinguished (or otherwise) provenance. At the bottom of the tree were the dozens of dealers who dealt from the back of a van and, in the case of Raymond de Romare, from a caravan; this, badly parked in Duke Street, St James's, narrowing an already narrow street, was ripped to shreds one day by a passing army lorry, leaving his stock of ghastly paintings lying in the road among the splintered timbers. One of them, on a quite large sheet of copper, was badly bent; unwilling to pay the cost of a restorer's attempting to flatten it, he gave five shillings to the driver of a steamroller to drive slowly and ever so gently over it — of which the consequence was a much larger and much thinner sheet of copper with not a flake of paint adhering to it.

Between the top and the bottom were dealers who specialised in some particular aspect or genre — lap dogs and carousing cardinals, paintings of ships, horses, fox hunts and Montgolfier balloons, nineteenth-century Dutch landscapes — some of whom were respected as experts in their fields; and there were a handful who, like old Oliver Brown, had dealt, often face to face, with artists who were becoming a new generation of old masters, among them Sickert, Soutine, Kisling, Klee, Kokoschka and even Monet. How extraordinary to have been able to record in his journal, as Oliver did, 'John Sargent called with Claude Monet to introduce him and arrange an exhibition.'

Such respected old boys as he set the best practical example for young dealers moving into the trade and there was never a more revered reputation. Usurping them, the young revived interest in British artists of the earlier twentieth century — an interest that had sunk so far that many were surprised to find, for example, Duncan Grant still alive. Anthony d'Offay, who had made a fortune selling the dismal but indubitably genuine scraps retrieved from the floors of great artists' studios, cornered the market in Gwen John, Robert Bevan, Roger Fry, the Omega Workshop and the Bloomsbury Group, and was overjoyed when his rediscovery of Duncan Grant and hundreds of paintings and drawings of male nudes (some quite obscene) turned the old dear into a gay icon. An early move into contemporary art was his becoming Lucian Freud's dealer, but this collaboration ended abruptly and in tears with Lucian writing, by night, on Anthony's windows in Dering Street, an expression of opinion too extreme ever to retract; it did Anthony no harm (nothing ever did) and he moved on to become a high-end dealer with Warhol, Basquiat, Richter and Koons in his stable, and, with astonishing sleight-of-hand on his retirement, a benefactor to the nation. I must argue that I too, at Christie's, in setting up sales devoted to twentieth-century British art, had played a not insignificant part in its revival and was for decades regarded as an expert on Augustus John and Charles Ginner; now, at a time when both are being distorted by the addition of forged signatures to inadequate canvases, my reputation in this field is largely forgotten.

Charles Ginner (1878–1952) is, indeed, the perfect example of my many failures to achieve. One of the circle of English painters who, with Gilman, Gore and Bevan, both overlapped with and succeeded Sickert, Ginner's work is distinguished by his almost mechanical application of evenly impastose strokes of paint so thick that they rarely indicate the use of brushes – Van Gogh tamed and neutered, as it were. 'I shall paint as thick as I damn well please,' he responded in 1914 to Sickert's accusation in his mischievously punning essay *The Thickest Painters in London*, that Ginner attached 'a somewhat doctrinaire importance to the value of impasto itself.' It was, however, the impasto that in the end undid me; once formulated and then unvarying for almost half a century, this deliberate laying-on of paint lent a dread sameness to his hundreds of paintings to which, ultimately, boredom was my reaction. Alone, a painting by Ginner can be exciting; in a company of two or three that excitement is enhanced and one begins to understand the man; but with twenty or thirty this response is hard to maintain and, with more, it ebbs away. Malcolm Easton, of Hull University, was first to wave a banner for him, but even he, privileged owner of Ginner's scrupulously kept notebooks, lost his enthusiasm for the proposed catalogue raisonné; he gave me copies of the notebooks and passed the task to me. There were, at first, enough of Ginner's old friends and acquaintances to interview to make the task seem interesting, but my enthusiasm waned when no publisher offered encouragement, and an introductory essay in a catalogue for the Fine Art Society in October 1985 is the only evidence of an enthusiasm that ran into the sand.

CHAPTER 3

Return to Kensington

By January 1968 the full year of unrelenting activity and travelling that I had inflicted on myself had exhausted me. The collapse was sudden, brought on, I later learned, by eating infected bratwurst in Aachen, where I had spent a melancholy day searching for the ghost of Charlemagne. It was meant to be a day of aesthetic and intellectual renewal before doing some work for Friedrich von Artus and, that done, driving on to Munich, where I was to deliver some drawings bought blind by a collector. On the autobahn, two hours or so south of Frankfurt, a mild sense of unease accelerated into the certainty that I was about to faint and should not be driving – that I should, indeed, stop at once. And so I did; I staggered to the shelter of trees above the snowy bank, wrapped my duffel coat close about me and lost consciousness. It was still light when I recovered and, feeling ghastly but no longer faint, I drove on to Munich, stopping at the first hotel encountered in its dreary outskirts, the Hotel Carmen, there to drowse for three days and nights, eating nothing, drinking only water. When, at last, I felt, if not well, less ill and fit enough to shave, I was puzzled to find the mirror strongly tinted yellow. There was another mirror in the dining room where I struggled to eat a little breakfast. It was not until, having delivered the drawings and driven on to the Alte Pinakotek that, again feeling faint, I went to the loo there to splash my face with water, and realised that it was not the mirrors of Munich that were yellow, but me. I was so jaundiced that my eyeballs looked like pickled onions. I have no idea how many days it took, but slowly I nursed the car back to London, making first for France where I knew it would be easier to find both overnight accommodation and roadside places where

I could rest flat on my back for a while to ease the dull but pressing pain.

I did indeed have jaundice – the comparatively mild form of hepatitis that is not sexual in origin but is pretty serious in its effect – and weeks later emerged from a dreary hospital in south London very shaken by the experience, not only cripplingly debilitated but aware of how insecure a solitary life can be. It was, I thought, time to renounce my hectic ways, but I did not, indeed could not, so heavily I felt the pressure to get out of debt. The hepatitis recurred and, my liver grossly enlarged and hardly functioning, there was a second long stint in hospital; for weeks on end I could not drive, could not carry heavy pictures, could not sit through auctions, indeed, could not even sit for any length of time so painful was my liver in any position other than prone with my arms by my sides. It was in many ways a wasted year, but even so, the little work I did enabled me both to repay Eliot on the very day two years since his £2,000 had propelled me into becoming an art dealer, and to accumulate enough of a stock of drawings for me to think of myself as the specialist I wished to be. I could afford to slow down; I could even afford to stop for a while.

It was at this point that Bill Martin came back into my life, Bill who had been my first boss at Christie's and, as the then head of the picture department (the most important for the firm), the prime target of Patrick Lindsay's enmity and envy. To put no fine point on it, Patrick thought him an 'ugly little toad' (his very words at a lunch of which the purpose was to make clear to me where my loyalty should lie), and was immediately instrumental in ousting him from the firm when stricken by a cerebral haemorrhage. Bill had then gone into partnership with Harry Sutch, an elderly dealer with a small gallery in Bury Street (in the same block as Christie's), and there they spent their days drinking sherry and closing for lunch, which meant that either they were asleep behind the drawn curtains or eating jellied eels in Overton's. They carried no stock other than the old master drawings that Bill put in the window when he was short of ready cash, and had no clients other than the few who relied on Harry to update their insurance valuations, but they enjoyed smoking and drinking all day with no one likely to disturb them. The only cloud over this vale of Lethe was that Harry wished to retire altogether, but the once long and very cheap lease was by then menacingly short and renewal would undoubtedly be more than Bill could afford unless the business became more energetic.

Bill proposed a partnership. My jaundiced brain suggested caution and after much doubt, prevarication and delay, I proposed a joint exhibition of drawings as a trial. Bill agreed and we fixed dates for it in the first half of May. Only then did I discover that over the past two years I had bought every drawing he possessed and he now had nothing to contribute. Our joint exercise was joint only in that he provided the premises and I the fifty-five drawings that could be accommodated. Nevertheless it worked well enough and I discovered the great usefulness of having an accessible foothold in St James's in which to do business, instead of a house in far away Barnes; and even if Bill's drinking and smoking were irksome, his presence gave me freedom to cover the salerooms and go about other aspects of my business. The exhibition brought clients new to both of us.

This slower pace suited my miserably slow recovery from jaundice, the loss of energy, the often overwhelming sense of fatigue, and six months passed before we again did anything active – a 'Christmas Exhibition' of English drawings and watercolours, almost all of them again mine. These were exhibitions only in the sense of revealing stock; with no common thread of origin or scholarship they were not didactic and to call them exhibitions was impertinent, but they were the custom of the day at all levels of the trade and they drew in the collectors. Bill and I agreed that ours had augured well and that we should enter into formal partnership. Harry, who to my great annoyance had been taking ten per cent of our profits, quietly withdrew, the names over the door were changed from Sutch and Martin to Martin and Sewell, and it was under that heading that in May 1970 we mounted another exhibition of drawings, all bought by me, that included seriously good examples that I was a fool to let go, for the market was showing the first signs of short supply and steepening prices. This I had predicted but had not expected so soon; there were, however, everywhere many more dealers in the field, more collectors too, and American museums had greatly increased their rate of acquisition.

Logistically it could be a very easy trade, for drawings, unlike paintings, need no frames and are not necessarily enhanced by them – many collectors keep them in solander boxes.* Rarely do they attract public interest enough to rouse demands to keep them as the nation's heritage, and any possible difficulty with export restrictions can be avoided by casually carrying them between the pages of a magazine. This is exactly how an American dealer, Stephen Spector, carried two important drawings by Watteau from London to New York. Very young, ignorant, insufferably brash, noisily queer, and rich with his middle-aged lover's money, Stephen declared himself a dealer in old master drawings by buying the best of what London's most eminent dealers had in stock, none more eminent than Wildenstein's, the source of the Watteaus at, he told me, £15,000 apiece, then a whopping price. I wondered how he could make a profit, but Stephen cultivated a market as influenced as himself by price, working on the assumption that the more punishing it was, the better the quality must be. His camouflage copy of *Vanity Fair* he carried nonchalantly onto the plane home to JFK and, tucked into the pocket of the seat ahead, forgot it. Passing through customs he was reminded that he might

---

* Shallow boxes of standard paper size for keeping safe maps, charts, drawings and pressed specimens, devised by Daniel Solander, a pupil of Linnaeus, who accompanied Joseph Banks and Captain Cook on their first exploration of the Pacific Ocean.

have something to declare, and there followed an episode of pure black comedy. The Watteaus were never seen again.

When travelling across Europe my disguise was as a working painter, the car crammed with palette, paints and apparently blank canvases, though of these a number were half-finished Alpine views that could be brought to the top on the return journey. Never once, at a time when no European border could be crossed without a fuss, did the ruse fail.

Bill and I, happy with our May exhibitions of 1969 and 1970, hoped that they might be an annual event, but in 1971 we could muster only half the number of drawings needed. Prices across the market were rising and we had far too little capital, all of which I supplied. Bill's only contribution to our still informal arrangements was the little left of the lease of the gallery. I had long since asked that this should be renewed, making its extension a condition of the partnership. Nothing was done – or so I thought – and only when I could contain my unease no longer did I learn from our joint solicitor that the landlords, at first sympathetically prepared to accommodate us with a new lease of twenty years for £20,000 (a bargain), had eventually cut matters short with a refusal to renew on any terms. For this Beatrice was responsible – Beatrice, Bill's ever-present mistress, his 'bringer of joy' if the name's Latin root is to be trusted; this stout, plain, bespectacled termagant had quibbled too aggressively with the landlords and all we had to show for it was the dying end of the existing lease, a year or so.

That this brought our uneven arrangement to an immediate end was perhaps for the best – there would never have been equal capital and equal work and Bill's old-fashioned responses to certain situations would never have been mine. He tended to judge unknown visitors to the gallery by their shoes; he had once been so appallingly abrupt to a young man in trainers that I had followed him onto the street to apologise, there to discover that not only was he seriously interested in drawings but, with an American newspaper magnate for a father, was well able to afford them. Bill also kow-towed to the great; when Edward Heath came in to inspect a pair of political cartoons by Henry Tonks, Bill gave him them – not 'I'll knock off ten percent,' not 'You can have them at cost price,' but 'We are happy and honoured to give them to you.' Happy and honoured, my foot. On the days when he was on his own Bill reverted to his old 'Out to lunch' routine and either snoozed behind the locked door or toddled on his own to Overton's, once running up such a whacking bill – £800 – that they sent a man round to sit in the gallery until he got the money; as Bill and Beatrice were away on holiday, it was I who had to pay. As for their affair, to this, if it suited them – as often it did – they gave sexual expression behind the drawn curtains of the gallery. Once, having lunched with Peter Langan, I took him and his wife, Susan, to see a Sickert in the gallery and found the curtains drawn but the door unlocked; inside was Bill, in shirtsleeves, braces down, his hair dishevelled, struggling to move the heavy 'picture chair' that unaccountably now stood, not in its customary corner, but in the middle of the room; not a chair, but a velvet-covered prop designed to support pictures when clients wished to engage in close contemplation, it had been used for a less aesthetic purpose. We caught a glimpse of Beatrice scuttling down the winding stair to the basement, leaving, widespread on the floor, her elasticated gripper-knickers. Peter, at once recognising these signs (for he too had a taste for cunnilingus), chuckled, said 'I might as well still look at the Sickert, now I've spoiled your fun', did so for about ten seconds, and then we left.

Without me poor Bill bumbled on with Beatrice for a while, but there was no business to support his cravings for tobacco, sherry, champagne and eels, and when he had not only to close the shop but leave his comfortable mansion flat in Westminster after falling asleep on a sofa with a lighted cigarette (a vigilant policeman saved his life), she deserted him for the husband she had never left. Bill then ended his days with his ancient mother in Roehampton, a house of very unhappy memories as a child, occasionally pleasured by a Soho prostitute and then, taking a taxi home, on the way calling on me for a sub to pay the fare. He once arrived without shoes and jacket; he had not had cash enough to pay the whore and she had packed him off without them to get the money and ensure his return.

I had to reorganise my life. I recognised first that I had not enjoyed, indeed disliked, being tied to premises that must be open five full days a week − impossible if I had neither partner nor employee. I knew too that in my way I was as tactless as Bill with visitors − I should not, in answer to 'How much is that?' have answered 'Oh that's far too good for you.' The enquirer was a manufacturer of shoes from Leicester who collected paintings of children; he had come to see a seriously good Victorian picture of children playing in a wood, the rare Henry Mark Anthony its painter, had spent almost an hour of my time talking about the paintings he already had, and then rejected mine on the grounds that the children were barefoot − a thing unacceptable to a man of his trade (I would now suspect him of being a paedophile with a shoe fetish); then, glancing at a seventeenth-century painting of a modest feast, he asked the question that elicited my inexcusable response. Many years later I saw the Mark Anthony in the window of a Duke Street dealer and was astonished to see that the children now wore shoes − but then this was a dealer who had earlier bought from me an important landscape by John Linnell of which the principal dramatic feature was a great dead oak, and in his restorer's hands the oak sprang into spring leaf. I had also begun to question my future as a dealer: I liked buying because I liked the disciplines of looking, questioning, arguing, researching and identifying, for these were close to the disciplines of the art historian and the curator, and above all I enjoyed discovering things of art historical interest, but though I was happy to sell at auction, I had no instinct for adding a margin of profit and selling face to face. When Kenny Thomson, now Lord Thomson of Fleet and then Chairman of Times Newspapers, offered me £800 for a still life by Jan Vonck for which I had paid £900 and was asking only £1,100, I refused it with 'And shall I pay fourpence for your sixpenny *Times* tomorrow?' – another potential client lost. The third problem, working from a house in remote Barnes, was, however, easy to resolve – I exchanged it for one in middle Kensington that I had known since my toddling childhood.

Number 19 Eldon Road had an intriguing history. The first house of an intended terrace speculatively constructed in the 1840s on the southern edge of what was then the kitchen garden of Kensington Palace, it had been much extended in 1929 to accommodate Chester Beatty and his growing collection of Impressionist paintings, of which more than eighty were bequeathed to the National Gallery of Dublin. In spite of covering the entire garden with a lofty and very grand studio, his rate of acquisition exceeded the rate of expansion and neither he nor his pictures moved into it or any other part of the house which, despite its very good and pretty fireplaces, remained a typical London terrace house with two decent rooms on each floor and tiny rooms for servants in the attic, windows onto the staircase landings here and there making it light and airy; the roof of the studio was paved with York stone, and ivy, honeysuckle and wistaria clambered about high fences that offered considerable privacy. Beatty moved into a suitably larger house in Belgravia and, unable to sell Eldon Road in the great slump of the Thirties, lent it to his peripatetic, penniless and irascible friend, the painter C.R.W. Nevinson, for whom it was a reliable address until his death in 1946. Beatty then sold it to Arpad Elfer, an Hungarian photographer with (at least among my new neighbours) a reputation for soft pornography.

The studio was perfect for housing books and paintings (even for painting pictures myself – as I occasionally did in idle moments), and, exceeded in size only by Agnew's vast first-floor gallery, was a wonderful exhibition space for a private dealer; unlike Barnes, it was only a short taxi ride from central London. Working from it I would need no business partnership and be completely independent, and no dealer or collector from abroad could complain (as they did of Barnes) that it was too far from his hotel. The main house offered the additional advantage of splitting easily into two halves so that I could comfortably accommodate my mother and, in her doctor's parlance, 'keep an eye on her'. This was a terrible mistake far worse than leaving Christie's or the partnership with Bill. As old as the century, she played the game of being physically too frail to remain alone in her house in Castle Hedingham and I was weary of the need to go there, cut grass, prune roses, lop trees and fill the refrigerator; it would be altogether easier, we persuaded ourselves, if we lived independently in the same house – but there is no such thing as a bachelor's independence from his mother, for inexorably the relationship reverses and the ageing mother becomes his child without, however, relinquishing anything of her original authority.

Of my mad life after leaving Christie's and the failure of my venture with Bill, Anthony Blunt had been a constant observer, amused, benign and ever helpful, prompting friends and public art galleries over which he had some influence to buy drawings from me. Seeing that my career (for want of a better word) was again tottering, he first persuaded Toronto University again to offer me a teaching post – 'You don't have to ask for it, you have only to say yes.' But fifteen years on from the first offer and for all the old misgivings, yes I could not say; so late, I could neither leave my mother nor carry her there as baggage. Then he suggested to Jacob Rothschild (with whom his role was distinctly avuncular) who had just bought Colnaghi's, the only art dealers in London of never questioned respectability, that I had experience enough to run the firm for him. We met over drinks in Anthony's flat in the attic of the Courtauld Institute. When asked by Jacob how I would change things at Colnaghi's, I answered that I might change nothing, that James Byam Shaw (1903–92), its retiring head, was universally recognised as an honest scholar at least as much as an honest dealer, and that in buying the firm Jacob had bought that most precious of commodities, a long unblemished reputation, difficult to achieve, arduous to maintain, impossible to restore once sullied. Thus I dowsed any interest he had in me. I was not given the job; instead, there was a good deal of shifting and shunting among the bright young men of Christie's and Sotheby's, and for a day or two my former assistant, Noël Annesley, seemed to have been appointed, but in the event remained at Christie's. Slowly, in the hands of the unqualified and inexperienced young coxcombs whom Jacob eventually chose, Colnaghi's reputation faded away, and the great name became, as it is now, nothing more than the identification of premises in Bond Street.

Doors had opened and I, always my own worst enemy, had closed them. I reconciled myself to life as a solitary dealer and bought a bicycle. 'Oh,' said Renée Fedden, my new neighbour, wife of Robin Fedden who had years earlier offered me a job with the National Trust, 'a bicycle' — as though it were the most extraordinary thing in Kensington; and then she followed it with, 'We're off to Leningrad.'

*   *   *

Almost to the day it took two years to settle into Eldon Road, so much had to be done to the house to accommodate my mother, the contents of her house and of my own, and not quite all my books – for some of these, mostly from my schoolboy years, I shed; what extraordinary pleasure there has since been in finding other copies in old bookshops, even as far afield as Dresden and Oslo, and replacing them, for as sure as eggs is eggs, once a man has had a book he will again return to it, even after decades. I read Kinglake's *Eöthen* when I was twelve at the command of an enlightened schoolmaster; returning from my first journey to Turkey more than thirty years later, it was the first book I sought on my shelves – and then I remembered that I'd sold it for tuppence in a tea-chest with a hundred others.

I was right to buy the house, but in error to install my mother in it. She had, to some extent, moved into the house in Barnes, but half-heartedly, still clinging to her own house in Castle Hedingham; but this, with the return to Kensington, which we both thought of as our native village (as it certainly was in my case), she sold, and our coming together became irrevocable. She at once sought to tame my freedom. She watched, and recorded what she saw. She must have responded to every creak of the heavy iron gate, every click of the front door lock when turned by the key, every greeting of a joyful dog, and may well have hung for hours over the bannisters to catch a glimpse of my nocturnal visitors – 'Past midnight and another man brought to the house – where will it all end?' a typical wail in her diary.

Until I began to write about my life and turned to her diaries to supplement my own, I had no idea how vigilant she had been, how disapproving, commenting on every friend who came to stay and almost every casual bed-mate I brought back. Occasionally she attempted to make trouble – 'You're not the only one,' she said to a Danish friend, a museum curator, not a bed-mate. 'He's got a little Scottish boy, you ought to know.' The Scot, a six-footer and far from a boy, was another professional visitor.

Gloucester Road, nearby, had nothing of the sense of danger that so heightened the experience of sodomy on the Thames towpath, but it was a very happy hunting-ground for bodies, many of them American servicemen in a local hostel, in transit or on leave. Susie, one of my dogs, half-Hungarian pointer, brown coat, brown nose, brown toe-nails, offered them their opening – 'Taking your dog for a walk?' Why else would a man be out with his dog in the hour approaching midnight? But one night, without Susie, walking home from the High Street Underground, I was propositioned by an English bloke in his mid thirties or so, rather too old for me, but tall, very well put together, and with the animal magnetism that is occasionally immediately obvious in a man. 'Yours or mine?' was his presumptuous opening line. 'Mine,' I said, 'It's near.' His response – 'Mine's nearer, it's in Church Street' – clinched it. Crossing the road, within a hundred yards, with a nod to the guards and to my dismay, we entered the Barracks (demolished 1987). My companion was a sergeant in the Royal Military Police there. He took me to the room he shared with another sergeant, already a-bed, and without much in the way of introduction, fucked me; there was no alternative. Finished, but holding me down, he woke his mate with 'Do you want to take over? I've got to piss,' and off to piss he went, once his mate was comfortably ensconced. And so they changed and changed about until near four in the morning when, sated, my sergeant dressed to take me, I thought to the gate, but instead it was to the Mess where other sergeants were still drinking and, holding me by the ear, as it were, he offered me with 'Anyone want him before I let him go? – he's a bloody good fuck.'

Every man who risks a sexual encounter with another must expect, occasionally, to find the roles determined by the physically stronger. I felt not the least humiliated – the very reverse, released of inhibitions indeed, exhilarated by the pornography of an experience to which, once begun, I had abandoned myself, and that had been a match, not only for any of the experiences of officer cadets recorded by young Simon Raven,* but for the fantasies of porno magazines and films that I had seen in New York. My grudging willingness lent pleasure to what, long before and unwilling, had happened to me as a National Serviceman. Is it unreasonable to assume that these pleasures were perhaps nightly pursued, not only in this small barracks, but in others, and that to the vaunted heterosexuality of the armed forces there a constant homosexual undercurrent?

It is, perhaps, to many a mystery beyond understanding that sodomy can offer pleasure to the sodomised, but to some - by no means all – it does. 'You haven't lived ,' said Edward Montagu to Petter Kolrud during lunch at Beaulieu some summers ago, 'until you've been fucked up the arse.' He was being mischievous and wished, I think, to move the conversation on from poetry and

---

* Simon Raven: *Sound the Retreat*, 1971.

ballet, the preoccupations of two other guests, and Petter, every inch the brawny Nordic blond, was sitting next to him, munching away in silence. It was a sudden leap, the consequences quite uncertain, but Petter took the assertion in his stride and it was I who spluttered with surprise, amusement and anxiety. Petter is a skiing friend, a tennis friend, a clambering and climbing friend, twice married, a father, whose only flaw in our enthusiastic days of fierce activity was the frequency with which he attempted to telephone home for a sentimental chat when we were in places far away and international communications were fragmentary and unpredictable – I, when travelling, have always had the cold capability to leave my home behind. Petter, an analyst aware of all the sexual aberrations to which men are subject, said only, 'Yes, of course,' and went on munching and conversation remained in the control of the poet and the dancer, unaware of the interruption. The assertion was, nevertheless, worthy of debate – though perhaps not over lunch – for it is to some extent true that anal coition with a man (but not a woman) can involve, for the recipient, sexual stimulation and climax so intense that it is addictive – Lawrence of Arabia gave an honest and oddly innocent account of it in *The Seven Pillars of Wisdom*. Now, of course, this anal stimulation is no longer exclusive to the homosexual – heterosexual men are now aware of it and turn to female prostitutes for 'fisting'.

In the summer of my fortieth birthday I juggled three more or less steady lovers – an Indian student at the London College of Fashion who became tedious and irascible when drunk (too frequently), a young American art historian who was to desert me for John Pope-Hennessy (far more influential), and Angel, a Spanish waiter of such erotic allure that I had to share him with a dozen others; to these comparatively gentler souls my Military Policemen lent fierce variety. There was another soldier, a Horse Guard, equally determined, and he, capable of conversation even if mostly about the notes with condoms that tourists tucked into his boots and the chocolate bars that melted into his socks, lasted several months, as did a footman from Buckingham Palace, but most encounters were of the moment only, and that is how most wished them to be – an extended, more thrilling and often wonderfully enriched form of masturbation, with the huge advantage over the heterosexual fuck in that it had no consequences, no obligations.

These encounters, wholly consensual, were no longer illegal if both parties were twenty-one – that much, and only that much, had been achieved by the long fought for Sexual Offences Act of 1967. As the armed forces were excluded from this new freedom and it applied only to two men in private, my Military Policemen broke the law on both counts, and so too did the Lotharios of the Putney towpath, but this judgement of Portia, this pound of flesh but not a drop of blood, was better than nothing and something of a defeat for the Gwyneth Dunwoodys of this world. Mrs Dunwoody, a Member of Parliament of ancient Labour caste and childbearing hips, contributed to the debate both within and beyond the House in such flogging and castration terms that even I, who had no wish to suffer again from being labelled queer, wrote to her in protest. In the consequent correspondence she was so crudely unrepentant that I felt I had to do something: I joined the Campaign for Homosexual Equality (CHE). This I found to have its headquarters in Manchester (then, and still, another country), and to be run by the kind of men who are always dubbed 'old women'; a pro-London coup engineered by a handful of members of whom I was one, more or less succeeded in achieving independence, but then it too succumbed to what we unkindly called 'the couch parties' – the uncomely middle-aged and middle-sexed, turgid of mind and body, who wanted every word of every meeting addressed to the chair, and who could never reach agreement without setting up a working party. I and the other revolutionaries left and CHE eventually died of self-inflicted suffocation.

CHAPTER 4

Salvador Dali in Cadaques

It was to recurrent attacks of jaundice that I owe a brief, extraordinary and enriching friendship that ended as suddenly as it began. Although the type of the virus was identified as mild and fairly harmless, further bouts of jaundice were, for well over a decade, triggered by butter, oily fish, all forms of animal fat and alcohol, and sometimes, I thought, by anxiety and overwork. For a while, bread and salt were all that I could eat without reaction, and bouts of exhaustion unpredictably interrupted work. After several incomplete recoveries, and with Bill Martin able to hold the fort for a while, in September I left, exhausted, with three acquaintances rather than friends, for the south of France, the unfashionable coast of Hérault and Aude. It was an impulse prompted by gossip at a dinner party, four near strangers feeling sorry for themselves for having had no time to plan holidays with more familiar companions – and one of us had seen advertised in that day's *Times* a flat for four near a *plage* between Montpellier and Perpignan.

We booked it for two weeks but stayed one night. It was filthy, and so too was the featureless, bleak and shadeless *plage*. Cutting our losses we drove into Spain in search of a more friendly place in which to take an autumn holiday, to swim, eat, read and do nothing. We were bound further south, but the signpost to Cadaques triggered some more than half-forgotten memory and without another thought I turned the car onto the winding track that led down towards the sea. In the Sixties it was just that kind of Catalan coastal village – no crowds, no fashionable shops, no smart hotels, and one family restaurant for peasant and plutocrat alike, serviced by and serving the local fishermen. The cactuses in every garden were heavy with their prickly fruit, but within their armament of spines – the very devil to extract from fingertips and lips – lay flesh irresistibly sweet and succulent, free to anyone brave enough to pick them. Sand edged the deep bay, wild rocks enclosed it, and some welcoming spirit whispered, 'This is it.'

Simple rooms were to be had in the dilapidated Villa Tortuga and within hours I had been adopted by two beach dogs, Scipio and Hannibal; it was they who got me from my bed each morning, and with them at my heels I walked the length of what passed for the main street to the butcher's shop. Every day he found something unspeakable for the dogs, and the three of us then returned to the restaurant where, while drinking coffee, I fed them bloody morsels sliced with the knife that has travelled everywhere with me since National Service. And that is how I encountered Salvador Dali.

On that particular morning the butcher gave me the windpipe and lungs of a sheep, complete, intact and very bloody – and there it was, bloodying the wooden café table and my hands, the dogs slavering at my knees as I sliced it for them. I was scarcely conscious of the great green pre-war Cadillac as it whispered to a stop, car nerd though I am, and took no notice of the two people who'd got out of it, a tiny woman and a much taller man, both dressed from top to toe in velvet of a dark green to match the car. They sat in the sun a little way away and watched. Then the man came over. 'Do you know who I am?' he asked, his attitude imperious. 'Of course. You're Dali,' I replied – and to this day I do not know whether he was flattered that I knew, or disappointed that he had been denied another opportunity to announce to all in earshot, 'I am Dali.' 'And you've been waiting for me' – half question, half accusation. He seemed surprised when I said that I had not. To me, but not apparently to him, it was a preposterous notion that anyone would lie in wait for him with the dogs, the blood, the knife, the windpipe and the lungs as an elaborate ruse to draw him into conversation, but that is indeed what he supposed.

The encounter ended with an invitation to his house that

evening, but when I asked for the address I was given no more than a wave to the north-east. Then I recalled why it was that Cadaques was in some unknown sense familiar – in my work at Christie's, the best part of a decade earlier, I had damned a painting signed *Dali* as a fake and had, after a very long delay, received a note agreeing from his secretary in Cadaques.

Cadaques was not the place of Dali's birth – that was Figueras, twenty miles inland – but it was the spiritual and instinctive home to which he returned every summer, but for those of his absence in America, as driven there as the swallows and the swifts. As a boy the village and the wild coast flanking it were imprinted on his visual imagination, nourishing it with light and colour, form and fantasy. It faces east, the easternmost point of Spain, a place of thrilling dawns, and in the evening, looking out across the perfect symmetry of the deep bay, the compensation for never seeing the sun set behind the shoulders of the hills that shelter Cadaques from the west, is the eerie and compelling tranquillity of the skies so high and distances so gold and blue that are caught forever in so many of his paintings.

If Cadaques offered Dali the serenity of perfect natural balance, Cape Creus gave him the chaos of rocks once molten and erupting, stilled in their dying energy for the past billion years, eroded by the elements into age-old forms so animal, so human, so monstrous and so hallucinatory, that they engendered in him and embodied for him fantasies beyond our comprehension.

And it was at Port Lligat – no port, but a poor place of half-a-dozen fishermen's cottages tumbled together – that Dali put down his roots when, at twenty-five, with cash from his first commission, he bought one of these shacks. Piecemeal he bought the others, and piecemeal they grew into a single house, an organic thing leaning into the low cliff behind, a labyrinth of corridors and stairs, of rooms and spaces that lost their functions and became the repositories of would-be Surrealist objects, most of which remained obdurately kitsch. The moment the door opens, the twists and turns within the house mirror the erratic complexitiies of Dali's mind, the unexpected intuition, the fortuitous banality, the paradox of high intelligence and quite appalling taste.

These, not Figueras, were the real places of his birth, the womb from which he sprang, the womb to which he consistently returned. Here, if the exhibitionism did not quite go into abeyance, he was prepared to see the truth about himself, and occasionally to speak of it. Long after he had ceased to be a practising Catholic, Cadaques was his confessional.

A servant opened the door. The house was like a Schwitters *Merzhaus* leaning into the cliffside, climbing, a few stairs here, a wayward passage there, with glimpses into rooms and, through windows, repeated views of another, more complex, bay, more a long inlet of the sea, subtly changed as we gained height. As we emerged onto the roof, less a terrace than the clifftop, Dali seemed to be lurking in wait and not at ease; he mispronounced my Christian name – Brrreon – the *r* absurdly rolled. 'What shall I call you?' I asked, thinking Salvador impertinent and Dali even worse.

'What would you like to call me?'

'Majesty,' I suggested with a questioning lift to the last syllable. And Majesty it occasionally was, wryly, when he had been particularly lofty or absurd.

He ushered me to a giant eggshell, broken open as though boiled for breakfast, indicated that I should duck through a low hatch and sit inside. Of these there were three; Gala was already installed in one, Dali ducked into the third, and there we sat, at such a distance as to make conversation difficult; from mine in the middle I had to lob prattle over the jagged serrations of white cement at either Gala or Dali, knowing that the other could not hear it. Gala never responded; at that stage I did not know that she was deaf and thus thought her staring straight ahead, never uttering a word, a stratagem to make me go. Never have I been more uncomfortable.

Dali at last said, 'Let me show you my Christ.' Scrambling out of our respective eggs we set off, not back into the house to see a painting – as I expected – but away from it, past garden ornaments so kitsch that not even the nouveaux riches of Billericay would have bought them, and into an arid olive grove, to discover a gigantic figure lying on its back, arms outstretched as though crucified, its ribcage an old fisherman's boat, its curling pain-wracked fingers hacked from car tyres, its long limbs heaped earth and rubble, broken bricks and tiles, with fragments of glazed drainpipes that were, disconcertingly, the colour and texture of old medical prostheses.

I had not worked for Christie's for a decade without learning the ambiguous words of astonishment that to the gullible easily pass for praise. I uttered them, thinking myself a hypocrite, a shit.

This *Debris Christ* is perhaps Dali's least regarded work. It was fully finished in the autumn of 1968, but most authorities put it in 1969. In its use of materials it anticipated Italian Arte Povera by a full decade and Joseph Beuys by rather less, and I must argue that as Dali had made it in a mood of high seriousness and regarded his making it as an unconscious and ecstatic act, we should take it more seriously, not, as he thought it, as a work of ultimate Surrealism.

'Let me photograph you with my Christ,' said Dali.

'Yes, of course,' said I.

'There in the left armpit.' I obeyed. 'No, no, not standing; curled up as though asleep.'

Wearing my only decent trousers, I demurred.

'Take them off. Be naked. It will make a better photograph.'

And 'What the hell,' I thought, a little drunk, bemused and, I admit, awed.

'Lie down,' he ordered, and lie down I did, with grit and rubble biting into my skin as, responding to more commands, I turned this way and that in foetal positions and listened to the clicking camera.

'Now masturbate' (again the excessive rolling of the *r*) – and

'What the hell,' I thought again, but did, wondering where all this might lead.

Starting from scratch and in so un-erotic a situation, this took some time, Dali all the while clicking the camera and fumbling in his trousers.

When I'd done, I had to brush the grit from my skin, grimly thinking that masturbation can be remarkably unrewarding and mechanical. We went straight back to Gala, who was still sitting in her egg.

Dinner, an hour or two later, was in the village restaurant where we had met that morning, not in the house – and, indeed, I cannot recall ever eating in the house, or ever seeing the kitchen used for anything more than making coffee and producing ice cubes – both kitchen and dining room were, like most other rooms in Port Lligat, no more than theatre sets in which Gala and Dali put on their show.

In the restaurant they were treated as something between old and expected friends and feudal nobility; food and drink were brought, we consumed them, and then left. Neither Gala nor Dali asked for a bill and no payment was offered – they arrived and left as though food was their due. Next morning, there again for coffee and the dogs' breakfast, I asked if I might pay for what we had had, and was refused with the explanation that bills were totted up for a while and then paid by Dali's secretary. Perhaps this was the case in Paris and New York too, for not once did I see either of them pay for anything.

I was mightily pleased with myself when at last I went to my bed, for Gala, who had warmed a little over dinner, had asked me to come again the following day. But lying on the sand with Scipio and Hannibal, what did I see in the distance but the great green Cadillac sweeping into town and Dali gathering the hippy flotsam of the night – it was the weekend and there was plenty of it. I went to the house, as asked, and so did twenty others, and when most of the boys were taken off to see the *Debris Christ*, I stayed with Gala.

They were away far longer than I had been and the terrace was in darkness when they returned in dribs and drabs. Which of them, I wondered, had been in which armpit, which had masturbated for him, and which, perhaps, had done for Dali what Florentine boys had done for the last real Medici, and buggered each other for his delight?

If there was ever film in his camera – which now I doubt, for I think it was a camouflage for a voyeur who, though brazenly addicted to the habit, was still, at his age, both embarrassed by residual shame and unwilling to admit to homosexuality – then in his archive there must be thousands of photographs of unidentifiable young men in much the same situation as he put me.

I realised then that Dali, for all the fawning interest of strangers, was alone and could not bear his loneliness – Gala, his anchor in Cadaques since 1930, was not enough. Used as a child to the indulgent approbation of his family, as a young man to the profound affection, even lust, of Lorca, as a precocious Surrealist to the envy and curiosity of the older founders of the movement, and used above all, as a celebrity painter, to the patronage and adulation of the rich, powerful and equally celebrated, he could not, in his dotage, live without a daily dose of hero-worship – and if it did not come, then he was quite prepared to go out onto the streets to get it. Again and again I heard him go through the 'Do you know who I am?' routine and, whatever the answer, invite strangers to the house.

Dali at the end of the Sixties was perhaps not quite six feet in height; at sixty-four he had begun to stoop a little and, conscious of it, had the habit of often straightening his spine, squaring his shoulders and puffing out his chest. His hair was thinning, receding and, I think dyed, for there was no hint of grey or white; it was by no means fastidiously clean. His face had sagged enough to blur the once emphatic line of his chin, and only the moustache with its ridiculous waxed spikes remained as vigorous as in his prime. The moustache was, I think, important as some sort of delusory monument to an equally delusory virility. He could still widen his eyes to show a startling white all round their irises.

His breath was always foul, sometimes so foul that I wished he farted more and breathed much less – not that I ever heard him fart, but the subject fascinated him and he *claimed* to fart a lot, his farts as sweet as the perfumes of Arabia. He knew his breath was foul and claimed that it was foul enough to keep flies from perching on the wings of his moustache; when one once did it was made immortal in a photograph.

Dali spoke English with perfect ease, often with a dramatic sense of interval and emphasis, but sometimes, in public, he spoke very slowly and affected a heavy Spanish accent, elaborating diphthongs into syllables. In spite of eight continuous years in the United States, his Americanisms were few – but then he rarely spoke of anything that had happened there and seemed to have blanked out what had quite certainly been his most flamboyant and commercially successful period.

Dali must have had a dozen velvet suits in his favoured green, for he was always immaculate when out early in the day, the velvet never crushed or crumpled, the jacket never greasy round the neck, the trousers never discoloured by the urine dribble of the elderly man in boxer shorts. I wish he had been as fastidious with food, but he ate greedily, shovelling as though he had only seconds to empty his plate into his mouth, and this strain on his digestion may well have been the cause of his mephitic breath. He was one of only two men I have known capable of sputtering, not only on himself with a napkin tucked below his chin, but over every neighbour at a table for four with napkins on their laps. The other man was Bernard Crick, founder of the Orwell Prize for political journalism, who, on the occasion of awarding it to me, ruined a favourite tie in plain green silk, bought because it perfectly matched (or so I thought) the green of Dali's velvet. I now know never to wear a plain tie to lunch or dinner – only one that is heavily patterned can survive a gravy stain. At Port Lligat, not putting on the style (or rather, putting on another – that of the rich and ancient hippy), the velvet suits were never seen late in the day; then he took to jackets that were either marginally ethnic or operatic military, with cotton trousers and immaculate white shirts of loose Byronic elegance, and went barefoot or wore the classic sandals of the ancient Greek.

There was not much to do in Cadaques forty-odd years ago. In the village there was no exploitation of Dali's nearby presence – no museum, no kitsch souvenirs at which to giggle. Nor was there much to do at Port Lligat, for the phallic swimming pool had not been dug and many of the kitsch features of the garden had not been installed. Gala still swam just below the house and sunbathed on the terrace, but Dali did neither. Fully clothed he sat in the sun like an old lizard. Nor did he paint. Others claim to have seen him painting in these lean years, but I did not. It was as though his mind had emptied.

We occasionally walked a little on the beach, but his steps were the sandal-dragging slither of an aged Japanese. He must once have been lithe and careless enough to clamber those uncomfortable rocks with ease, but not in my day. The beach, however, had an astonishing effect on him – as though he had never been on it before; I was at first dismayed by this Alzheimer effect but I think now that he was overwhelmed by so dense a palimpsest of memories that he could not speak. Any other man would have given me a time and place to childhood recollections, and have said that here he saw a woman empty her bladder, that there Lorca had first buggered him, and on that rock Gala in his arms had talked of death, but Dali kept these things to himself.

I once suggested drawing a bead on the house and walking back in a straight line – perhaps a kilometre – instead of following a track. Taking no account of his flimsy sandals, off we set, but however much he thought that he belonged to that wild land-scape, he knew nothing of it and was helpless among the thorny shrubs that tore at his trousers. Like a child, he had a tantrum and we returned to the track, he in a furious sulk and me in disgrace.

Salvador Dali in Cadaques

The swimming pool was a calculated attempt to extend the social life denied him in Cadaques. The more serious of his friends in his early years had seen the point of being there with him – but that was long ago and his coterie in the late Sixties were neither serious nor sincere, and few of them were prepared to be his courtiers anywhere but in Paris or New York. But it was naive of him to think that a pool in the shape of an erect penis would make Cadaques another Babylon. It seemed to me a kind of madness when the sea was within spitting distance of the terrace – though it was sometimes clogged with weed – and the village had long since outgrown its natural water supply and ran dry when the water tanker that steamed into the bay every few days was delayed – but Dali was nothing if not utterly selfish. I did not see it finished, but the Hollywood embellishment of the garden with hideous objects had begun in my time, and they all made the point that not even Dali could make an actuality of Surrealism, that this genre of fantasy wore very thin very quickly unless, filtered through his hand and eye, his wit and imagination – all of which he still had in abundance – they were translated into a painting.

Dali had read the works of Freud long before meeting him, but when that meeting at last took place in London in 1938, he was obsessed by the skull of the old and ailing analyst; he likened it to the shell of a snail, to be winkled out with a needle. But he had already winkled out as much as he needed; thus the inspiration of his Surrealism became the active process of cultivating fantasy and grafting it onto reality. Dali proclaimed that his art grew from hallucinatory energy, and that he must paint like a madman, documenting the functions of his subconscious mind and, again using his own words, 'completely discredit the world of reality'.

Through the obsessive contemplation of objects it was possible for him to enter another plane. By painting them the subconscious was liberated and the object freed from conventional associations – and at that point it became possible to introduce distortion, decomposition and putrefaction, and take the object so far from its original state and meaning that it must mean something new. This is where shock and horror may disturb the viewer, but if he is to share anything of Dali's private eye, he must engage in Dali's experience of obsession and transmutation. This is visionary experience, fantasy imposed on the world of natural appearances, psychological derangement, sexuality and metamorphosis, all in an infinite space recognisable from our own dreams and from Dali's 'hand-made photographs' of Cadaques. Everything that Freud knew, Dali knew better – and from his own experience.

Perhaps the most important thing that Dali did – apart from becoming the supreme Surrealist – was to confront the taboo that made masturbation quite unmentionable; but the polite society that was the art world in Britain and America seemed not to notice. In 1929, to call a painting *The Great Masturbator* was to provoke outrage – but outrage came there none, probably because so few who saw the picture, if any, understood the imagery and could not discern in its complexities any action resembling self-abuse, as was then the euphemism for it.

Self-abuse was widely recognised as 'impure'; psychiatrists advised anxious parents to tie their sons' hands to their bedsteads, or fit the strange preventative contraptions that could be bought in shops that sold rupture trusses, artificial limbs and condoms. It was a practice that could devastate the mind and debilitate the body; the boy who masturbated would go blind, become so enfeebled that he might not reach adulthood, and almost certainly not have children if he did; he must 'save' himself, all adults (who, lying, had abused themselves without these consequences) said, for the night following his marriage.

Dali would have none of this, but the picture was too obscure to become the great masturbator's manifesto, polite society ignored its implications, and the impolite society of the Surrealists, who knew all about fellatio and sodomy (Gala, they discovered, could not, because of some deformity, be fucked and buggered simultaneously), took masturbation in their stride. Had Dali been a member of the

New English Art Club or the Royal Academy in 1929, he'd have been drummed out of their premises with hypocritical bellows of disgust.

Did Gala and Dali ever have the straightforward sex life of a married couple? I doubt it. When they met in 1929 he, in hetero-sexual terms, was still a virgin, terrified of the vagina, disgusted by menstrual blood; she, on the other hand, was the sexually voracious wife of Paul Éluard from whom no orifice was safe; he found her 'the most intense incarnation of love, desire, and erotic pleasure', but was content to share her with other men to heighten the experience. Éluard was a French poet who, with André Breton, led the Surrealists in Paris.

What could Gala see in timorous Dali, at twenty-four a decade younger than herself and manifestly uncertain of his sexuality? Was she remarkably more prescient than all the Surrealists put together in recognising Dali's oncoming superiority? Can she really have thought in 1929 that he would make her rich beyond her greed and avarice? Can she really have gambled on his celebrity becoming the flame to which myriad moths might be attracted so that she could take her pick? That was certainly what happened and went on happening, and there must have been hundreds of young men who briefly bedded Gala and masturbated for Dali, thousands even, wondering which they might please more and from whom they might milk something of a fortune, only to find themselves milked for a day or two, then to be utterly discarded – but for Gala it was a hell of a gamble.

Some young men lasted longer. Gala had infatuations that cost tens of thousands of dollars to initiate and maintain, and if Dali never suffered the same hopeless sexual passions, there was always a legion of freaks and misfits that cost fortunes to amuse, the hunchback, the dwarf, the identical twin, those who surgically changed sex when this was rare and strange, the boyish girl and the effeminate boy. Had he discovered the ladyboys of south-east Asia he might well have been in his element, for to him the ideal body and the ideal state were those of the hermaphrodite, able in every way possible to be simultaneously hetero and homosexual. It was a fantasy: I asked him if he had ever encountered an hermaphrodite and he had not.

There is every indication that he disliked, even feared, the genitals of women and harboured some primeval distaste for menstrual bleeding. Excrement, however, fascinated him. He examined his stools for form and consistency and admitted to a profound sense of loss when flushing them away. This interest was, perhaps, the one lasting stimulus to his imagination engendered by his hated father, for this feared monster of a man had once returned home far later than expected, unashamedly announcing as he dismounted from the taxi, that he had crapped in his trousers; Dali, ten or twelve at the time, felt humiliated and ashamed, claiming later that this had been the turning point in his relationship with his father. Faeces became so much an open obsession that by the time Dali reached Paris a decade or so later, the established Surrealists suspected him of eating shit. 'Are you a coprophage?' they quizzed him, compelling Gala to ask the question; he was not, but in asking, the Surrealists succeeded in expanding Dali's deep-rooted but naive preoccupation with the business of his bowels into more sophisticated fields.

Dali was, however, fastidious to the point of squeamishness. Not for one moment would he have *touched* a stool, let alone eaten it. I doubt if he even touched semen, another product of his body and therefore a subject of fascination; and I know that he would not touch blood, though he could watch it flow with pleasure from a wounded bull at bullfights, the perfect combination of blood and homoerotic beauty.

I once saw Dali paralysed by the sight of blood. We were wandering on the deserted shore to the north-east of the house when a boy emerged from the sea – Dali's slim-hipped, brown-skinned ideal, twenty or so – and if that were not enough, he was bleeding heavily from one foot, staining the sea. The cut was deep across the sole, the pumping loss of blood considerable but almost stemmed if I held the foot firmly in both hands. It was then that I saw Dali utterly still, just staring. Staring was the one thing that he did more intently even than masturbation – and often they were the same thing, for he claimed that he could ejaculate merely by looking (that is when he wasn't claiming to be impotent).

'Bloody man's coming in his trousers again,' I thought, and shouted at him. This was not an occasion for addressing him as Majesty. Breaking into his trance took every word of abuse that I could muster, every obscenity, and at last I could offer him the choice of holding the foot and getting blood on his fine linen trousers, or running for help; he chose to trot off with a little more urgency than his customary shuffle. I have seen men paralysed with fright, but never before or since have I seen a man rendered insensible by sheer aesthetic pleasure; any normal homosexual would have taken hold of the bleeding foot and let me, much younger and much fitter, run for help.

By the time I knew him he claimed almost daily to be impotent and yet there was the almost daily fumbling in his trousers by his *Debris Christ*, and the not infrequent invitation to young women to withdraw into some other part of the garden and watch him masturbate. He preferred to watch men and be watched by women, and in 1929, in Paris, wild with excitement at having been embraced by the Surrealists, he wrote a vivid account of watching himself masturbate in the mirror of his hotel bedroom. It is something that most boys have done by the time they are fifteen, but immature Dali left it till he was twenty-five – a 'rhythmic and solitary sacrifice' that he prolonged for fifteen minutes before 'wrenching out the ultimate pleasure with all the animal force of my clenched hand'. Forty years later, impotent or not, the sperm and blood of other men still excited him as much as the abattoirs and butcher's shops that had by then been the sources of so much luscious imagery, of severed heads and viscera, of flies and putrefaction. His first interest in me had sprung, I was often to remind myself, from the lungs and windpipe of a sheep.

Dali was fascinated by the *idea* of sodomy. He knew how it was done, and believed that a harder erection was required, but never in any active sense had he been a partner in it. His penis was small, and cruelly mocked for it at school, he was embarrassed by it as an adult; he was, moreover, subject all his life to premature ejaculation. As is so often the case, the child Dali was father to the man in that at his first school he developed an affectionate obsession with the buttocks of another boy compacted into 'pants that were excruciatingly tight . . . an invincible curiosity compelled me to look at these tight pants each time a violent movement threatened to split them open'.

As the recipient, he had found sodomy impossible, he claimed. His friend in early manhood, the poet and playwright Federico Garcia Lorca, Dali's 'twin soul', dazzling physically and intellectually and probably his only true friend in a long lifetime, attempted it in 1925. Openly homosexual and unembarrassed by the taboo that in Spain in the 1920s made this virtually unmentionable, Lorca tried twice to bugger Dali, and failed – or so, for years, Dali maintained, asserting that he himself was not and had never been homosexual, and, significantly, that the attempts hurt. Forty years on, and less guarded about it in the more relaxed atmosphere of the late Sixties, when Spain was notorious for the willingness of men to be casually homosexual, he felt able to admit that pain rather than absence of desire had been the deterrent. If it hurt, then Lorca had at the very least begun to penetrate him, and Dali had permitted it.

Lorca left only one observation on the matter: when in 1930 he heard that Dali had found in Gala a woman with whom to spend the rest of his life, he exclaimed, 'It's impossible – he can only get an erection when a man has stuck a finger up his arse.'

I observed that as some arseholes are tight enough to make emptying the bowels almost impossible, proper medical remedies had been devised, and the following year took him the very instrument, gift-wrapped as it were, from John Bell and Croyden in Wigmore Street. But I was forty years too late with this formidable piece of polished steel machinery; Dali chuckled over it and then showed me a drawer full of rubber phalluses – not an academic collection like those held in the Thorwaldsen and British Museums, but a sorry little band of working tools to be employed by one boy on another in the more exciting preliminaries in the armpits of the *Debris Christ*, as I then learned. Did he use them on himself? Who knows? – he had such a phobia about being casually touched that intimate sexual touching by anyone other than himself had become impossible, and anal masturbation with a dildo may well have been all that he had left if he was indeed impotent by then. The lifelong trouble with Dali is that so much was fantasy and so little the whole unvarnished truth.

Of all the painters of whom Dali spoke at length and frequently, Velazquez I am certain was to him far the most important. He even toyed with the idea that he might be the great man's reincarnation and was delighted when I told him that I knew a woman who claimed to be Delacroix re-born and painted watercolours to prove it. 'She is also,' I said, 'the head of a coven of witches in West-minster' – and that really did get him going. But beyond their both cultivating particular moustaches, both wearing their hair in styles sufficiently close for Dali, when his grew thin, to commission a wig modelled on Velazquez, their both having fathers who were notaries and both craving to be identified as of noble lineage, Dali could find too few parallels even to convince himself.

Even so, were he to be in the Prado at the unlikely moment of its bursting into flames, Velazquez's *Las Meninas* would be the one picture that he'd rescue. I considered him, frail and shuffling, struggling with all nine square metres of the famous canvas, and as everything that Dali thought or did was tainted with ambiguity, I wondered whether rescuing this greatest of all Spanish masterpieces would have suited him better than dying in the attempt – what a grand *Götterdämmerung* it would be if, shrouded in the great canvas, he and it were engulfed in the inferno, leaving not a shred of either to posterity. Would that not ensure his lasting fame?

Why did I stop seeing Dali? After four long visits to Cadaques I felt that we had exchanged as much as we could and that the friendship – if that is what it was – had run into the sands. It was clear that he had recovered sufficient energy and impulse to revive much of the international life that had been his before what I perceived as a doldrum had set in in the later Sixties, and was impatient to return to it, plans already made. It was as though he had stepped off a merry-go-round and now felt compelled to get onto it again, to recover the earlier pace and serendipity.

In 1980, when the Tate Gallery mounted an encyclopedic retrospective exhibition of Dali's work, it seemed an attempt to justify everything that he had ever done, to sanitise the man and his imagination, to be a Dali-can-do-no-wrong piece of propaganda, to counter the critical dismissal that had been the informed view of him for, by then, a generation. I wanted to shout that I knew another Dali, a dirty Dali so to speak, a Dali who had always since a boy had a filthier imagination than any army sergeant humiliating raw recruits. I wanted everyone to know of the hundreds of drawings that could never be published or exhibited, revealing the depths that he had plumbed.

I wrote the necessary note when Gala died, but when he followed her – and I am certain that he thought of it as following, for he had followed her every day since their first meeting, there was no one to whom I could express my grief – except myself – and I did genuinely grieve. For once the wider public had been right – and is right still: Dali deserves his reputation with them as the last of the great old masters.

CHAPTER 5

Joseph McCrindle

This was the point at which Joseph McCrindle began to play a major part in my life. Eight years my senior, but seeming much more, very rich and very lonely, though rarely solitary, we had drifted into friendship through the frequency of his visits to Christie's and his wayward enthusiasm for drawings by old masters. His father, Ronald, a British flying ace who had – as had my stepfather – fought with Allenby in the Mesopotamian and Jerusalem campaigns of the Great War, had married Joe's mother, Odette Feder, an American socialite, her wealthy family very jealous of their status in the Social Register, the American equivalent of Debrett's and the Almanach de Gotha. Divorce was swift; Odette immediately married a French Count, Guy du Bourg de Bozas, departed for Paris and the south of France, and little Joe became the charge of his maternal grandfather, Joseph Feder, and, particularly, of his formidable grandmother, Edith Mosler Feder, growing up in their Stanford White mansion on Fifth Avenue, privately tutored in boxing and the violin (for neither had he any aptitude), precociously collecting rare books and manuscripts with his pocket money. As measures of the Feder wealth (much of it subsequently his) it is worth recording that to entertain him on a long vacation when he was eight, they despatched him on their yacht to the eastern Mediterranean with Lanning Roper (later to be a distinguished expert on gardens) as his tutor and the crew for company as they explored the Aegean coast of Turkey; at eighteen he set off for Yale in a Duesenberg, the very grandest of American cars, with a chauffeur at the wheel and a footman to handle his luggage.

Joe was thus very much part of the American establishment, and yet an escapee from it, living in both London and New York in untidy circumstances that seemed less obviously wealthy than donnish and scholarly, oddly down-at-heel. His passionate interest in the visual arts may have stemmed from his grandmother's genes, for she was the daughter of Henry Mosler, in his day a fashionable American Salon painter of portraits, landscapes and genre. Joe spoke and read French, German and Italian, and when travelling in Europe was never without the local newspaper. He ate very well but dressed appallingly, not because he bought his clothes in charity shops (though that is how they looked), but because his perspiring bulk – he was built as robustly as a Doric portico – and the spilling of food and drink combined to camouflage their much loftier origin; he was a tailor's nightmare. Repeatedly he fell in love with young men, his ideal the flannelled fool of the Ivy League, though he settled for many far less glamorous and far less suitable. Never predatory, he could be reckless – his cry of 'Don't stop, don't stop' at one of his own dinner parties when he had locked himself in the bathroom with Ted Pillsbury, the archetypal flannelled fool who was later Jacob Rothschild's grotesquely unsuitable nomination as Director of the National Gallery, still echoes in the ears of all who heard it. To his dying day he was driven by infatuation, and when it ended in wretched disappointment, as it always did, the few faithful friends, female and male, with whom he had never been in love and who played the dependable Nicklausse to his Hoffmann, were always there to console him and haul him to his feet.

His less formal dinners were notorious. At these, the mismatch of young men acquired through his literary interests as editor, owner and publisher for twenty years of *The Transatlantic Review* (a magazine of short stories, poetry and criticism) with those, fewer, discovered through the visual arts, seemed wanton. I might find myself with Mario Amaya, a clever young critic of the day, Mario Dubsky, Keith Milow and Mark Lancaster, all more or less forgotten bright young painters of the Sixties, or with Nikos Stangos, Brian Johnson, David Plante and other equally forgotten

writers, and with strangers who came from neither camp; Brian
Epstein, for example, of whose miserable affection for John Lennon
Joe knew more than most – as did I through my tiresome com-
pulsion to comfort the miserable (the Seven Works of Mercy,
once dinned into a boy, become impossible to neglect).* Joe
simply could not recognise that we were all sorts of oil and water
and that our interests would not mix, and, smiling benignly, eating
more than most of us, happy with second helpings as large as the
first, was always puzzled that we did not clamber into bed with
each other or, occasionally, with him. Joe was for more than forty
years my very close friend, but whether in London or New York,
his dinner parties were always the same, always bathetic for his
guests and himself.

All this, everyone in his other world, the grandees of American
museums, galleries and universities, knew very well and, in spite
of gossip, they embraced him on their various boards, positions
for which he did not greatly care – 'I never say anything at these
meetings,' he despairingly confessed of the American Academy in
Rome, nevertheless admitting that they were the perfect excuse
for jaunts to a city in which he felt almost at home and where
the Sestieri family (dealers, discoverers and, alas, restorers) found
him something to add to his ever-increasing collection. To all
these panjandrums he was known for his impulsive yet always
inconspicuous generosity, and it was to their world that he
introduced me so discreetly that I did not realise how subtly he

* Brian Epstein, the Beatles' manager (1961–67), haplessly attracted to John
  Lennon and tormented by his flirting, was eventually – when they were
  alone on holiday in Barcelona in the spring of 1963 – allowed to fellate
  him, with the usual heterosexual excuse 'just to see what it is like'. Brian
  took this as a sign of promise; Lennon, on the other hand, married, his
  wife Cynthia in hospital recovering from childbirth, soured the relationship, not only by refusing further performances, but by mocking Brian
  for his homosexuality. It was from Joe that Brian got his 'houseman',
  Lonnie Trimble, the very tall and handsome black man who served him
  in the years 1964–66.

was steering me away from the direct dealing that I had grown to dislike. His *Transatlantic Review* was a vehicle for promoting writers whose early promise was invisible to other publishers, and that talent he now applied to me. I became, as it were, the curator of his collection, three times responsible for hanging it as three times he moved to larger apartments in New York, and three more times in London, responsible for guarding its condition, responsible for maintaining its inventory; as there was never time to catalogue it properly, the task that I might most have enjoyed fell to the constantly disgruntled Fred den Broeder, another of Joe's shorn lambs. I was never able to slow his rate of acquisition; an obsessive traveller, he could go nowhere without attempting to buy paintings and drawings, and in their absence, such objects as Pre-Columbian sculpture and Tanagra figures, returning with as many embarrassments as successes. Nor could I ever persuade him to rid himself of the many things that he should not have bought; these were crammed into the servants' rooms of his Central Park West apartment, never to be seen by him again.

I already knew a number of American directors and curators, but Joe ensured that I knew many more, and for some of them I drifted into the intellectually and morally much more comfortable position of becoming their London and European errand boy. I was already in that role for museums in South Africa, reinforcing collections there of twentieth-century British art, paid small annual stipends rather than working on commission, and with similar stipends from American museums I eventually had an income that relieved me from all that I most disliked about being an art dealer, while retaining the extraordinary pleasure of having – at least in some small part – ensured that museums had been properly and suitably enriched. Freedom from the commission system on which most advisers worked meant that my advice on price or auction bid could never be interpreted as for my own benefit. It also meant that when negotiating with a dealer he could reduce his figure not only by the then widely acknowledged 'museum price' some ten or fifteen per cent below the asking price, but also by the percentage that he would normally set aside for an agent introducing a buyer (I had indeed learned my lesson from Geoffrey Agnew). For a small museum that extra percentage reduction often meant the difference between buying and not buying. This was a very different pattern of practice from that current now, when agents have been known to take commissions from both seller and buyer and even to add ten or twenty per cent to the initial asking price, pocketing the difference as well as the commissions.

I relished this combination of freedom and responsibility, hunting through auction rooms and the stock of dealers for my particular quarry, the ability to work almost like a curator filling gaps in a collection or opening new fields for a museum. Decades later I still experience a thrill when coming upon a painting or drawing in the acquisition of which I had a hand. I felt that no part of my experience as a student art historian with some practical knowledge of cleaning, restoration and forgery, as a precocious cataloguer of international exhibitions and a dogsbody for so long at Christie's, had been wasted and that all were now being applied in a wholly worthwhile way.

Four or five times a year I flew to New York, stayed with Joe to recover from jet lag and then moved on, if not inland to Chicago or Minneapolis or Cleveland, then up or down the eastern seaboard, even to Key West, its southernmost tip. There Joe had arranged for me to advise the redoubtable Mrs Frances Mitchell Wolfson who intended to found a museum devoted to John James Audubon (1785–1851), the celebrated French Creole naturalist and draughtsman who spent most of his life in America recording birds. As he had passed 1831 researching in the Florida Keys there was some justification for her ambition, and before I met her I foolishly hoped that this almost *tabula rasa* project might be to some extent mine as well as hers. In London I had known, briefly, her son Mitchell II (Micky), a collector of Eric Gill material and similarly stylish erotica, and should have been warned by his mercurial behaviour that his mother might be dominant and difficult. She was.

The Wolfsons were Florida aristocracy engaged in politics and philanthropy, and in 1958 had saved from demolition the mid nineteenth-century Classical Revival house that Frances intended to convert into her museum; talking to local builders and the local architect, considering the compromises compelled by her very proper wish to preserve the outward appearance while providing internally all that even a very small museum must prepare for its visitors, she was imperious and much less agreeable than the Marschallin at her levée in *Der Rosenkavalier*, with which her morning inspections of the site had much in common. We seemed to resolve nothing. After a week or so she invited me to dinner, letting it be known that I must be properly dressed – in levels of temperature and humidity that cook the pale-skinned Englishman – and sent the Cadillac. Did she own, I wondered, the hotel in which she appeared to live? For perhaps half an hour we got on well enough on the verandah and then went to her table. 'The usual?' enquired the waiter (whose hand she required me to shake), to which she assented, obviously for both of us. 'What is the usual?' I asked while he was still shuffling our chairs, 'Turtle' the answer.

'I won't eat turtle.'

'Why not?'

'Turtles are endangered.'

'This turtle is dead.'

So were my chances. 'Give him anything he wants,' she said to the waiter, which meant having to read the menu while she glowered in silence. My subsequent attempts to make conversation were blocked by her monosyllabic checkmates, and the letter that was delivered to my hotel early the following morning, she must have written before she went to bed. She had had second thoughts, she wrote, no longer considered her choice of building to be suitable, and was now uncertain that she would continue with the project. Nothing of this was true but it served her purpose in getting rid of me; the project was eventually completed on a rather larger scale than first intended and very neatly too, but on a considerably increased budget. Considering that I had paid for my flights to Miami, the hired car and the hotel, she enclosed with her letter a wretchedly ungenerous cheque.

I paid my hotel bill and drove the monotonous and often dead straight line that is the road to Miami and the flight to New York. I was now at a loose end and could have stayed, swimming in the warm Atlantic among the diving pelicans, or in the disconcertingly cooler Gulf of Mexico, but I did not care much for the hotel and even less for keeping my own or any other company there, for, booked by Joe in a moment of mischief, it was an hotel of particular reputation, not just queer but where the then still infant Fist Fuckers of America held gatherings. It was out of season, but with the handful of other guests shaven-headed, black-leathered, studded, belted, harnessed and chained with Harley-Davidsons between their thighs, it was no place for me to idle.

I could hardly reproach Joe; I could have upped sticks and gone to another hotel but was too indolent – yet I did wonder if Frances Wolfson had known of its reputation and let this colour her opinion of me, for the turtle tiff seemed a thin reason for my sacking. Back in New York and with time to waste I could explore the then much sleepier museums, the Metropolitan a Vale of Lethe, Brooklyn fallen into desuetude and selling its duplicates and trivia in the souvenir shop, fifty people in the Cloisters, none in the Hispanic Society. I trawled the dealers and bookshops and found drawings; I trawled the baths and discovered sex beyond my wild imaginings. New York in the late Sixties and throughout the Seventies was a blatantly sexual city. Live sex shows and printed pornography were everywhere; one might have to search a little for the queer variety, but it was hardly hidden, and even between lunch and tea it was possible to see a live burlesque show of boy strippers as a preliminary to astonishingly queer films.

There were too the time-honoured and occasionally menacing places for immediate sex in Central Park and the derelict docks, and there were steam baths the length of the town, in which, for the price of hiring a thin old towel, sex could be had with a chosen partner or an entirely random half-dozen, standing, lying and in positions studied by Michelangelo for his *Last Judgement*. All these, long-established, once served an honest purpose for a physically hard-working population living in tenements, but with widespread improvements in domestic hygiene had become superfluous, surviving on the sexual appetite of men for men; some had particular populations – younger, older, tougher, rougher or   inclined   to S and M – and all but one were seedy.

The Continental Baths were smart. In the basement of the Ansonia Hotel, they were the bright idea of an entrepreneur who saw that the sleazy older baths offered scant discretion or security; his, much more expensive, maintained the air of fashionable public rooms into which the passer-by might casually drop for drinks and cabaret – Bette Midler its most celebrated performer (once with Barry Manilow). Women as well as men went there to see who was about and it was not uncommon to see couples in evening dress after a do sharing a table with an old friend in a towel. I was surprised, even a little dismayed (for he had always seemed so much in coy denial about his sexuality that I and many others had long assumed him to be still pre-pubertally innocent), to encounter at a junction of corridors the length of which he could easily be seen, Bruce Chatwin on his knees alternately fellating two equally beautiful young men – but this was, after all, a place designed for the delight of aesthetes, one way and another.

Recourse to the baths – any of them – was hardly necessary unless in search of the particular thrill that accompanies leisurely sex with anonymous strangers to which no obligation is attached. Men in New York seemed everywhere to flaunt their sexual heat, and if it was not always easy to identify their sexual direction, this, bewilderingly, often did not matter, for it seemed that sex was sex, required no classification by gender, could be had urgently any-where at any time, and orgasm was all. I had experienced something of this in Italy and was to see more of it among South African whites, but in New York it was rampant and straight men seemed as much on the hunt for it as queer. The Seventies were, how-ever, not only my second decade of fervid, impetuous, careless, abandoned and perhaps dangerous sex, the appetite only ever briefly sated, but my cannabis years – and the effect of this on me was sometimes sexually debilitating, pitching me lower if my mood was depressed. In New York we not only smoked it but ate it as a salad vegetable, chopped it into goulash and baked it in cakes and cookies, its effect on tempers and tensions wonderfully soothing, but on my libido quite disastrous. When a young curator from Princeton took me to Andy Warhol's Factory for the first time it was in anticipation of finding beautiful boys from among whom to identify a sexual partner for the night, but the cannabis on offer there was of sublimely powerful quality – and though the boys were there in number and were indeed quite beautiful, there was nothing to be done but, embraced with them, lie euphoric and incapable like Arcadian shepherds on the banks of Lethe, smoking, stroking, murmuring mindless gibberish.

Andy himself made very little sense at night. The Factory was his court but he made scant effort to hold it in any sense that Charles II might have recognised, though there were courtiers with minds as bawdy and depraved as Rochester's. He was not much more sensible by day and, apart from his notorious and much quoted quips, was largely inarticulate. My abiding impression of him at work on his now ludicrously expensive screenprints is that he was so indecisive as to how they should proceed that adjustments, interventions and colours were far more often determined by his assistants than by him, and that the finished works are more theirs than his – 'You decide,' his only instruction after fifteen minutes pondering; this, however, was in the Seventies – of his practice earlier I was never a witness, and never after 1979.

I cannot recall taking LSD at the Factory, but it was very much part of life in the Seventies, best taken in very small doses on cubes of sugar or tabs of, I think, blotting paper laid on the tongue like the Host at Communion, and certainly best taken in reliable company in case the effect was dangerously strong – though I doubt if there was ever an antidote. I had been introduced to it in London by a boy at Christie's, Ricky Daniel, who had been extraordinarily sensible in controlling the dose so that the visual effects were as good as Kandinsky's abstract paintings in the years immediately before the outbreak of war in 1914 (his earliest and best). Whether in London or New York these sessions lasted for six hours or so, during which one was not much good for anything, and always ended with a rabid hunger for food and sex – effects quite contrary to those of cannabis. There were tales of takers leaping out of windows convinced that they could fly, and of madness following drips of LSD into the eyes, but I saw neither and suspect that both are urban myths. I was once persuaded to take it in an eye – the right – on the grounds that the effects were more immediate than through ingestion, but it wrecked my focus for some days without in any way improving on the Kandinsky effect and was not tried again.

CHAPTER 6

The Seventies

I was in New York twice in the bitter winter of 1973–74 when the Arab-Israeli War and the oil crisis brought about by a quadruple increase in oil prices unsteadied the economies of the West. The art market was astonishingly slow to react and remained buoyant throughout the late autumn, but collapse, when at last it came, was sudden and devastating, destroying confidence. Prices at auction fell; no one, unless compelled by misfortune, sent fine things to market; dealers pulled in their horns and derived their cash flow from selling old stock at a loss; museums, their patrons directly affected by alarming inflation and rates of exchange at which only the Deutschmark and Swiss Franc held steady, bought virtually nothing.

This slump lasted until Sotheby's mounted the week-long Mentmore sale of May 1977. This dispersal of one of the world's most outstanding nineteenth-century collections, formed by a Rothschild and extended by a Rosebery, sumptuous pomp and circumstance their aim, unseen by art historians and untouched by the grubby fingers of the trade, could only be irresistible to both and it helped bring the art and antiques trades back to active life. That recovery, however, was more than three years away and I had to find something to do with my life. I resumed painting – a rusty business at first but, recovering the hang of it, I enjoyed myself enough; when the chance was offered – usually prompted by a valuation – I repaired and restored paintings that involved no greater difficulty than light cleaning, retouching here and there, and finishing with a sympathetic varnish.

On Friday 13 September 1974 my idleness was interrupted by John Hulton, Director of Arts at the British Council, who had in

1958 asked me to catalogue the British contributions to Europäisches Rokoko, the Council of Europe exhibition in Munich that year; he asked me to work for him again. The exhibition this time was Pittura Inglese 1660–1840. As it was the City of Birmingham's exchange for paintings lent it by Milan the year before, Lombard Painting 1595–1630, I was surprised, for the curator of paintings there was Peter Cannon-Brookes who, since he knew from our very first encounter in 1960 or so that I thought him a pompous ass, was very unlikely to agree to my cataloguing an exhibition that was essentially his; that I did so was at John's insistence, for he knew that I could work to a tight deadline without skimping scholarship. Peter had selected one hundred and fifty-three paintings to be borrowed from many sources and I had barely three months in which to complete my work; most I knew, some that I did not could easily be visited,* but others, in private collections, I was compelled to catalogue unseen, working from photographs – something no art historian should do. I never did see them: this was Birmingham's affair and though the Mayor and all his worthies were, in January 1975, invited to the celebrations in the Palazzo Reale, all expenses paid, I was not among them and times were far too lean for me to spend my fee on the vanity of such a jaunt.

I have just read some of that catalogue and am astonished by how good it is – my present sense that the essentials of all writing on art should be clarity and thoroughness was obviously well-established long before it became my sole occupation. My brief essay on the Grand Tour, written thirty years before I made a

---

* A small group, stored in the roof spaces of the Victoria and Albert Museum, where I had noticed here and there gaps through which the sky could be seen, were, later in the very day that I went to catalogue them, damaged by torrential rain that drenched me to the skin as I walked home and forced open the heavy iron drain covers in the streets. In some cases irreparable, the loss was never made public and is now forgotten and unknown. There was too little time to repair the less damaged paintings for the exhibitions.

television film on the subject, is evidence of a grasp of the history of Italian influence on all English arts that I would now be hard put to summon, and on every page there are observations and facts that I no longer know, but know that I once knew. It is a melancholy reminder of a wasted life that should have been spent looking, thinking and writing – though that is, of course, exactly what I have done for the past thirty years, but for a daily newspaper in which interest lasts not even the twenty-four hours of its date and to which there can be no posthumous reference. Was there ever a more futile vehicle for perception, scholarship and sensibility?

There was one other exercise in curatorial respectability for me before the Mentmore sale; it was a commission from the National Theatre in the spring of 1976 to prepare for exhibition the theatrical paintings and drawings bequeathed to it by Somerset Maugham in 1965. Prompted by Hugh Lane, the perceptive collector of French Impressionist paintings who was drowned when a German U-boat sank the *Lusitania* in 1915, Maugham bought Zoffany's *Garrick with Mrs Cibber in Venice Preserv'd*, swiftly followed by Samuel de Wilde's *Bannister and Suett in Sylvester Daggerwood*, and began to haunt all the salerooms of London. Thus was born his idea of furnishing the walls of the National Theatre with portraits of great actors of the past. The Theatre itself, throughout his lifetime never more than a hope, was first conceived by David Garrick, but not until 1908 was it taken seriously, a committee formed, a site found in Gower Street, a foundation stone laid and substantial funds (to which Hugh Lane was a contributor) raised in the hope of building it by 1916, the tercentenary of Shakespeare's death; but the outbreak of the Great War in 1914 thwarted a proposal not revived until the closure of another war.

On his death Maugham's pictures were put in store and, as when the store was flooded no one noticed, they stood in an inch or two of water for some years, rotting; fine carved and gilded frames of the eighteenth century rotted; original stretchers rotted; the paper of watercolours rotted; and worst of all, the canvases of considerable paintings rotted. This was not discovered until January 1976; by then Denys Lasdun's National Theatre on the South Bank was nearing completion, its Lyttleton stage almost ready to open, its Olivier stage scheduled for a grand opening by the Queen on 25 October, and the authorities on suddenly recalling the existence and purpose of Maugham's gift 'to adorn the bare walls of the theatre and give it a pleasant intimacy', went to inspect the paintings and were horrified. I cannot imagine that I was the first 'expert' to be consulted, but the decision to give me the task of repair and restoration was made on 11 February after (I was told by Geoffrey Ashton, the theatre historian) a fiercely acrimonious meeting of the board.

I was, of course, sworn to secrecy. No one connected with the theatre or the bequest wished the evidence of its neglect to be exposed, and so, with one exception, no one in the team that I assembled knew to whom the paintings belonged or why there was such urgency for their repair. Ivor Jones was the exception; he I had first encountered through friends at the Fitzwilliam Museum, Cambridge, where, on returning from years of training in Rome, he had begun to establish a reputation for skilled and sensitive under-cleaning – that is never going too far with swabs and solvent, never removing even a smidgeon of original paint – and while I was at Christie's he had performed near miracles for us on fragile early German panels. Unlike my close friend Joan Seddon, he would not be diverted by the science of the task, nor be tempted to try new solutions, but would slog on until it was done; there were forty-one oil paintings on which to work and, at most, thirty-five weeks in which Ivor and I must get them ready. The forty watercolours were not a problem – all I had to do was get them to Cambridge where Doreen Lewisohn was ensconced at the Fitzwilliam as a conservator of works on paper and leave the decisions to her; no other restorer of drawings and watercolours was as capable and sensitive as she, nor as reliable in working to a delivery date.

The Seventies

My studio was suddenly more a war zone hospital for the wounded than a comfortable repository of books and paintings; almost all Maugham's pictures had first to be relined and the flaking paint secured before we could consider cleaning them and restoring the extensive losses. As for the frames, most of them of the same period as the paintings they contained, what parts that had been immersed in water had either lost their gilding and all embellishments in moulded plaster, or rotted away altogether, and what had not rotted was infested with active woodworm. Replacing them was virtually impossible, for sod's law is that no antique frame is ever the same size as the canvas one wishes to put in it, and there was, moreover, neither time nor budget for such perfection. Even so, the impossible was in eleven cases achieved and fine period frames replaced the wrecks. Two staunch friends, both expert assistants of Gibello (then perhaps the most celebrated frame maker in London) came to my rescue – Christina Leder, who is still gilding and framing in London, and Johann Peter Riemensberger, a Swiss boy, who could be trusted to restore a carving by Grinling Gibbons, and was as expert as a caster of moulds. Between them they worked miracles and the restored frames looked as though they had, for two centuries, been affectionately dusted by tender parlour maids – discreetly worn.

By the beginning of April Ivor and I had done much more than we thought possible – all the relining, that is the laying down of old canvases on new, was complete, and old stretchers had been repaired or replaced, so that all the paintings were ready for restoration. Of this we kept a scrupulous photographic record, for in some cases the damage and the loss of paint was so extensive that we had to invent solutions. We broke for ten days at Easter because, earlier in the year, the British Museum had been invited to send a party of twenty scholars to Albania, then intensely proud of what it had achieved by its archaeologists and historians in illuminating the Illyria of antiquity. Among its own experts the museum could find too few who wished to go, and even with others from the Courtauld Institute and Birmingham University, the party was short in number until I was asked to tag along, and then Jill Allibone, my contemporary as a student, tagged on too, though neither of us had any classical qualifications other than Latin enough to read inscriptions. On my return, Ivor and I set to work methodically and with total concentration until, at the very end of August, every one of the Maugham paintings and drawings was back in its frame and ready to be hung in the National Theatre.

Displayed in my studio, a posse of panjandrums, including Denys Lasdun, the architect of the Theatre, came to see them. It was not, for me, a happy experience. The panjandrums seemed bemused, as though paintings were alien objects of which they knew nothing (nor did they). Lasdun hated them and said, 'Of course, you'll have to remove all these ghastly frames – if these pictures are to hang on my walls, they must be in simple aluminium strips.' He and I subsequently had a blazing row and I feared for what might become of my children. In the event, and in their original frames, the paintings were hung in the theatre's restaurant and rooms reserved for VIPs, and looked very well, giving exactly 'the pleasant intimacy' for which Maugham had hoped – but not for long. Seven days before the official opening on 25 October, one of the Portuguese waiters in the restaurant threw a raw egg at another; it missed him, but hit a painting, and they had then attempted to wipe away the egg as it dribbled down the canvas. Raw egg and young varnish do not go well together and should not be mixed – their molecular structures change and, emulsified, they become opaque and very hard. By the time the picture was returned to me its disastrous condition had become impossible to remedy before the opening. This mishap and the almost immediate theft of the smallest things in the collection, lent strength to Lasdun's arguments against hanging paintings in his architecture and, on the grounds of their safety and security, all were removed from the theatre and have not been seen there since. They were first shuffled off to Mottisfont Abbey, supposedly on public view there, but the circumstances were impossible, then to the Theatre Museum, but when that shut down, neither the Victoria and Albert Museum nor the National Portrait Gallery would take responsibility for them, and they are now wretchedly divided between the Theatre Royal, Bath, and the Holbourne Museum there, the frames now fudged to make them look like modern fakes. I nourish a seething anger that Maugham's bequest should have been so betrayed by its supposed Trustees. There was a further, almost amusing deceit: a catalogue of the collection, written by the theatre historians Raymond Mander and Joe Mitchenson (engaging old rogues with a collection of their own, much inferior), was so long in preparation that by 1980, the year of its publication as a 'National Theatre Paperback' recording the 'remarkable collection of theatrical paintings, now on permanent display in the National Theatre's foyers' (as claimed on the cover) was long gone; this catalogue is now a rarity – the National Theatre, to prevent curious enquiry, ordered its destruction and very few copies escaped.

*   *   *

Life as a dealer did not entirely shut down during this doldrum; Joe McCrindle still bought drawings and so did Ted Pillsbury, then at Yale, though for himself rather than the University collection; there was, too, an importer of cheap Russian watches who seemed suspiciously anxious to spend money on paintings by Sickert and his ilk – rather good investments in the long term. And there was Peter Langan, the considerable restaurateur, confidant and friend: Susan, his wife, was later to describe me as a 'friend of long standing, though much tried and tested in his friendship, Peter's tutor in art appreciation and artistic merit, his guide through saleroom viewing and his adviser on what to buy, the friend . . . who was in at the beginning. He remained as a friend'.

We met through Nicholas Vilag, whose so-called Fine Art Gallery at 25 Devonshire Street in Marylebone was next to Peter's first restaurant, Odin's Bistro. He was an Hungarian Jew whose

career as a photographer for *Picture Post* (the great magazine of the
1930s) had been interrupted by Horthy and Hitler, and broken by
internment in England. After the war he settled in rooms over a
shop in Croydon, the dreariest of boroughs in the distant south of
London, and began to scratch a living by buying and selling
topographical prints; willy-nilly he became an art dealer of sorts
and opened the gallery – far less gallery than junk shop. It was hung
to the ceiling with pictures of appalling quality, and racked and
stacked with unframed prints and drawings obscured by filthy
polythene that kept them clean but dirtied the hands of curious
customers. Downstairs, where no visitor was allowed, the basement
store was in part a dark impenetrable confusion of frames, canvases
and bulky folders of yet more prints and drawings, labelled London,
Paris, Prague, Fruit and Flowers, and Erotica, and it was on these,
in the one lit part of this Hades, that Muriel Kay and other women
worked, turning penny plain into tuppence coloured, tinting back
into new life any watercolour that had faded in the sun, and
making gay with gouache any simple outline print of European
cities, Italian peasants dancing the Tarantella, and every sort of
souvenir brought back by tourists before the invention of the
camera. It was in rescuing from their attentions a fine and very
valuable Canaletto etching of Padua, and paying Nicholas a proper
price for it, that our affectionate friendship was established.

When Muriel became Nicholas's mistress and the urgency of
their affection required immediate satisfaction – to be achieved
only in the basement – the others had to go. Muriel blossomed; she
became more and more the hostess of the semi-picnic lunches that
Nicholas gave in the back office to his fellow expatriate Hungarians,
his Mafia, and, as an improver of his prints, more ambitious, more
characteristic of herself as a sometime graduate of the Croydon Art
School – sweeping blue skies overwhelmed the faded greens and
browns of distant forests and meadow foregrounds, Paris was roofed
with bright red tiles rather than black slates, ancient Rome became
a riot of rouge and yellow marbles, and from Dresden to Madrid

no city was safe from her irrational enchantments. Even the gullible great doctors of Harley Street who were the regular customers, spending their untaxed Arabian cash-in-hand, began to express doubt and, eventually, Muriel had to go, banished to her home in Putney, never to be seen again.

There was, however, an overlap in her role as mistress. Muriel was small and neat and mouse-like, her replacement twice her size, ample and overflowing, useless as a watercolourist but smothering when it came to accommodating Nicholas. She came in to buy a print and stayed to inherit the business, and to the onlooker, the way in which, like a cuckoo, she edged Muriel out of the nest, was a fascinating performance, brutal and brief.

He had another friend who contributed mightily to the gallery's success, Robert Dumont-Smith, a one-eyed grandee of the Croydon Contemporary Art Group, piratically black-patched, an occasional exhibitor at the Royal Academy who, for a small fee, added signatures to oil paintings or replaced signatures with others more ambitious, occasionally so often that, after much wiping away, the final name stood proud upon a bald patch. All were culled from a dictionary of signatures that Nicholas cunningly pressed on any customer who asked for confirmation that the signature was genuine. When Peter Langan, who had bought a number of these masterpieces, asked me what I thought of them, I felt compelled, miserably, to tell the truth; some days later, with the excuse that a knowledgeable diner had doubted its authenticity, he returned one of the pictures to Nicholas and was so charmed by his immediate willingness to take it back, that he exchanged it for another at twice the price and just as much a forgery.

Peter's refusal to let rancour taint his relationship with Nicholas, who was always happy to take in early deliveries of food and wine, led to a topsy-turvy trust between them. Both were libidinous – Peter openly boastful, speculative, enquiring, Nicholas grunting and secretive – and there were times when one of the amateur watercolourists played amateur in another sense, making both of them happy among the frames and parcels in the basement, though not at the same time. Peter's 'I'm just going next door for a quickie', said in Odin's to anyone who cared to catch the phrase, meant that he would return to the kitchen in ten minutes with a strangely intense expression and a sheen of sweat.

The tale of our unlikely friendship, fierce, loyal and generous on both our parts, I recorded in a memoir written for Susan, his widow, to supplement the fragments of an autobiography on which Peter had worked from time to time as the Leitmotiv of a book of recipes.* On re-reading it I feel inclined to think it not only a fair account of a rumbustious and often roistering relationship in the course of which I learned enough of food and drink to qualify as a restaurant critic, but one that offers wry insights on David Hockney, Patrick Procktor and Ron Kitaj, all of whom were his customers, all of whom exchanged their wares for his and contributed mightily to the collection of paintings hanging in Peter's first two restaurants; moreover, it corrects assertions made by other writers, particularly those in Hockney's camp. My contribution was, yet again, to play a Nicklausse to a Hoffmann, to find what could not be found, to mend what should never have been broken, even to play waiter when, as was so in the early weeks of the larger Odin's, he had no money with which to pay professionals; but I could do nothing to remove the twin demons always at his elbow. That he drank wine in every waking hour of the day, I could do nothing to influence – he could not function without it; I could do nothing to restrain his insatiable speculation, voiced loud and unmistakeable, over the sexuality of the women he encountered, no matter how casual the occasion – even across a street – nor what their role or status, nor, so promiscuous myself, could I curb the prodigious sexual drive that compelled him, without a moment's notice, to turn to the nearest prostitute – wherever we were in London, he seemed always to know of one

* See Peter Langan, *A Life with Food*, Bloomsbury 1990.

nearby, and when he bought the old Coq d'Or and turned it into Langan's Brasserie, there was rejoicing, open-mouthed, among the whores of Shepherd Market.

Without Peter's introduction, would I ever have known David Hockney the little that I do, would I have known Kitaj and his wife (steadily overtaking him as a good figurative painter), would I have had Patrick Procktor as a confessional friend? It was my friendship for Patrick that prevented me from writing the biography that was looking for an author; I was his choice, but I knew that I would tell the truth as bluntly as in any review of an exhibition, or, indeed, as of myself in this autobiography, and that in doing so I would risk destroying our friendship. I valued it far more than the vanity of critical opinion and never once reviewed his work, for I felt so strongly that the robust promise of his early years had swiftly declined into a mannered delicacy from which he seemed unable to escape. It was through Peter that the formality of acquaintanceship with Lucian Freud was relaxed – the effect of my witnessing their competition for a girl from Fortnum's looking for a lover for the night. We were in Beth Coventry's bar, just south of Piccadilly, when in she came; within minutes Peter was telling Lucian what his pudgy hand could feel up the girl's skirt, and when they took to a tonguing kiss it seemed that both were in some sense challenging the older Lucian, already saurian – indeed, I suspected that she knew him and that what she did with Peter was done solely to arouse Lucian's libido, for it was he who effortlessly got her simply by opening his arms in welcome. I imagine that it was the fingering rather than the kiss that did it, together with Peter's commentary, for what his fat fingers found was as lubricious as a ripe persimmon, his word for it the blunt Teutonic radical that for centuries no polite literary man has dared to use. Lucian observed it often enough, always with deliberate scrutiny as though he were a kitchen-boy looking for slugs in a lettuce; he drew and painted it too, and let such studies leave the privacy of his studio to decorate the bedrooms of rich men – but, as art, even the crudest erotic fantasies of Keith Vaughan and David Hockney have more merit.

With the Fortnum's girl on Lucian's knee and not to be got off it, Peter raged obscenely and got drunk – but then he always opened his arms in welcome to whichever of the Deadly Sins was appropriate. His Sloth was indeed the spiritual torpor that undoes the active man, the Black Dog of depression that walked at Winston Churchill's heel – it had nothing to do with God, but it effectively excluded Him. His Envy was of prestige and popularity and the power they might have brought him in his field; and he was covetous of fine things finer than his own, vain enough to drive a coachbuilt Bentley. With Rage his face suffused with blood, shouting at cooks and, occasionally, customers; and serving Gluttony was his career, however delicately dressed in quality. As for Lust, night and day she jogged the elbow of this unquiet soul. A decade after his death, in a chance encounter with Lucian, I confessed how much I missed Peter. 'You must be mad,' he said, and I could see in his eyes that he meant it.

I once thought that in recollections of such small events as these lay an immortality of sorts, that in our chuckling over them Peter's bulky presence might be revived, but that was soon after his death in December 1988 – foul temper, alcohol, fire, self-immolation, *Götterdämmerung*; now, a quarter of a century on, I wonder, for I hear no one speak of him and, as with Simon Raven (considerable novelist), when I raise his ghost I must explain the who and what of him to provoke the response: 'Oh I remember . . . wasn't he the man with the bloody chopper wandering round Odin's?'

* * *

For me, 1979 was a very crowded year. At the end of January I was asked to give evidence for Tom Keating, the to-be celebrated forger, in his trial at the Old Bailey. I gave it willingly, for since February 1970, when I had first encountered one of his pastiches of Samuel Palmer in a modest auction room in Woodbridge, Suffolk,

I had been astonished by the behaviour of the art market and curators who should never have been duped. Half the trade was at the Woodbridge sale, £9,400 was paid for it, and at the end of the year it was exhibited by the Leger Gallery with a price tag of £15,000. That Leger accepted it as genuine was heavily significant, for the firm had dealt with Palmer until his death in 1881, and subsequently with his son Alfred Herbert, who continued to live in their Kensington house (6 Douro Place) until 1940 or so, constantly supplying Leger with original Palmers never before offered in the market. The gap of thirty years mattered not at all, for the head of Leger (a boastful man whose Rolls-Royce bore the number plate ART I) bridged it, and that was enough to lend his firm a reputation for peculiar and particular expertise with which they quelled the nay-sayers. As Tom's expert witness I argued that his pastiches had been given authenticity by the specialist art dealers and museum curators who had acquired them, and had they the expertise they claimed, they would at once have rejected Tom's imitations as impertinence – as did most experts at the British Museum. It takes two to make a fake – the faker and the grandee who declares it to be genuine – and in one early case, *A Barn at Shoreham*, Edward Croft-Murray, no less than Keeper of Prints and Drawings at the British Museum, supported a drawing bought by John Baskett, grandee of Colnaghi's, and saw that it passed into the collections of the Cecil Higgins Museum, Bedford, of which he was a trustee.

Tom in the dock was a pathetic figure: the flushed complexion suggested problems with heart and blood pressure, and he sat hunched and bleary-eyed, seeming to ignore the goings-on around him. He had the bladder of a mouse (sans sphincter), and had with miserable frequency to ask to be excused – recall the wretchedness of childhood disasters at school and then transpose them to the majesty of the Old Bailey; it irritated the judge, who did not care to be interrupted midstream. In the early stages he sketched in a palm-sized notebook – as did Sickert at the theatre – until authority discovered the reason for his downcast head: defendants are supposed to pay attention and not distract themselves with irrelevances, but the sketches were not irrelevant; they were of Christ's trial and trudge to Calvary inspired by recollections of Rembrandt and Tiepolo, and were quite beautiful.

In the end Tom was not crucified: there were delays because he had bronchitis and then, one morning, side-swiped from his Vespa on the way to court, the case came to an inconclusive end. I suspect that the judge had little sympathy with the prosecution and was grateful that a *deus ex machina* had relieved him of the embarrassment of sentencing a frail old man – there was, indeed, a general feeling that the wrong man had been brought to court. He returned to Dedham, penniless, to the comfort of four thousand letters of sympathy from strangers, and one from the Inland Revenue that spelled total, inescapable, ruin. Their demand was based on the assumption that all his fakes – of Rembrandt, Constable, Renoir, Degas et al – were worth the £15,000 paid for one of the many pseudo-Palmers in a sale at Sotheby's (27 June 1973, lot 68). This hammering for income tax reduced him to living in an unheated shed and more bouts of bronchitis interrupted the burst of activity through which he hoped to respond to the demand. I thought it would kill him, but a kindly soul in Dedham lent him a cottage for a while – though the ceilings were so low that he had to work on his knees to finish the foreground of a new Constable six-footer.

We became friends of a sort, though I preferred to take a picnic to the cottage rather than experience yet another garrulous performance from Tom in the Marlborough Head; all Dedham must by then have known what he thought of Bridget Riley: 'All talk and watered vino – she works out the rhythms and migraine-stricken assistants do the job.' He claimed to have once been one of them, but when his hand wavered she excluded him from her canvases and made him paint the stairs instead – all white; that done, she sacked him. He grew in celebrity; on Independent Television he taught us the techniques of the old masters and complained about cleaning in the National Gallery, but when a young man from the BBC made an approach with 'I am a Jew and a socialist . . . ' Tom's response, 'The one is obvious, the other you must prove,' caused such offence that, whatever the project was, it was not pursued. In the summer of 1982 we were both enlisted by Winsor and Newton to celebrate their one hundred and fiftieth year in the production of artists' materials, and in a pair of marquees on the lawns of the original Tate Gallery, I lectured on panels, canvas, copper, paints, brushes and all the other things that painters use, while Tom set up a still life of flowers and taught amateur ladies how to paint. His was far the more popular marquee, but by lunchtime, drunk, he was no longer capable of holding a brush and the Winsor and Newton men were blushing at his vocabulary; I had to take over and let the materials look after themselves.

On his death in 1984, a partial clearance of his studio gave rise to an outpouring of respect by the art market in the only way it knows – it paid absurd prices at an auction. Christie's had already held one sale, presumably to settle taxes, the year before, and this second sale was thought to be the last chance to buy a Keating. It was not – sales continued until at last the penny dropped and the salerooms recognised that there must now be a forger of Keatings: the forgery of forgeries in the case of Elmyr de Hory, very recently exposed, should have warned the market of the possibility with Keating.

*　　*　　*

The following months of 1979 were filled with journeys to museums, collectors and dealers in France, Germany, Switzerland and the Netherlands, and on 1 May I left for a long stint in America – my last (though I did not know it would be so) and far and away most ambitious in terms of work to be done as a consequence. On my return there was one of those jolts to memory and sensibility that are felt hard by the too sensitive soul – an invitation to the memorial service for Michael Jessett. I had not seen Michael since he left school and we had not parted on good terms. We had had schoolboy sex a hundred times before my sixteenth birthday, the night on which he, a few months the elder, fucked me for the first time; losing my virginity so painfully I interpreted as love (as indeed it was, of a kind, on my part, but not on his, and I was emotionally bruised by our swift drifting apart). More than thirty years had passed; I had later come to terms with my homosexuality and had recklessly enjoyed, at one extreme, its passionate engagements and, at the other, its madcap carelessness, its risks, its thrilling folly – indeed, one of the compensations for having to work in New York, Frankfurt, Geneva or anywhere else was that sex with new partners was everywhere available and became a matter of course. I had for some years been in love with a younger man, conveniently abroad and conveniently married, with whom I could indulge my occasional bouts of broody paternalism without the curse of having a family and with little risk of the relationship growing stale, the bedevilling characteristic of all homosexual relationships. I was therefore content with what seemed the best of both worlds and the disadvantages of neither. Michael's death was, nevertheless, a footstep on my own grave, not only in that, at forty-eight, it had come so soon, but in that he had become a distinguished musician (once my ambition too), his life celebrated in death by musicians in the church of the Royal College of Music, Holy Trinity, Prince Consort Road, a service to which I received an invitation. As our paths had never crossed again, who knew that I had known him and known him well enough to perhaps need to know of his death? That he left a wife and family reminded me that the homosexual pleasures of the boy are, for most of them, the transitory convenience of the heterosexual. Before the glorious Bach came to an end, I slipped away; were the tears that I wanted no one to see for Michael, for me, or for something indefinable that I still felt, even still feel?

In 1979 I did not go to Turkey.

CHAPTER 7

Turkey

If, 'In 1979 I did not go to Turkey' seems an odd conclusion to my recollections of the Seventies, it is not so, for the land beyond the Bosporus had developed, willy-nilly, into an obsession and was to become a Leitmotiv of my life for fully fifteen years. To go there for the first time in the doldrum summer of 1975 had been a whim prompted by a sudden sense of the familiarity of Europe and a weariness with the discipline of trudging round art galleries; what I did for a living had become, if not quite a Dantesque circle of purgatory, an inevitable drudgery – what, I wondered, had happened to my sense of adventure, to plans once made to drive round the Mediterranean, to explore Ethiopia, Persia or the Spice Islands that once belonged to the adventurous Dutch (this last a madness when I was eight)? Paintings had become, and are, a drug, and without them I suffer withdrawal symptoms; as my skiing companions know only too well, the question 'How far is it to Vienna?' – or Munich, or Geneva, or Turin – murmured at breakfast on the third day of a planned fortnight in a ski resort, was a clear signal that I had already had enough of piste and schuss and needed a quick fix of paint on canvas; so too would it be were I lying on a beach somewhere. Of Turkey, however, I thought that if, for paintings, classical ruins and Ottoman architecture could be substituted, then we might have a solution to my addiction and we might satisfy my longing for adventure. The lurking recollection of a book read while in the Lower School at Haberdashers' – Kinglake's *Eöthen*, a now forgotten young man's travels in the Ottoman Empire, published in 1844 – though I could not find my copy, put flesh on the bones of the idea. I have often damned that school for its not being Eton, as it were, for its low church bias and dull-mindedness, but the English master who, in the grim and bitter winter and so-called Little or Second Blitz of 1943–44, set cold and hungry boys of twelve on a journey through the Balkans to the Grand Porte, was, without knowing it, a man of lasting inspiration. How many boys at Eton then read Kinglake? How many boys anywhere now?

From this first unprepared journey I returned with a jumble of impressions and the conviction that I must go again, but with serious intent. Relics of the Ottoman occupation of the Balkans – five centuries of it – increased in number the further south we went in what was then Yugoslavia, competing with those of Byzantium, and across the water into Asia, Byzantium gave way to ancient Greece and Rome, the Aegean coast and hinterland a wondrous palimpsest of cultures. No sooner back in London than the serious reading began – or so I thought it, but it was largely the chatty books of such travellers as Freya Stark that informed me until I discovered those of George Bean, a great man of Greek, Latin and archaeology at the University of Istanbul. His four introductions to south-western Turkey* were to be my *vade mecum* on all subsequent journeys; they opened my eyes not only to the subject but to a manner of writing that informs the reader of the present while bringing to life the distant past, functioning, not as a guide book, but as a guide, the writer – having seen and done everything himself and thus immune from the errors of the copycat – a lively and informed presence always at hand or in one's knapsack. Respected by the guardians of sites, many of whom had laboured for him on his excavations, to carry a Bean book in its bright orange wrapper was to carry a welcomed passport, 'Ah, Bin Bey,' their greeting. Some might reach high above their heads, palm down, to indicate his gangling height, so memorable to stocky Turks, and all would show me more recently excavated finds.

---

* George Bean, *Aegean Turkey*, 1966; *Turkey's Southern Shore*, 1968, *Turkey beyond the Maeander*, 1971, and *Lycian Turkey*, 1978.

Turkey

All that I know of the eastern spread of Greek and Roman influence is founded on Bean's scholarship; when, a decade later, I wrote a brief and slightly frivolous memoir of my, by then, many journeys in south-western Turkey,* the serious parts of it were in homage to his imagined tutelage. My intention was not to replace Bean but to bridge the gap between his scholarship and an ignorance (mine) that was then typical of most British travellers in Turkey; it was not that Bean's books were in any way difficult – they are far from stern in their approach, but they require a level of background classical knowledge that is no longer what 'every schoolboy knows', so much have the old essentials of education withered away. In the event – many events – the book fell between every possible stool and was not kindly reviewed; even so, it has been twice reprinted. I turn to it still when I need to recall such arcane matters as the customs of the gladiator, the extinction of the Caspian tiger, the Boy Bishop, the Mass of the Ass and the Wandering Jew.

My new enthusiasm I was foolish enough to disclose to Jill Allibone, who lived five minutes' walk away and was a constant borrower of books (always returning them). Before the year was out she had taken charge of my plans, was coming with me (or rather, I with her, for her husband's Range-Rover, not my Peugeot 404, was to be our vehicle), and we were to extend the journey far to the east, for she had spent her girlhood in Persia and wanted to see how Persian eastern Turkey might be.

In April 1976 I had a taste of what might be to come for Jill attached herself to the Albanian jaunt that briefly interrupted my work on Somerset Maugham's paintings. Even as a student she had been a little too dependent on alcohol (she came from drinking parents), and as a neighbour I had often seen her amiably sozzled, but one evening in Tirana she was in a foul temper and during dinner her response to my arguing some point was an almighty

* Brian Sewell, *South from Ephesus*, 1988, reissued 2012.

under-the-table kick that skinned my shin and bloodied my trouser leg. I should have taken it as a warning that the determined and purposeful girl whom I admired years before had, perhaps, become something of a shrew – but I did not.

We flew to Ochrid, a town of wonderful Byzantine churches then in southern Yugoslavia and on Albania's eastern border. This we crossed on foot over a stretch of no-man's-land, to be greeted at the barrier with a cry of 'Welcome to Shqiperia' from Rexhep, the English-speaking schoolmaster who was to be our *cicerone*. 'Abandon hope, all ye who enter here' might have been more suitable, for customs officers deprived us of all books, even our notebooks, a recording machine, binoculars and anything that roused suspicion. The procedures of formal welcome ended with a beckoning finger addressed to me; I was taken into a large room in the centre of which was a single chair with whatever it was that dangled on a wire from the light socket above, held in the hand of the guard who stood behind its back. Ordered to sit, I sat, a guard behind me, a guard on either side, and thus held down, the buzzing began and the clipper, cold on my neck, set off on its business of cutting rough swathes through my hair. Not even on my first day as a National Serviceman called to Aldershot had I been so crudely shorn. Thick and curly, but by no means long, my hair was, it seemed to the border guards of Shqiperia, evidence of moral turpitude.

Ten days in Albania in the inescapable company of scholars (we were allowed no freedom and were always in Rexhep's sight) provided enough experience to fill a book. By the oldest member of the party, a man who had spent his youth repairing the mosaics of Hagia Sophia, I was instructed, while waiting to board our plane at Heathrow, never to touch a Balkan door handle if I wished to avoid sickness. 'It is pointless to wash your hands in a lavatory,' he said, 'if you then open a door.' I learned from one expert how to read a wall and was astonished by the amount of information that can be gleaned from a stretch of re-used material converted into a defence; all that I knew of Byzantium was consolidated and extended by the amiable knock-about of professors from Birmingham and the Courtauld who knew the streets of Trebizond better than the Bullring and Piccadilly Circus; and by a youngster from the British Museum my eye was swiftly tutored into distinguishing the centuries of provincial Roman sculpture. All the while there lurked the violent Albania of the Dark and Middle Ages under the Serbs, Bulgarians and Normans to be elucidated with lubricious pleasure by historians, and half a millennium within the Ottoman Empire, to which even I could contribute a little; and all the while there was too the present of the present day, with three blue-clad Chinese under every Judas tree and the admonitions of the Communist tyrant Enver Hoxha writ 'HOLLYWOOD' large across the landscape that we should 'praise the labours of the freedom-loving people of Shqiperia'.

These freedom-loving people turned mute to the nearest wall if we approached them and, at Butrint, the most beautiful of archaeological sites, a place for Turner and Lear to paint, a palimpsest of cultures, where peasants were retrieving what they could from the beached jetsam, our Party Member drove them into the sea, thigh deep, so that we could not speak to them. We spoke to no one; archaeological sites were emptied of their archaeologists, museums of their curators, and even hotel staff fled if our presence coincided with their duties. Our Party Member drove us on dusty unmade roads past primitive oil wells, the air heavy with their stink, the land sodden with it, grazing sheep mired in it; but we also travelled through an Alpine hinterland where valleys were dense with Judas trees, their bark as sooty black as the stockings of Toulouse-Lautrec's can-can dancers, their blossoms as bright as their frilly underskirts. We saw meadows of wild flowers and upland fields so steep that their ploughed furrows could only be broken by ox-drawn wicker harrows weighed down with laughing women and children. And we encountered gun emplacements, always facing the enemy to the west.

This Albanian journey, coming so soon after the confusions of my first Turkish jaunt and a winter of making a nuisance of myself in the bowels of the British Museum, was Confirmation after Baptism; it lent sense to so much of what I had seen blundering about in Aphrodisias and Pergamon, Side and Termessos, and to have spent ten days so alert in the company of devoted and generous scholars had been an astonishingly educative experience. I was not arrogant fool enough to think myself their peer, but I was confident that my second Turkish journey, if researched and planned, would be far more intellectually revealing than the first.

It was not. Jill's husband, David, accompanied us on the outward leg, intending to return by air – as he did – from wherever we were at the end of the third week, while we drove on for another month or so. The Range-Rover was a pig to drive, nose up and down-at-heel with the weight of their whisky and claret, its steering light and vague, not helped by the case of Pedigree Chum on which I insisted, knowing that I would need to allay my misery whenever we encountered a starving dog – a futile gesture, I know, made more for my benefit than theirs, for all the tinned dog food in the world could not feed the feral dogs of Asia. We planned to drive fast, but the Range-Rover was unmanageable beyond sixty; we planned to be up with the lark, but stayed in proper hotels, ate proper dinner and proper breakfast, and eleven every morning was time for the first whisky of the day, David and Jill keeping each other tippling as they drove; it was on our picnic lunches that they downed their claret. On subsequent journeys, driving alone, sleeping and showering in camping sites, my Peugeot could be in Istanbul by mid afternoon on the third day, but in the sluggish Range-Rover we covered as little as two hundred miles a day and a full week passed before we crossed the Dardanelles. Diligence was at once abandoned: my plan had been to visit all the sites that I had not seen the year before, and revisit all that I had, but Jill and David soon declared themselves exhausted and decided that we should press on to Side, to an hotel that I had scheduled as a break before setting off for the east. I surrendered without argument for I was by then convinced that the expedition was doomed.

There had been two disconcerting incidents. We had been close friends for more than twenty years, but one evening, when we were alone, David had suddenly remarked, 'Even if I didn't know, I could tell that you're queer – you never look at women walking past.' The observation seemed charged with notes of deprecation and superiority, even aggression, and had nothing about it of the well-meaning but blokeish clumsiness of a womanising friend – I did, do indeed, have such friends, kindly in their attitude to my sexuality, if occasionally given to unseemly curiosity about the mechanics of the business. I wondered if David resented the ease with which Jill and I slipped into prattle of art history, felt excluded from it and blamed me for it; did he know that immediately after his proposal to her she had asked me my intention? Worse was to come: in Güllük, a pretty place on the wide bay north of Bodrum, Jill made what I interpreted as a clumsy attempt at seduction while David was away hunting for whisky. She called me to their room, and there she lay, flat on her back, in the tired pink of underwear much washed, the material broderie-anglaise, her pubic hair curling through its apertures. She offered no seemly reason for her call and I, determined not to enquire, left after some empty conversation. Perhaps I did her an injustice, but I have known other women suffering the conviction that with very little effort they can reorient a man's errant sexuality. Years later, persuaded to attempt a novel, I based the central character on Jill and enhanced this episode, but the more I wrote, the more monstrous and real the fictional character became – so much so that, preferring the Jill I knew rather than the Jill I had invented, I felt compelled to destroy the manuscript and retain the friendship.

The Turtel, in Side, was an hotel of high European standards, run with old Ottoman courtesy by Mardin Bey and Prussian efficiency by his German wife; to Jill and David it promised as much whisky as they could drink, and to me it offered respite from their bickering. There we found, with his entourage of staff from London, Bernard Breslauer, a notable antiquarian bookseller who occasionally picked my brains about old master drawings and the only man courageous enough to destroy a portrait by Lucian Freud. This he had commissioned, but Lucian had made the worst of his Fagin nose, his glasses (thick lenses in a hefty frame of horn), and the thin hair, dyed black, grown long and combed over his bald skull; I thought that such pure cruelty betrayed a commission that Lucian should have refused; Bernard loathed it and, reassured by friends that it was not a masterpiece of Goyesque mockery but a spiteful caricature that by any other portrait painter would have been damned as anti-semitic, he turned it face to the wall and would not hang it. I thought it an act of kindness to say that if he hated it so much that he could not bear to live with it, could not bear even to give it to either of his two devoted assistants, then he must do what Clementine did for Winston Churchill in the affair of the Sutherland portrait. Very carefully he cut the canvas into tiny rectangles that would not block his lavatory.

Imagine this procedure. Bernard was not a man to know or understand the physical structure of a canvas, the fabric stretched taut on a wooden support that is invisible once the picture is in its frame; this support, the stretcher, makes it rigid only when two triangular slivers of wood (pegs) are driven into slots in its four corners; nor was he a man to have in the house a pair of pliers with which to remove these pegs and collapse the stretcher so that the canvas could easily be removed from it. He must have cut the strained canvas with a knife; did he trace the blade along the edges of the image or slash it across the centre and tug at it with his delicate pale hands? Did he confront his image as he destroyed it, or attack it from behind? Had he by then stopped dying his hair and, reconciled to the grey of it and the shiny pate, had it cut *en brosse*? Had the portrait thus become the image of a man he no longer wished to be, no longer was? Only one thing is certain – that he cared not a damn what he'd paid for it.

Bernard was a disaster for my relationship with David. His noisy greeting and the hug were bad enough, but in Side he was as unrelentingly flamboyant as in London he was grave, the scholarly bibliophile to his bones. His hair suddenly grey and cut *en brosse*, narrow of shoulder, pot-bellied, the withered buttocks scarcely proud of his spindle shanks, the pouch of his tiny Parisian bathing slip far too loose for what little it contained, he can hardly have roused the appetite of the hotel boys, but I suppose he paid them well enough to do their duty on the deserted beach to the west where the straggly edge of the forest almost reached the sea and the village boys idly buggered each other in the heat of the afternoon. We saw him go and we saw him return, the perfunctory conjugation apparently enough to satisfy – but it was rarely with the same boy; having been with him and taken his money, each tended to avoid him, discreetly disappearing as only the Turk can. One, older and more a man than a boy, unfortunate enough to be put immediately on bar duty on his return, did his damnedest to avoid eye contact with Bernard who, weary of snapping his fingers for attention, shouted without shame: 'You fucked my arse ten minutes ago – now do me the courtesy of bringing me a drink.' Jill, for days in a bloody-minded mood, broke into helpless giggling; David, silent, walked off with his whisky and gazed at the sea.

Male travellers beyond the boundaries of Anglo-Saxony and the Austro-Hungarian Empire should, if homosexual, be monkish, celibate and chaste if any Islamic country is their goal. Whatever the prohibitions of the Prophet and his acolytes, the actuality is that though homosexuality may not be prevalent, homosexual activity particularly with western strangers is found all round the Mediterranean and in Pakistan (I have been no further east) – it may even be, or have become, culturally traditional. Where European men are part of the occasion it is largely opportunist, mercenary or even triumphalist in the sense that he who fucks a European despises him as a mere trophy. On every outward journey, once across the Turkish border, I had been advised by a now renowned venereologist and historian of sexual behaviour, Michael Waugh, to make myself asexual, to make no signals and show no interest that could be misinterpreted, and this sound counsel I had the will to follow; on the return journey, a busy night spent in the stews of Frankfurt or Cologne could assuage the released hunger. Young heterosexual men too can be vulnerable; in the course of my Turkish studies I have encountered several cases where misread signals led to extreme embarrassment, and two where the acceptance of hospitality at home led to gang rape. Bernard, of course, might have enjoyed that, but one boy in question certainly did not and, psychologically, seemed to have been permanently infected by hatred of both Turks and homosexuals, utterly failing to understand that homosexuality played no part in what was probably no more than common sexual opportunism by men in a family where casual sex with girls and women is forbidden by both society and religion.

Journeys to Turkey in 1977 and 1978 were made alone and possibly at risks that I did not recognise. Away for months, I planned to cover in detail quite small areas, all dealt with by George Bean, and do so thoroughly, adapting the car so that I could sleep in it if necessary, and learning a smattering of Turkish with which I might initiate a conversation, if not maintain it (it is not an easy language). I can recall no misadventures of any kind – only the pleasurable drudgery of wandering in ruins and occasionally sleeping in them, and the ease with which I adapted to activity by daylight hours and sleep as soon as it was dark. I had long known the importance of well chosen books to transport me, in adversity, elsewhere, and I learned that a portable chess set provokes conversation in the most improbable of places.

In 1977 the long journey back to London was punctuated by halts at every art gallery celebrating the fourth centenary of the birth of Rubens – wonderfully instructive; and the following year, north of the Greco-Yugoslav border, I paused to offer a lift to a hitch-hiker who would, I knew, if not picked up, find nowhere to spend the night. Joseph his name, Croatian his nationality, his parental home was some way off my route to Zagreb and Ljubljana, but I had time in hand and was rewarded, not only with bed and bath when we reached his home, but by his father's suggestion that we should take off into the hills to explore churches, monasteries and mansions within reasonable reach. For five days we hiked and I was introduced to the enchanting periphery of Austrian baroque architecture and painting, much of it, having survived the German occupation in World War II, soon to be damaged and destroyed in the Serbo-Croat war of the 1990s.

*　　*　　*

The strong revival of the art market prevented my going to Turkey in 1979, and Anthony Blunt's exposure at the end of that year had such repercussions that I felt in 1980 bound to stay within his reach, at least by telephone and within a day's journey. In March skiing took me to Norway with Colin Darracott (an established custom), and in August we walked for ten days along the great fence that then divided Germany – an episode of great pleasure and relaxation, though feasting on blueberries close to the wire provoked East German guards into an hilariously exaggerated response with armoured troop-carriers. In 1981 I noted in my diary that my income had fallen to a point at which I could no longer afford to run the house in Eldon Road and must consider leaving London for the country, and did indeed look at houses within reach of Bath and Marlborough, only to find the prospect utterly depressing – I am, I think, a Londoner to my bones and essentially a Kensington villager. In 1982 I had recovered enough to return to Turkey, but not for another deliberate exploration of a limited area; instead, with Michael Waugh, my useful doctor friend, our objective was the far south-east, the furthest point of the journey that Jill and I had thought to make.

It was plain idiocy. We failed to take into account the then two-

year-old Iran-Iraq war, the floods of refugees, particularly of Kurdish
origin, that crossed the mountains into Turkey, and the response of
the Turkish army (then more or less the government), which was
to make that corner of the country a military zone. We flew to
Erzerum, intending to travel by bus to Van and south to Hakkari,
where Robin Fedden had climbed as a young man before World
War II and recalled wonders to behold – Robin had, indeed, given
me all his large-scale maps of eastern Turkey, including those of the
border with Russia, all printed in Germany in the 1930s and perfect
for military purposes. Bus schedules were in chaos and only by
sitting for hours in the bus station could we be sure of leaving
Erzerum, though with no certainty of reaching Van; halted by
soldiers at checkpoints, passports inspected, luggage unloaded, these
delays repeated and repeated, we reached Van at two in the
morning, after a twenty-hour journey. We fell into the filthy Hotel
Kent because a light was on and we could see someone sleeping at
the desk.

Two in the morning is no time to discover that the contents of
one's knapsack are sticky with ginger marmalade. All my life I have
suffered from travel sickness, particularly in buses (I have even
managed to be sick on skis among the moguls), and it was Robin
who advised a spoonful of ginger marmalade as a sovereign preventative; foreseeing the breakage of glass jars, I had transferred two
pounds of it to a stout plastic container – alas, not stout enough to
withstand the rough handling of my knapsack by Turkish baggage
handlers, and marmalade had seeped into everything about it.
Michael mocked me for a fool, only then to find that his luggage
was as soaked in a kaolin and morphine remedy for diarrhoea.

We saw something of Van, but as a garrison city we were much
restricted. We were allowed to go by bus to Aghtamar, the best
known of Armenian churches (though far from the best in quality),
but our return transport was a lorry driven by a man almost blind
with conjunctivitis. Hakkari too we reached by bus, only to be
trapped for days by a military clampdown, staying in an hotel full

of refugees in which there was no water and use of the lavatories was inhibited by the stalagmite of shit accumulated in the tray. We saw what we could – the landscape is spectacular – and waited; I had with me John Pearson's *Facades*, five hundred wonderfully distracting pages on the Sitwells to divert me from the dust, delay and Michael's temper. Eventually the departure of a bus to Diyarbakir was announced and we began another nightmare journey, this time with mechanical breakdowns between the military checkpoints and, over some wild stretches of road, armed soldiers ready to do battle. With the army constantly in evidence, Diyarbakir was not a comfortable place to be and a sequence of day-long bus journeys slowly took us back to the south-west.

Michael, moustached and gravely saturnine in emergency, attracted no attention from the Turks (indeed, he was often taken to be Turkish), and at one checkpoint stood watching a soldier butt me with his rifle when he found Robin's maps in my luggage – only the arrival of another bus laden with Kurds diverted him. To my protests that he might have come to my assistance, Michael responded that had I been arrested he could then have done something through diplomatic channels, but if we were both in a concrete cell, that might be the end of us. I was reminded of this on a later journey when unwittingly I crossed the porous and unmarked border with Iraq and did indeed spend some hours in a concrete box wondering what the hell might happen to me. The sheer funk that I then experienced brought my solitary adventures to an end, and Petter Kolrud, my other redoubtable and constant skiing companion, became the stalwart prop of all but one of my later Turkish follies.

*   *   *

It was with Petter that I tied the loose ends and filled the gaps of south-western Turkey; without him my one book on that country would never have been written (though mean publishers, worried about length, forced the elision of several chapters), and with him I set out to write two more, of which only the skeletons were developed. In 1984 we made an inventory of all the rock churches in Cappadocia that we could find. These, excavated from the soft volcanic deposits of an overwhelming pre-historic eruption, are ingenious conventional church interiors, cruciform, arched, vaulted and domed, but windowless, and many have paintings or wholly painted surfaces, ranging from the crude and primitive to the sophisticated, the style uniformly Byzantine pre- and post- the iconoclastic controversy of the Eastern church that began with the first destruction in AD 726 and fizzled out in the middle of the following century. Some are no more than isolated hermit churches and burial sites; a handful are extensive enough to deserve identification as monasteries (Christianity in Cappadocia reaches back to the second century AD). Harsh winters, with snow as deep as four metres, induce rock falls that bury some churches and reveal others, so that no inventory can be perfect; their gross number has been estimated at five hundred, but the number accessible in any summer is far fewer. Those most visited, usually by accompanied groups of tourists, are at risk from sudden changes of humidity brought about by their perspiring presence, the brushing shoulder and caressing finger.

One of the long-buried churches, revealed in the 1960s at Tağar, south-east of Ürgüp, devoted to Theodore Tyro, a local soldier saint, hideously tortured, led to our being invited to witness a village circumcision. The boy, Ahmed, six, was in the uniform of an army general, pinned about with banknotes, the gifts of family and friends; we pinned more on him. His mother came to talk to us; enormously stout, in baggy breeches of green velvet and a cardigan that spoke of Marks and Spencer, she chattered in broken German; home for a month from Berlin, her answer to my questioning was a melancholy, 'Was machen muss.' We were given ayran (a thin yoghurt) and Turkish delight; young men brought us cigarettes and were, as usual, amazed to see Petter roll his own (another useful knack for making contact); a band arrived –

violin, clarinet, guitar and drum – and teenage boys began to dance, slow, graceful, statuesque, intense, remote, pair by pair as though Nicholas Poussin was their choreographer. They were swept aside by young men in a dance that jostled shoulders in a forward-thrusting shimmy of aggression, the prelude to a single dancer, his first movements slow and spiritual, his eyes unfocused, but as the musicians increased their pace, his turns became a whirl that ended with his spinning on his knees in the dust.

Another ring of dancers replaced him, a boy in their centre seeming to adopt a feminine role with mischievous hip-wriggling and knowing glances – he would provoke them all and then concentrate on one who would eventually replace him. Both clowning and provocative, it was not without humour, but one particularly lithe boy could bend back so far that his face was upward at the crutch of his choice, continuing to dance until kissed by his victim. He it was who drew Petter from the painted farm-cart on which we stood for a better view, grasping his hand so that to refuse would have been churlish; Petter joined the ring and all was unremarkable until the wily boy once more got into the middle and bent his back until his face was at Petter's crutch and danced, it seemed interminably, while Petter gazed down at the upturned face too embarrassed to give the required kiss.

We ate yoghurt soup and macaroni, crunchy beans in crushed tomato, vine-leaves stuffed with rice, and crisp red water melon, the quantities enormous and not a sheep's eyeball to be seen; dancing was replaced by song and the musicians' clamour struck a softer note until cut short by a sudden silence in the crowd – the man with the knife had arrived, a doctor, not the Imam who had been present most of the day, who would do the deed. Ahmed's father insisted that we go with him to the upper room where the family elders gathered; he sat on an upright chair and the wary child in pyjama trousers was passed to him. The father loosed the cord and settled the boy on his knees, looped his forearms under and between the child's thighs and gripped his wrists so that, his bottom hanging low, knees wide apart, his crutch was thrust forward. The doctor swabbed behind the foreskin, pulled it over the corona and teased the little penis to tumescence; with the foreskin now painfully stretched forward by an instrument resembling pliers, a swift sweep of the knife removed it.

An astonishing quantity of blood spurted from the wound, much of it over my white trousers. Ahmed screamed and men called his name and snapped their fingers to distract him, but he screamed the more. Then the stitching began, a cat's cradle of a business with the tiny bloody penis tugged here and there as the stitches tightened and the profuse bleeding was reduced to a welling ooze; we watched in silence as the last drops of blood gathered and fell away. The penis, straight before this surgery, now veered to the left. The offending foreskin was tipped into the lavatory. That may well have been the fate of our inventory of churches: sent to the Ministry of Culture, I was thanked for it, and Cappadocia became a holiday resort.

*   *   *

Our report on the state of early Armenian churches in the north-east was probably as pointless. 'Armenia' is an unutterable word in many Turkish circles, but a century ago Armenians were a significant element of the population in eastern Anatolia, probably indigenous but certainly rooted there five centuries before Alexander the Great made his way across their lands on his way to Persia – that is some two millennia before the Ottoman Turks arrived. Now much reduced and land-locked in the southern Caucasus, its ancestral territory once reached far further to the west, to the Pontic Alps on the Black Sea and the mountains of Cilicia on the Mediterranean coast. Among the earliest Christians, they declared Christianity the state religion in c.314 and the Church has ever since lain at the core of their national identity and culture. The classical period of their art was from the fourth to the seventh century, then abruptly halted by Arab invasions within a decade of Mohammed's death in AD 632.

With the establishment of a Christian dynasty, the Bagratid, in
AD 884, there was a brilliant cultural recovery, particularly in architecture, until the invasion of the Seljuk Turks in the 1060s. The
cultural heart of the people then moved west to Cilicia, the kingdom
of Lesser Armenia that played so important a role in the Crusades
and built such impregnable castles.

Any boy of my generation, and particularly one brought up by
as educated and enquiring a parent as my mother, was likely to
have known something of the Armenian diaspora and the great
tragedy of 1915 that was its climax, when far more than a million of
all ages were driven from their homes to die of starvation and
exposure in the desert of northern Syria. My long dormant interest
was roused by a modest book given me by Robin Fedden much
worn in the re-reading.* By Denis Hills, an old-fashioned traveller
without objective, but for whom travelling itself, together with
curiosity and the surrendering to impulse that enlivens everything,
were enough, it is not a polemic, but to his continuous narrative he
added eight appendices, of which one was on the Nestorians
(Christians of whom I had hoped to find some evidence in my two
attempts to explore Hakkari), and another, rather longer, *The
Georgian Churches of Turkey* (as one is required to call these considerable monuments of the Armenians) – and it was with this that
the seed was sown.

Hills himself, by the time I met him to compare notes, was
seventy and still travelling, but only in Europe – Poland mostly –
and long past his Turkish wanderings. He was a quiet shadow of
the man who had been brave enough to dub Idi Amin a 'Black
Nero' ten years or so before – the one thing for which writers of
history may recall him. Teaching at Makerere University in
Kampala in the early Seventies he had been appalled by the
dictator's butcheries, and when the typescript of a critical book
was leaked to the authorities he was, without formal trial but after

* Denis Cecil Hills, *My Travels in Turkey*, 1964.

a confrontation with Amin himself, holding his ground, condemned to be shot. After Harold Wilson and the Queen became humiliatingly involved, James Callaghan (then Foreign Secretary) was sent to bring him back to London. He died, aged ninety, in 2004, fretting at the penury that forced on him the institutional life of the Star and Garter Home for indigent old soldiers – he had been an officer in the King's Own Royal Regiment for most of World War II, his adventures as derring-do and humorous as any. Few men deserve less to be so forgotten.

It was not easy to expand Hills' notes, so many village names had changed beyond recognition and association – Keleşot to Filizli and Arkunis to Ilikaynak, and all Robin Fedden's maps had the former Armenian names – and it is an area not much written about in any language, but we set off for Trabzon (Trebizond) armed with notes garnered from all sorts of sources and were, we found, far better informed about the churches that we sought than any of the local 'guides'. It was a melancholy journey, for we found too many churches that, left neglected, might have centuries of survival left in them so soundly built were they, so accurately cut, trimmed and decorated their masonry, but, carelessly quarried (always from the bottom) for hearthstones and doorsteps, tumbling had been the consequence. At Dörtkilise (which means, literally, four churches) we found the fourth that other travellers have supposed not to exist; the main church was dilapidated and overgrown in the same sad beauty that obtains in many a Piranesi print, with two smaller churches close by, but the fourth is below it and across the valley, invisible so heavy is the overgrowth, but from it the main church can be seen. A fifth church, Bayirkilise (which means ascent or hill church), is two hours' climb to just below the summer snow line at ten thousand feet or so, a breathless finger and toe clamber with a local shepherd; at one point I felt the nausea that signals altitude sickness and clung for minutes with my face pressed to the rock, thinking this a beautiful place to die and not be recovered. Too far from any village, transporting a doorstep quite impossible, the tiny chapel, a thousand years old and still in perfect structural condition, must have been built for the loneliest of anchorites.

Penek, once a circular church of sophisticated magnificence, had long ago been used as an armoury or magazine and an explosion had destroyed its dome and upper walls, but the lower were still stout and beautiful and it was still possible to imagine a procession in the ambulatory, still possible to be as in awe of it as of S. Vitale in Ravenna. In Nikoma, where Denis Hills recorded nine well-preserved murals of saints between the windows of a chapel abutting a cowshed, we found the arches and the roof fallen and only three weather-worn figures left, the shell occupied by shepherds brewing the tea that was our only reward for a march of twenty kilometres. As stewed and bitter as any tea that I drank as a National Service-man, they demonstrated how to drink it while holding a small slab of sugar between our teeth; I noted that not one of them still had the central teeth of either register. At Barhal, because used as a mosque, the church was in fine condition, the masonry as crisp as on the day it was cut, the arcaded outer walls as mathematically perfect and proportional as any of Bach's *Goldberg Variations*, but close to the apse two poplar saplings had rooted and must by now have brought about its fall; I tried to convince the not unfriendly Imam that they should be dug out and that simply cutting them down would only delay calamity, but his response was very much 'what the devil has it to do with you?' and that the church's fall would enable him to build a proper mosque. In the north we followed part of Rose Macaulay's supposedly fictional journey to Lake Çildir – at six thousand feet the highest stretch of water in all Turkey, swarming with mosquitoes, teeming with seagulls, a place of six-month winters, Russia within sight. Reviewers damned her novel of 1956, *The Towers of Trebizond*, for its landscapes of fantasy, but every word of her descriptions was true and I was filled with admiration for her intrepidity thirty years before.

We strode, thigh-deep, through the meadow flowers that were the joy of the English countryside when I was a boy. Offered a lift in his trailer by a tractor driver, we found our feet in the grave soil of one Haydar Öz, his gravestone identifying the projecting bones. In Olur, where for some days we lodged in the fire station (no locks to the lavatories, no doors to the showers, the custodian part Quasimodo and part Argus fascinated by the blond nakedness of Petter), the Deputy Governor lent us his fluorescent peacock-blue Land Rover to shorten what would otherwise have been a two-day trek over the mountains, and insisted that a local man with a shotgun go with us. 'Why the gun?' I asked, 'To shoot bears' the answer – to which my response was to buy a large plastic container of honey and insist on leading the expedition. My trust in the gratitude of bears for gifts of honey, no doubt ridiculous, was quite beyond their comprehension (and Petter's), but A.A. Milne's Pooh Bear, my contemporary as a child, was pathetically lurking. There were no bears, but at one point I disturbed an eagle on a ledge – and perhaps have seen nothing more beautiful than the one lazy flap of its wings that set it on a seemingly effortless vertical flight up the sun-warmed cliff behind it.

It was in Olur too that I encountered a handsome young bitch, part Alsatian perhaps, but lighter, taller, rangier, her dugs heavy with milk. She sheared away from me, as do all feral dogs at first, and I had nothing to offer her. An hour later I found her again, dead, garrotted by thick wire; kneeling to remove it, she was still warm; rage kept back the tears and I did not believe the excuse 'rabies', offered by an uncomprehending passer-by trying to be helpful; I could think only of her desperate struggle (had I witnessed it, what would I have done?) and her pups slowly starving to death.

*   *   *

Dogs are the fiercest memories of other journeys. Walking round the Sea of Marmora – a drab and rubbish-strewn experience with scarcely a hint remaining of the marbled past from which its name is derived – Petter and I were in one dreary little town reputed to have a Roman ruin enthusiastically greeted by a small white terrier;

we found the wretched ruin and then returned to the town centre in the hope of lunch, just in time to encounter him again, this time a corpse chucked in the back of a rubbish truck. With Polly Hope, painter, sculptor, theatre designer (far better known in Germany than here) and others, wandering the Aegean shores of Turkey in a gulet (a timber sailing-boat with an engine), we came upon a dog chained to the roof of its bleak shelter by so short a chain that only its hind paws touched the ground, a great fly-blown wound on his brow; I swam back to the gulet for ointment, but the only food I could find was bread and milk; these we gave him and dressed the wound as best we could, but were unable to remove the chain – Polly and I were for desperate measures, but the gulet's Turkish captain would not allow the dog on board and we had to leave him. Did he starve to death? Did the infected wound eventually kill him?

We found an old donkey, alone on a deserted island with no obvious source of water – he trotted to us as though we were his friends and would not leave us as we searched for the antique fragments reported to be there; he must have been transported there to die, and we could do nothing for him. We did, however, rescue two full-grown turtles from the shallow, stagnant garden pool of an hotel where we had a drink while the gulet took on fuel one evening before mooring off-shore. I was so appalled by their condition, their shells shaggy with green weed, the larger a metre long, the water only half a metre deep, dead fish floating on its surface, that I begged the others on board help me to release them. At the first glimmering of light, four or so, we took the dinghy to within fifty metres of the hotel, abducted the turtles and returned to the gulet; the captain, thinking that we had stolen them to eat, could not understand the urgency with which we asked him to up-anchor (always a time-consuming business that involved his wife's swimming down to dislodge it), but eventually we sailed some miles from the coast and let the turtles drop into clear deep water; to see them dive at forty-five degrees, down, down, down until invisible, was our reward.

Outsider II

One dog I did bring back to London. In 1987, mystified that Freya Stark, in her book *Alexander's Path*, thirty years before (extolled by the *New Statesman* as 'as near perfect as such a narrative can be'), had written what seemed nonsense, I set out to prove her either wrong or right. I liked her, admired and envied her, but late in life she came into the category of 'dear old thing' and often fell asleep over lunch and oftener still in mid conversation in her unconventional house in Asolo – always to be forgiven, for she was, in my time, approaching her centenary. She was the last and latest of the heroic English women travellers in the Near East, a generation younger than Gertrude Bell, and her many books on Turkey are invaluable records of how things were there before the country became a holiday destination, but *Alexander's Path* did not live up to its title and served neither its subject nor Freya well. Armed with her account and those of Arrian and Quintus Curtius Rufus as correctives, David George, considerable photographer, my companion, we attempted to follow Alexander's leisurely meandering marches along and across Asia Minor to the site of the great battle of Issus and the defeat of Darius of Persia.

I had travelled before with David, in Denmark from the windy tip of Jutland where, at Skagen, Danish painters set up their easels and recorded the raw life of fisherfolk, imagined history and were seduced by light, to its far south bordering the territory of Schleswig-Holstein, that bane of history lessons long ago, where Sickert was born a Dane before being compelled to become an Englishman. Who now recalls, I wonder, the Eastern Roumelian Question? We had also been to Tunisia, concerned much more with Carthage and ancient Rome than anything Tunisian, and I knew that we would work well together in Turkey, for his eye was very much in tune with mine (and mine with his, as a photographer) and he had a wonderful capacity for being interested. The journey, which ended in chaos at Heathrow and across London, for we returned on the night of the great tree-felling and light-extinguishing storm of October 1997, so cemented our friendship and so educated us both – it was David who saw so clearly where the Battle of Issus must have been, to the south of Toprakkale, for only from that hill could Darius have commanded a view of the plain, the coast and the flanking hills, and have been sure of his line of retreat – that I think we could have walked the Silk Route together. He was subsequently my lodger for a while in Eldon Road, and often came into my study to say that he was off to do some shopping and ask if he could bring anything for me. Milk, I might ask, or bread, or oranges – but to no point, for often days might pass before his return. To my 'Where *have* you been? his answer was always 'I met such a pretty girl . . . such legs . . . such hair . . . such eyes . . . ' I could never say how much I wanted him myself.

I could have written a book on Alexander in Anatolia as long as Freya's, but did not, and all that remains of that aspiration is the grave, under a black pine in my garden, of Mop, the pup we found in the ruins of Mopsuestia, an ancient site in Turkey's armpit. Her right foreleg was broken, the shoulder dislocated, and she was so dehydrated that death was not far off. I should have broken her neck: instead, I emptied my knapsack enough to carry her with ease and, eventually, returned to London with her. She stands, *pars pro toto*, for all the dogs and donkeys whom I failed.

*   *   *

As only an enquiring amateur I have no academic root in any of this enthusiasm for Turkey centuries before the invading Turks arrived in Anatolia, but one small practical experience of digging, identifying and cataloguing in the field I owe to the late Dr Kenan Erim, Professor of Classics at New York University, who for years (and not without envious opposition) led the excavations at Aphrodisias, the site in western Turkey that supplied much marble and sculpture for Augustan Rome. He it was who, in 1979, uncovered the remains of the Sebasteion, an unique (so far) ceremonial approach to a temple, in this case that of the Julio-Claudian emperors, and a treasure of such narrative reliefs as Claudius seizing Britannia and

Nero annexing Armenia. After hearing him lecture on the subject in May 1983 at The Anatolian Civilisations, a vast and astonishing encyclopedic exhibition mounted in Istanbul by the Council of Europe, I asked him if I might join him as a neophyte later in the year. He set me to work on the defensive wall erected by the Byzantines round the old heart of the city, a higgledy-piggledy structure of fragmentary sculpture and masonry dragged from tumbled buildings. There was something about him that spoke of gentlemanly Ottoman Turks at ease with a dozen languages, alive and dead, with European culture, philosophy and politics; we slaved all day and in the evenings sat at his feet, much as did the students of Xenocrates in the olive groves of ancient academe, astonished by the polymathic range of interests demonstrated by this vigorous and autocratic aesthete who could not suffer fools.

Working with him that autumn was the remarkable Professor Juliette de la Genière, taking time off from the marine archaeology that she was pursuing on ancient vessels shipwrecked off the coast near Reggio, Calabria. She entertained us with a tale of interference by the Mafia and their having to be bought off with a share of the antiquities retrieved (a daily bargaining), and then let loose the notion that they were in possession of Caravaggio's *Nativity with Saints Francis and Lawrence*, stolen from the Oratory of St Lawrence in Palermo in October 1969 and subsequently housed in a church known as Santa Maria della Mafia in the hills of Aspromonte, to the east of Montalto (Monte Cocuzza); the large-scale map that she subsequently sent me identified the village as Sant di Polsi. Rodolfo Siviero, the honest Italian policeman most interested in such matters, had died only two weeks before and as there was no one else with whom I could discuss such a dangerous matter, I had to let it pass.

Two small things at Aphrodisias remain with me – the true taste of pomegranates bursting on the tree after a day in the sun, and, living in one of the ramshackle showers erected in the garden of the site, the family of toads that crowded onto my feet when water streamed down my body.

CHAPTER 8

The Blunt Affair

In 1979 I did not go to Turkey. Two years earlier, with the sensational Mentmore sale mounted in a marquee at the house, Sotheby's had confirmed the recovery of the depressed art market – indeed, had I not been asked to go to the USA for a month or so in January 1977 to discuss the wants of several museums, and to Paris in February, I might argue that the Mentmore sale had been the trigger of that recovery, so outstanding were the prices, so huge the crowds, but I now realise that it was the first major beneficiary of a new certainty that the slump was over. With my working life back on track after three bleak years, it seemed that I was spending more time abroad – mostly in the USA – than at home, and after a particularly intense stint in New York and the East Coast in May 1979, I was not in the mind to plan and execute another Turkish journey, and certainly not one that would break new ground, for I had by then learned the value of scrupulous preparation. Instead, with an old friend, Colin Darracott, and two of my dogs, Schubert and Gamage, at the end of August and for the first eight days of September, I walked first on Dartmoor and then along the shoreline to the south of it – at more than twenty miles a day, as exhausting an exercise as any trek in search of Greek and Roman ruins. Back in London on the evening of Sunday 9 September, I found messages from Anthony Blunt, more than anxious to talk to me – but not on the phone. I went at once to see him, and that, for me, was the beginning of the Blunt Affair.

At this point I must turn back to May 1970 when I sold a drawing by Constant Troyon, sight unseen, to Andrew Gow, an elderly Cambridge don of whom I knew nothing other than that he was Anthony's friend – and that I knew only because it was Anthony who told me of his wish to buy it and, further, that I was commanded to deliver it to Gow in Cambridge. He struck me as the coldest man I had ever encountered, a man of calculated silences, intimidating, and, beginning with 'Anthony wishes you to know . . . ' he told me the tale of Communism and espionage that now everybody knows; he offered no other reason for doing so. His account of the business was as dry, succinct, orderly and clinical as that of a pathologist recording the condition of a corpse, but I sensed that not only did he know more, but that he had eliminated from the recital any part that he had played, and took him to be mentor rather than confessor. I was not required to respond – nor did I quite know how to – but as it lent an armature to old Courtauld Institute gossip and mythology, I was not surprised. I sensed too, precaution against events unspecified and unpredictable but could see no particular point in the timing, and Gow's telling me rather than Anthony himself, I interpreted as Anthony's unwillingness to discuss the matter (though, surely, he must have been certain of my loyalty) or involve me more deeply. Were it ever to be raised, perhaps in some emergency, he had had the foresight to cut out the need for explanations. Now I wonder if this was Gow's laying-on of hands, telling me a truth that after his death and Anthony's disgrace might, if untold, be impossible to disentangle from rumour, blame and spite.

I said nothing of our encounter; Anthony asked nothing and everything he knew of it he knew from Gow. The only change in our relationship was, throughout the Seventies, an increasing warmth and, on his part, a relaxation in his essential privacy – his long relationship with John Gaskin, for example, though now in steep decline, affection reduced to the iron shackles of duty and responsibility, was something about which he felt able to talk freely. John, once handsome in the conventions of Thirties cinema, did not age well; as his body thickened and his skin grew coarse and red, the rich post-menopausal women who bought jewellery from Armour and Winston, the shop in the Burlington Arcade where he worked, found him less attractive and his well-paid occasional work as a *cicerone* on their Mediterranean travels fell away. So did his work for the shop and his last role there was more an act of kindness than employment – they let him act as a runner with unfashionable things taken in exchange, and these he pressed on scarcely willing friends until they had no more elderly relatives to whom such expensive trinkets could be given. Sinking into boredom and inactivity, he could spend hours slicing carrots very thin and whining on the telephone in the vile slang of the malevolent queen, often vicious about Anthony. He was not interested in any cultural pursuit – music was a mystery to him, he found it impossible to read a book, and what little curiosity he showed in art was only in the profit that might be made from it. When Armour and Winston's jewellery died away as a source of pocket money, it was replaced by Eric Hebborn's old master drawings, and John became a familiar figure in Old Bond Street and its environs, touting fakes that, by association, were eventually to menace Anthony's reputation. Anthony dreaded retirement: as long as he had the attic flat in Portman Square, with constant access to the library and his study, he could escape from John and ignore the great and growing gulf between them, but in the sort of flat he could afford when no longer Director of the Institute, life would undoubtedly be unbearable. How, he asked, could he get rid of him and live on his own?

It was I, not John, who ferried Anthony into hospital in August 1972 for surgery to remedy bowel cancer. Though serious enough for the Cabinet Secretary and MI5 to prepare themselves for what disclosures might follow on his death, he made a strong recovery – brave, even, for so fastidious a man – but the lurking menace of cancer made him think more purposefully of retirement. He had no savings, owned no property, and his pension was to be so small that he could hardly live on it. Completely out of touch with the realities of life in London, he was appalled to find the price of property so high and realised that one of his precious Poussins must be sold. As the then Director of the Cleveland Museum of Art had repeatedly told him of his serious interest in the larger, *Eliezer and Rebecca*, worth, he thought, much more than the smaller and likely both to buy him a larger flat and establish some investment income, the decision was easily made.

It was at this point that John Brealey caused havoc. Brealey was then a young restorer of the modern scientific school, by whom Anthony was charmed and to whom he had entrusted, with Joan Seddon, the conservation of Mantegna's *Triumphs* in the Royal Collection, which, though extensively and deeply damaged, have some claim to be one of the two most important works of Renaissance art in Britain (the other the cartoons for tapestries by Raphael, in the Victoria and Albert Museum). When, sitting below the *Rebecca* in Anthony's flat, Brealey learned that it was likely to be sold, he offered to lightly clean its surface, removing perhaps more than a century of the nicotine and household grubbiness that dulled its brilliance – a simple and straightforward job perhaps requiring no more than distilled water and cotton wool swabs – arguing that this might increase the price.

It did the very opposite: it wrecked the sale – as any old hand in the market might have guessed. A grubby picture is one that has hung undisturbed for decades, perhaps never touched by restorers, perhaps in perfect condition under the grime, its grubbiness an indication of long ownership, a denial of recent trafficking in the trade, and most museums, buying such a picture under the old rule *caveat emptor*, prefer to clean and conserve their purchases them-selves. This painting had hung for years in an obscure house in Cheshire until bought by the London dealer Duits in 1933, from whom it was immediately bought for Anthony by his close friend Victor Rothschild for a very few hundred pounds (the amount, variously recalled, was either £200 or £300), and in his ownership it remained in its seemingly sound and undisturbed condition, growing only a little more dimmed by yellowing varnish and the air we breathe – not even when he lent it to the great Poussin exhibition in the Louvre in 1960 had it occurred to Anthony to have it cleaned.

When Brealey phoned Anthony to tell him that the painting was now clean and that he wanted to discuss the next step, Anthony phoned me and said that he feared something was wrong – no next step should have been necessary. Together we went to Brealey's studio in Hamilton Terrace. 'My God' was Anthony's immediate and almost only response. Brealey had gone far further than remove the surface dirt, and for the first time I had an inkling of the difficulties that Joan Seddon had experienced with him as a collaborator on the delicate Mantegnas. This was not achieved through delicate swabbing with pure water; this was an acetone job with a Brillo pad. He had cleaned the surface radically, revealing every crack, bruise and other ancient damage, of which the worst were massive losses of original paint from the central subject of the canvas. After a long silence in which Anthony seemed physically bowed by the blow – for blow it was – without a word of reproach he asked Brealey to make the best that he could of it. On the way back to Portman Square he said, 'I can't possibly sell it to Cleveland now: in fact, I can't sell it to anybody, knowing what I now know.'

This painting was his prize possession, his ownership not only an earnest of his devoted scholarship, but of his lifelong homage to Poussin the intellectual and affection for Poussin the man. In having discerned nothing of its true condition he was not alone; in 1960 every Poussin scholar in the world had pored over it and seen nothing amiss – not even Denis Mahon, for whom this picture's date had been a matter of crucial argument, had doubted its condition. For Anthony this was no consolation and the sudden disclosure of such a major flaw was the cause of great distress. His protégé had turned what seemed a kindness into a betrayal that wrecked the hope of a comfortable retirement; worse, it made him doubt his eye, and in this he could not be consoled. Later, installed in far too small a flat, where it dominated the room, he confessed that he sometimes felt the same hatred for the picture as he felt for John Gaskin, and that in being compelled to live his last years at close quarters with the possession and the man he had once most loved, but for which and whom he now felt only profound distaste, was a circle of hell of which Dante had never thought.

Brealey effected a restoration that to me seemed obvious, his reconstruction of the draperies less defined than they had been, as though – in tune with the restoration philosophies of the time – he did not want his work to be mistaken for original and yet recognised that the camouflage of tonal hatching then practised by Italian restorers would disrupt the spectator's reading of the composition and divert him from the narrative. I could never understand how so many art historians, and particularly Denis Mahon who was responsible for the erosion of Anthony's status as the oracle of Poussin studies, when they saw the painting after restoration, failed to recognise that significant changes had occurred, evident even in photographs. When, after Anthony's death, I spoke out about the painting's condition, this was put down to disloyalty – an oddly critical and negative note, as his biographer, Miranda Carter, put it some years later; but I did so for the sake of John Gaskin when the probate value of Anthony's estate was published as £800,000 or so, the *Rebecca* valued, on the assumption that it was in sound original condition, at a far higher figure than it should have been. I hoped for John's sake – he was in considerable distress over the sum of death duties to be paid – that the valuation would, in fairness, be revised; it was not and I was scorned for denigrating Anthony.

Instead of the *Rebecca*, to fund his retirement in 1974, Anthony was compelled to sell the small Poussin landscape that for £12,000 he had bought from Duncan Grant only a decade earlier. That he made a profit of almost £100,000 gave spiteful gossips the opportunity to run to Duncan and make mischief; but he – whom Joe McCrindle and I were then regularly visiting with food parcels – was at eighty-nine in amiable dotage and beyond their manipulation;

it was, nevertheless, the first inkling I had that some in Anthony's wider academic field were inspired by malevolence.

Anthony did not know that he owned a third painting by Poussin. His confidence was so much sapped by the persistent undermining of Denis Mahon in the early Sixties that when he identified a to some extent uncharacteristically small, dark and highly emotional *Agony in the Garden* on copper as possibly by Poussin, he could not bring himself to believe it, anticipating another destructive attack on his connoisseurship if he published it. I had bought it for him for very little money but could hardly reassure him – he, in spite of all the Mahon artillery, was still the expert in my loyal view. After poring over it in the good light of his study in the Institute, he took it up to his flat and hung it in the dark corner by the door of the dining room that was so little used, almost ensuring that no visitor should even glance at it. He refused to let me give its filthy surface the lightest possible cleaning, refused to let the technology department examine it, did very little work on it himself and in his catalogue of Poussin's paintings* dismissed it as 'a Poussinesque composition in the writer's possession', perhaps connected with a painting now lost but known from records. I have not seen it since his death, but in 2001 it was, I understand, cleaned and found to have an inscription on the reverse that proved its authenticity as by Poussin.

The sale of Duncan Grant's Poussin brought not enough for Anthony to do what he most fervently wished – to discharge the responsibility that he felt for John, and live alone. Without John the small flat he found in Portsea Hall, a block within easy walking distance of the Institute, would have been comfortable, but with John, the disruptive enemy of the work he wished to continue, comfort of any kind was out of the question. The attic of 20 Portman Square, its servants' quarters, was nobly proportioned in

---

* Anthony Blunt, *The Paintings of Nicolas Poussin*, 1966, Critical Catalogue, p. 160, L 30.

comparison with the rooms in Portsea Hall, and the two men were inescapably on top of each other; moving there was the most serious of many measures of Anthony's long detachment from the practicalities of life. That in June 1974 he himself found the flat was almost astonishing, but having found it, he did not know how to buy it and I commended a solicitor to deal with the business, David, husband of Jill Allibone, and of David he became fond enough to appoint him his executor. I found him a carpenter to build bookshelves and sent him John Buttle, a gentle giant of absolute honesty, to remove his furniture, books and paintings. The beautiful big desk on which, for more than a quarter of a century, he had spread his books and papers to think and teach, was a Courtauld piece and belonged to the Institute and he had urgently to replace it with one much, and uncomfortably, smaller to fit in the new quarters; I found one, a plain English piece, early nineteenth century, with practical extensions to pull out, almost doubling its size, should he wish to spread a hundred photographs; it was hardly Hepplewhite. In all the preparations for the move John played no part, but for the move itself Anthony planned, well in advance, to be in Peru, leaving everything for John to do so as 'to avoid disagreements – it's a job better done by one'. As is always the case, things long settled in old circumstances did not fit in new, and on the morning of the move, John made, from Portsea Hall, the first distress call of the day. On Anthony's return the flat was still in chaos and John's mood poisonous; I know no other man who could for so long sustain a bitter sulk and by the end of the year, exhausted with stress, Anthony was in hospital again.

They eventually made what they could of their new quarters, but, so close together, the gulf between them widened. Anthony went often to the Institute to telephone his miseries; John used a call-box round the corner from Portsea Hall; neither, unless on some trivial matter, called from home, wanting not to be overheard; John foolishly mistook me for his ally. Occasionally all three of us dined with Anthony's old friend, Moore Crosthwaite, in Crescent

Grove, one of those patches of Clapham that pretends to be Kensington, but John was always petulant in his boredom, his only interest there not Moore's collections of ancient Roman glass and other small antiquities (he had long been ambassador to Lebanon), but his boyfriend, Dick Spalding, a stocky American ex-sailor in the US Navy, an able seaman so to speak, of such abundant sexuality that neither woman nor man could have resisted him – he was, as it were, a Tom of Finland figure in small, without seeming the least queer; and if how Moore, querulous, secretive, ashamed and terrified of being identified as homosexual, first got him into his bed is a mystery, how he kept him is more mysterious still. To be bedded by Dick was to experience an irresistible exploratory force – and he preferred his subject territories not to have been bathed or showered for at least twenty-four hours.

John was by then given, even without alcohol, to humourless outbursts, tediously long, of queer bitchery about everyone whom he perceived as crossing him and Dick was always the trigger for these – Dick, who made his own choice of the body with which he might have a sexual adventure, but whose staunch, dumb loyalty to Moore John could never breach. John seemed incapable of recognising that he was further and further alienated from Anthony's friends (he had none of his own) by the unloveable behaviour into which he too easily slipped. His looks long gone, his spirit ugly, he had become an incubus.

Anthony used every excuse to get away. I drove him often to Waddesdon where he was not only much loved by the Rothschilds, but for ever working on the catalogues of the collections there; and on Thursday 12 May 1977, with Neil MacGregor (then very much his favourite student) huddled in the back (perhaps not quite the right word, but he seemed slightly scared by both of us and folded very small), we drove to Mentmore and spent a very happy day viewing the sale, breaking off for a picnic. Only two weeks earlier he had had his first cataract operation and was unsteady enough to need me as a prop, but that gave me the benefit of looking at everything with his deliberate diligence. At the astonishing gouaches of Blarenberghe he remarked that he had forgotten how blue they were (years later my response to light and sky after the removal of cataracts) and with some amusement corrected Sotheby's identification of a pretty hunting lodge as a view of Fontainebleau. It was one of those rare days when Anthony put up no sort of guard, but was funny, mischievous and boyish, much more of my age than his own. On 1 November 1977, five weeks after the event, he would allow no greater celebration of his seventieth birthday than a quiet dinner to which his friends John Golding (art historian, painter and teacher at the Royal College of Art) and James Joll (Professor of International History at London University) should be invited, together with John Gaskin; this went as he wished, without a disagreeable performance from the latter, though I had a disaster with an over-poached salmon. At nine in the morning of 28 December, Anthony telephoned to tell me that John, whose unremarkable birthday it was, was in a rage that I had arranged no matching celebration for him.

At the end of January 1978 both Anthony and I were in Düsseldorf for another Poussin exhibition to which he had lent his *Rebecca* and to the catalogue of which he had contributed two essays; the specific catalogue entry was by Pierre Rosenbourg, who repeated a remark made by Anthony himself very soon after Brealey's restoration – 'About my own *Eliazer and Rebecca*, I would say that recent cleaning has confirmed . . . that it is a very late work, dating from the Sixties.' What wry thoughts, I wondered, had passed through Anthony's mind as he considered the phrase 'a very late work.'* No one remarked on the new state of the painting, not Rosenbourg, the most eagle-eyed of French art historians, not even Michael Kitson who was there to support Anthony and who had as good an eye as any man I knew. Had any other scholar thought to

---

* See *Burlington Magazine*, 1974, p.761 for Anthony's review of Jacques Thuillier's *L'Opera Completa di Poussin*.

raise controversy over this, Anthony would not have fought, for increasing weariness made him gently indulgent here, accepting all, arguing with nothing. One little episode particularly amused Michael – in search of a restaurant we passed a McDonald's and Anthony murmured, 'How strange to find a Scottish restaurant in Düsseldorf.'

The years 1978 and 1979 too (at least until September) passed in a pattern of early morning calls from Anthony and late morning calls from John, each letting off steam about the other. We often had lunch in an Italian restaurant in Connaught Street, sometimes with Joe McCrindle, whose familiarity with Christie's and Sotheby's and the ease with which interesting things could still be bought for absurdly little, encouraged Anthony almost to haunt these auction houses. Sometimes, almost always unsuccessfully, he asked me to bid for him, and eventually it became clear that, having seen us together, too canny dealers supposed that every time I joined the bidding it was either for Anthony or for myself with his blessing. Proof that this was so came when Anthony identified an oil sketch for a banner hung in Notre-Dame, now lost, but known from a print; not by Poussin, but sufficiently close for Sotheby's to sell it under that portmanteau attribution, it was, though pretty enough, valuable only as an art historical document – even so, Anthony gave me a bid that he could ill afford. I asked him if he would mind my continuing to bid on my own behalf if I failed to get it within his margin – and that is what happened on the day. I dropped out at £5,000, far beyond Anthony's bid, but the bidding continued to £15,000 as two Italian dealers fought for it. Then I left the room, but was followed by the buyer with the question, 'What have I bought?' I replied that whatever it was he had paid far too much for it, for it was certainly not by Poussin, as I supposed he thought. 'But Blunt . . . ' he said, tailing off, crestfallen, as I shook my head.

In some ways 1978 was a terrible year for Anthony. On 2 February Andrew Gow, his mentor (my word for him) for half a century, died. From time to time I had driven Anthony to

Cambridge to see him while I spent time in the Fitzwilliam where friends told me that, into his nineties and restricted to a wheelchair and walking frame (both bequeathed to the sick bay of Trinity College), Gow had slowly exchanged his essential gravity for stingy bloodymindedness; on our return journeys we drove largely in silence, Anthony morose in mood and seeming physically shrunken. The net value of Gow's will was £357,736, then an enviably substantial sum; most of it went to the Fitzwilliam, and to Anthony he bequeathed only two Faenza vases, three small rugs and the £100 that was his trifling memento to several old friends. I found it impossible to reconcile so mean a bequest with so long and intellectually intimate a friendship, and was even more puzzled by our contrived encounter in May 1970, though confirmed in my then assessment of the man; with his death, had I become the only holder of the secret outside that secret world?

Worse, perhaps, was the death in the early hours of 6 July 1978, of Antoine Seilern, the greatest of benefactors to the Courtauld Institute – greater, I must argue, than Samuel Courtauld himself, so extensive, yet so severely art historical, were his collections. Any American university receiving them would at once have built new premises to house them, but the Courtauld has treated them shabbily in spite of knowing for decades that it was Antoine's heir.

Antoine, Count Seilern, born in London in 1901, holder of Austrian and British passports, was as discreet and retiring as he was rich and aristocratic. His mother, Antoinette Woerishoffer, who died five days after his birth, was the source of his Christian name and his American fortune. His childhood spent in England and New York, he settled in Vienna in 1910 and his years as a young man were spent there in a whirl of Straussian balls, horse-racing, great cars and private aeroplanes, and on African safaris of which the trophy heads and horns hung in what seemed hundreds on the stairs of his Kensington house as a reproachful reminder of his misspent youth. At the age of thirty-two, encouraged by his father to study the history of art, he enrolled at the University of Vienna, his courses there supplemented with private tuition from Johannes Wilde, ten years his senior, the great Hungarian art historian who was then curator of paintings in Vienna's Kunsthistorisches Museum and was later to be Deputy Director of the Courtauld Institute; it was he who steered Antoine towards his eventual doctorate on the ceiling paintings of Rubens, the painter who remained Antoine's passion for the rest of his life. This doctorate achieved in 1939, a year after the Nazi absorption of Austria, he engineered the flight of Wilde and his wife to London (and of other friends), and came himself with only weeks to spare before the outbreak of World War II in September. He volunteered to serve as a private in the Pioneer Corps but was eventually attached to the Intelligence Corps and given a commission.

He brought from Vienna his 'little collection' already important enough to send for safety to Aberystwyth to be stored in the National Library of Wales. Even during the war it grew, and it continued to grow until his death – thirty-two paintings by Rubens, a dozen by Giambattista Tiepolo, two by Parmigianino, two by Pieter Brueghel, fourteen by Teniers, and others by Van Dyck, Fetti, Crespi, Guardi, Ricci, Magnasco . . . and others still, by Cézanne, Degas, Manet, Morisot, Pissarro and Renoir that complement Sam Courtauld's pictures. Among old master drawings there were thirty by Rembrandt, nine by Watteau, six by Michelangelo, three by Dürer and one each by Bellini, Mantegna and Leonardo. 'A private collection,' he once said, 'is formed for no other purpose than the enjoyment of it.' In the foreword to his catalogue, scrupulously researched and written by himself, of Johannes Wilde he wrote of his 'deeply felt gratitude for many years of unfailing friendship, and for all that he has done for me . . . I have relied with the utmost faith – always rewarded – on his guidance . . . I have sought his opinion before acquiring every work of art, and have never regretted it. What merit there is in the collection is due to his counsel. So it is with the greatest sincerity that I say, Thank you'. It was typical of Antoine's modesty that he published his collection without his name, and that it is now known only by the address of his old home in Princes Gate, but in his quest for anonymity, Johannes too is lost.

Antoine was heavily built, with a booming voice and what seemed an overwhelming presence, but timid students he welcomed with unfailing kindly courtesy, young art historians too, leaving even the most raw and insignificant of them alone to contemplate his pictures, then comforting them with an elaborate old-fashioned tea. With one exception, art dealers and auctioneers were never allowed into the house, much to their annoyance – but James Byam Shaw was a dealer only by force of circumstance and much more a scholar whose role in forming the collection was significant. Antoine's connoisseurship was informed and passionate, considered and well judged, coherent and purposeful, never impulsive; his was an art historian's taste, educated and severe, yet enlivened by his response to emotion and sensuality – those who thought him a man more of head than heart were wrong. He railed against the misleading brightness of coloured reproductions, and for the over-cleaning and restoration of pictures in the National Gallery he had nothing but despairing contempt.

To some extent he remained a student all his life, attending many lectures at the Courtauld Institute, never missing those by Wilde on Michelangelo, Leonardo, Rubens and Titian. Sometimes he arrived on the heavy old BSA motorbike that in fine weather he used for tootling round London (replaced by a Vespa in his later years), and sometimes he came from his farm in Buckinghamshire in a wooden-bodied Austin Hereford shooting brake, a favourite pig sitting upright in the passenger seat beside him – the pair of them resembling a demonstration diagram from some eighteenth-century tome on physiognomy and expression. Long weekends on the farm gave him repose for reading and research, but from pig-breeding and orchids he derived great and simple earthly pleasure, and in his orchard he grew more fruit than he could give away.

Was there ever another art historian of quite such varied interests? Was there ever another connoisseur so intent on his privacy that his collection does not even bear his name? In his lifetime he gave the National Gallery its finest painting by Van Dyck and some one thousand, two hundred and fifty old master drawings to the British Museum; on his death his bequest to his beloved Courtauld Institute was given a probate valuation of £30 million, a figure that today seems utterly derisory; but he received no honours for his generosity, nor has the Lottery spent a bean on housing his collection as it deserves, and his modesty has been rewarded with oblivion.

Anthony, distraught – for Antoine had been the last live link with Johannes (who had died in September 1970) and what was undoubtedly the brief Golden Age of the Courtauld Institute – composed the most drab and unfeeling of obituaries for *The Times*, with not a hint of the emotion that he felt. I too was distraught. When I joined Christie's in 1958, Antoine warned me that I could not come to his house again – I was not surprised, for I knew of the general prohibition against all in the trade and, whatever the partners in the firm might think themselves, Antoine viewed them as no more than one step up from Bond Street dealers. Nevertheless, he came to me for information and occasionally asked me to bid for him; that he was particularly cross not to have bought the Fra Angelico in the Northwick sale,* in which the doctor saints Cosmas and Damian replace the diseased leg of a deacon with one taken from corpse of a dead Ethiopian, caused me, in the light of his own death, some wry retrospective (but unsuitable) amusement. In my dealing years he bought things from me and, I think, trusted me, for when he learned from Anthony that I had turned into museum runner, dogsbody, errand boy or what you will, I was let into the house again.

Since the beginning of the year I had been working for him on a valuation of possessions *not* to be included in his bequest to the

---

* Christie's 28 May 1965, lot 14.

Courtauld. His tax affairs were in confusion and the Inland Revenue would, he was certain, pounce as soon as he was dead; he was worried on two counts – that there would be some catastrophic interference with the bequest in favour of death duties, and that his handful of relatives in Vienna might be deprived of the modest inheritances on which he had decided. My task was to identify easily portable works not listed in any inventory of which the Inland Revenue might be aware, and then get them to Vienna without involving any formal export process. Looking now at the schedules I am appalled to be reminded that we considered fragile ancient Greek and Chinese antiquities as well as more manageable prints, drawings and watercolours by comparatively modern Austrian and German artists as well as by old masters. All these were to be packed into my unassuming Peugeot 404 and driven to Vienna, camouflaged by my pretence to be a landscape painter. That under a number of blank canvases, paintboxes, palettes, bundles of brushes and other painter's paraphernalia, should lurk unseen solander boxes crammed with treasures worthy of the British Museum was not that much of a risk (a hitchhiker would add further distraction) and Antoine was boyishly amused by the conspiracy.

Here I must stress how much Antoine meant to Anthony as a friend as well as a benefactor of the Institute, and how close they were. Anthony was among the first to know, late on 10 June, that Antoine's condition – he had for months been recovering from heart trouble and the amputation of a leg – had suddenly worsened and that he was again in hospital, threatened with the amputation of the other leg; and the early morning call on Sunday 11 June was about that, not about some tiresome spitefulness of John. When Antoine returned to Princes Gate, still in possession of his leg, he was again capable of roaring like a lion, to be heard in the basement from his bedroom, and he was every bit as clear in his mind about the business on which I was engaged, but this was not to last and, again in hospital, he died. At 8.55 am on 6 July, Anthony's morning call was bleak. Within twenty-four hours it was my duty to take him into hospital for his second cataract operation; it would camouflage his tears.

*   *   *

On the evening of Sunday 9 September 1979 Anthony told me, less as a friend, I thought, than formally, as his executor perhaps, that he might soon, in a book, be exposed as part of the Burgess-Maclean-Philby business. What should he do? 'You must have signed the Official Secrets Act?' I asked, and he confirmed that he had. This seemed to me to offer him some protection, at the very least allowing him to neither confirm nor deny any accusation or rumour. I reminded him that as many older students at the Courtauld had known of the suspicions roused by the flight of Burgess and Maclean and had taken them in their stride, others too, outside the Institute, must have heard the rumours and not responded to them, and suggested that he should, if anyone now approached him, simply say that there had been much gossip over many years and that now, as then, he was constrained by the Official Secrets Act. Pretend world-weariness was my advice, say nothing and do nothing that might draw attention to his interest in the matter. He asked David Allibone's advice and he said much the same, but another friend sent Anthony to the eminent Michael Rubinstein, a powerful lawyer altogether more practised in such matters. That I have no idea who this friend was, was typical of Anthony: apart from Moore Crosthwaite and John Golding, I knew almost nothing of his personal and private friends, nothing of old loyalties, encountered none beside his hospital beds, none when he was recuperating, and as he kept us all in separate boxes it is reasonable to assume that they knew nothing of me. Of his lovers I knew only of Peter Montgomery, so often staying at the flat in Portman Square, with whom in the late twenties he had had an affair at Cambridge, and the amiable 'bloke', married, with children, who had for perhaps twenty years coolly fucked him once a week. Montgomery came from a wealthy landed family in

Ulster and was something of a big-wig there; in the late Sixties he was a tall, bluff, amiable man, conventionally handsome, prinked and perfumed in a way that did not wholly conceal the boy who had, forty years before, enchanted Anthony; garrulous and given to heavy drinking, within a decade he was showing signs of senility and I thought he had become an unsafe friend for the Anthony I knew I might one day have to protect. As for the 'bloke', he and I were on no better than nodding terms, for on our very first encounter he had, I thought, betrayed Anthony by offering for a not insubstantial fee to perform the same service for me, and I had tartly cut him short with: 'I give as good as I get and I don't have to pay for it.' I realise now, of course, that we all pay for it one way or another, and that Anthony's sex life, uncluttered by affection, was very easily put away in its box once the fiver had changed hands.

In theory, Rubinstein was a well-chosen solicitor for Anthony: the present menace was a forthcoming book and, as he had fought for half-a-dozen major publishers in libel cases, and for Penguin when, for issuing an unexpurgated text of *Lady Chatterley's Lover*, the firm was prosecuted for obscenity in 1960, there could be nothing that he did not know about counteracting literary accusations. It was not so: he was far too eager to take the battle to the foe without quite knowing the complex nature of the enemy – a doggedly enquiring writer who could not quite prove what he supposed, a press informed by rumour, innuendo and the malice of all sorts of minor figures anxious to pull Anthony down in revenge for imagined slights, an MI5 and MI6 thrilling to the renewal of a long-frustrated chase, and a naive Prime Minister inspired, not by spite but by such aggressive provincial patriotism that she could neither ask nor answer the question 'Why?' These forces were far beyond Rubinstein's power to control and, once unleashed, they swept him aside. It was he who, as a preliminary to quashing it, asked the publishers of Andrew Boyle's *The Climate of Treason* to let him see the text. As Anthony was not named in it, Rubinstein's asking to see it was promptly interpreted as an admission of sorts (had he been fool enough to name Anthony as his client?) and the publishers leaked the request to *Private Eye*; on 28 September the tumbrils of the press prepared to roll. With the publication of extracts from Boyle's book in the *Observer* on Sunday 4 November, I had the first telephone calls – from Stewart Tendler at *The Times* and Chris White at the *Daily Mail* – but all that I, an unknown nobody wondering, alarmed, how the hell these journalists knew of our connection, could say was that I knew nothing. I was in genuine ignorance of the situation, for I had not heard from Anthony for days and he had not answered the telephone when, troubled by his silence, I had called him.

On the morning of Thursday 15 November Anthony at last telephoned, whispering, as for some days he and John had been pretending not to be at home, had not turned on the lights, not opened the curtains, not even flushed the lavatory in case the sound betrayed their presence. Michael Rubinstein had just been informed by the Cabinet Office that the Prime Minister Mrs Thatcher was that afternoon to make a statement in the House of Commons that would confirm the rumours of espionage and treachery. Anthony, with the consideration for others that was habitual, thought that the life of every resident in Portsea Hall would be disrupted by the mob of journalists bound to lay siege, and asked me to take him, with John Gaskin, to stay with John Golding and James Joll in Ravenscourt Park; but he could think of no way of leaving Portsea Hall unobserved, for a handful of reporters were already clustered at the door of the block, prevented by the hall porter there from entering. I took a suitcase with an old loose overcoat that had belonged to my stepfather, mufflers and a broad-brimmed stitched tweed hat that I wore when walking dogs in the rain. Leaving the car unlocked in the road, I went into Portsea Hall and, without hesitation, up the stairs to the sixth floor, suggesting, I hoped, to anyone who might be looking, that I was on my way only to the first. Anthony let me in. John I instructed to take their bags, walk down the stairs and, as unhurriedly as he could manage, put them in the boot of the car and then sit behind the driver's seat – the front passenger seat was already far back on its runners so as to accommodate Anthony's long legs. Squinting through a crack in the curtains I could see that he had attracted no attention. That much achieved I, with Anthony muffled as an invalid and leaning heavily on me, took the lift to the ground floor, tottered past the hall porter (who knew perfectly well who we were) and, deep in conversation, made our slow way across the forecourt to the car. There was an awkward moment with his long legs as I got him into his seat, but not once did I look back at the reporters and it was only when I started the engine that one of them began to run.

On the way to Ravenscourt Park Anthony gave me very clear instructions. He presumed that the running reporter had a note of the car's registration plate and that I would soon be besieged. I was to keep the press occupied and him informed if they lit on anything particularly ghastly – as the *Sunday Telegraph* immediately did with the claim that Anthony, in betraying them to the Nazis, had been responsible for the deaths of forty-nine British secret agents in occupied Holland. Colin Simpson of the *Sunday Times* – to whom I had been useful long before in his exposure of auction rings in the art market – was kind enough to tell me that my telephone was being tapped and that I should not use it for any call I did not want the authorities to hear, by which I supposed him to mean MI5 and MI6; thus I made my calls to Anthony from Joe McCrindle's flat in Kensington Court, nearby. Reporters and photographers massed in my front garden day and night, followed me to Kensington Gardens in the early morning when I walked my dogs, watched me shop in Gloucester Road, and one of them even brought a bicycle when I took to riding mine in an effort to evade them, discovering my use of Joe's telephone (he was away in New York) and bribing the porter of his block; nothing I did went unobserved.

In retrospect it would have been wiser to disobey Anthony, say nothing and do nothing, for every scrap of rebuttal to a mob of journalists determined on obloquy and odium served only to reinforce their savagery. It has been said that Anthony was displeased by much of what I said and did, but he said nothing at the time, offered no change of instruction and the exhausting pantomime continued. John Golding or James Joll could easily have told me of Anthony's displeasure – if any – but did not, and when, with the publication of Miranda Carter's book in 2001* I first learned of it, I sensed the voice of Golding, always more possessive of Anthony's friendship than I ever was, more exclusive – and by the time he talked to Miss Carter he had been the victim of my comments on him as a painter. At the time, I could not understand how Anthony's presence in the Golding-Joll house had been discovered – to be followed by a mad dash back to Portsea Hall and the televised press conference arranged by Rubinstein – and it was only from Miss Carter's book that I learned the reason: James Joll, in responding to a radio 'phone-in' programme, had revealed it. That I should be reviled by the Golding faction when it was itself responsible for betraying Anthony's whereabouts, seems particularly wry.

John Gaskin too could with one word have stilled and silenced me, but from him I heard nothing; from Anthony's brothers, on the other hand, Christopher and Wilfred, there was a deal of encouragement to continue the diversion – Christopher wrote: 'The purpose of this letter is to express the greatest appreciation from both of us for the defence of Anthony you put up – something neither Wilfred nor I is qualified to do. We want you to know how deeply grateful we are.' There was even more reassurance from Michael Rubinstein from whom, at the time, I had support almost amounting to instruction, with direct telephone numbers to his office desk and home. Years later, long after Anthony's death, when an odd sort of 'clearing the decks' friendship had developed

* Miranda Carter, *Anthony Blunt, His Lives*, Macmillan 2001.

between us, Michael confessed that his initial advice, based on the conviction that he could scupper Boyle's book, had been in error, that everything that followed had been an *ad hoc* response, and that the press conference he had arranged at *The Times*, far from settling the matter, had inflamed it. When I asked if the statement then read by Anthony, so uncharacteristic in style and temper, had been written, not by him but (as I suspected) by the Cabinet Secretary Sir Robert Armstrong, he deflected the question at some length, leaving it unanswered.

Anthony too left a question unanswered. Three of many letters of support for him were published by *The Times* on 17 November; they were from former students, loyal to Anthony as a generous teacher and great art historian, from Michael Jacobs, one of his last post-graduate students and subsequently a distinguished travel writer, Mark Jones, later an enlightened servant of the British and Victoria and Albert Museums and now Master of St Cross College, Oxford University, and from me. Mine concluded with a declaration that 'the Fifth Man is dead', for the press, having labelled Anthony the Fourth Man after Burgess, Maclean and Philby, were already busily hunting for the fifth. It was disingenuous of Anthony to tell the press that he had no idea who was in my mind – it was, of course, Andrew Gow, to whom he himself had sent me all those years before – and yet, in a tricky way it was true, for we had never discussed that burdensome interview at which I had formed the not unreasonable assumption that as Gow had clearly played Father Confessor to Anthony, he might well have been his puppet-master too – and possibly for others. Later, when the press had hounded Leo Long (again I saw Anthony weep), John Cairncross and others, it became evident that the process was not unlike paring away the layers of an onion and that each revelation exposed another, but the sleuths eventually lost interest and never exposed the onion's core. When, very shortly before his death, Anthony asked who my Fifth Man was, he did not demur when I said 'Andrew Gow', but broke eye contact and stared out of the window.

The Blunt Affair

On their return to Portsea Hall after the televised interview, Anthony and John were virtually imprisoned by the continuing attendance of journalists and photographers. Anthony could have braved them, but John could not and instead insisted on reverting to the regime of the days before their flight to John Golding's house, refusing to switch on the lights or pull the lavatory chain, pointless deprivations that deceived no one, and ended when Anthony could stand the stink no longer. Michael Kitson, Anthony's one loyal supporter in the Courtauld Institute, Anita Brookner, Joe McCrindle and I (and, no doubt, others too) took them food and drink until Anthony felt able to brave a local supermarket; Joe and I, having prepared the ground by telling the staff what we proposed to do, walked him to lunch in the familiar Italian restaurant and the welcome was wonderfully emotional. There were, he told me, episodes of jostling and shouting in the street that unnerved him, but when these died away he managed well enough. The cruellest blow was struck by the Courtauld, suddenly forbidden to him – but Anita Brookner broke the sanction and ferried library books to and fro. The Courtauld library was closed to me too, brusquely and publicly by the librarian; years earlier, before Anthony's retirement, I had made a will in favour of the Institute – a life interest for my mother, and then the whole lot, house, books, pictures to be kept or disposed of for its benefit – and for this my small reward was to be able to use the library. Banned, humiliatingly, a book snatched from my hand, David Allibone drew up a new will for me the following day, eliminating the Institute, but the wound it inflicted that day still suppurates.

John Gaskin's attempted suicide – if it was that, for he could well have been drunk – on 12 February 1980, caused some confusion in that it was widely reported as 'Blunt's friend' who had fallen six floors from the flat, and many in the press (and not in it), thought at first that it was I, not John; as I had gone to Germany and could not be produced, the misunderstanding was not immediately quashed. My mother attempted to phone Anthony but could get no reply –

but then no one could, for he had deserted Portsea Hall; he rang her two days later, full of apologies, and explained that he was moving from friend to friend and could not be contacted. John, he said, he had seen, a broken collar bone and damaged feet his only injuries, but (I quote her diary), 'This happening has brought him to his senses.' With John away for months recuperating in a convalescent home and, later, with his sister in the north, Anthony went to Rome to work on his *Guide to Baroque Rome*, described as 'the greatest architectural guidebook ever written' when it was published in 1982. On leaving, he passed through Heathrow without comment or obvious recognition, but on his return on 11 August there was some unpleasantness, the more shocking after months in Rome that had been entirely uneventful.

John had not been brought to his senses; he was, indeed, worse – wholly self-centred, whimpering and reproachful when sober, abusive when drunk, and tediously camp between. Both he and Anthony fell back into their routine of telephone calls, and when I was away they confided in my mother instead – and if ever there was a recording angel it was she. They had fewer friends now. Moore Crosthwaite, close friend and sexual confidant for half a century, could not bear even to speak of Anthony and was so shifty and furtive when he encountered me that I could only laugh at a man who had been an ambassador but seemed to have lost all his aplomb and social graces; Dick Spalding, however, remained loyal, and after Anthony's death was a stalwart help to me in managing John. Shrugged off by the Courtauld hierarchy and unable to use any of its resources, his successor as director, the useless Peter Lasko, did his best to suggest that Anthony's directorship had been no more than a trifling episode in its history, and the deputy director, George Zarnecki, frustrated in his ambition to succeed Anthony and blaming him for his failure, poured bile and vitriol on his academic achievements, matching those writers in the press who were determined to destroy him utterly. When the Institute moved to Somerset House and Anthony's manuscript notes (part of his bequest) were put out for the dustmen – some brought to me by dismayed students as proof of what the authorities there were doing – any hope that my once passionate affection for the Courtauld might recover, altogether died.

All this is ancient history to Courtauld students now, and there are, no doubt, new gods, just as art history itself is so much changed since Anthony's day that it is a different discipline. According to a recent prospectus first year students, knowing nothing of the European Renaissance art of which students of my generation were first made aware, took a course in 'Getting to Grips with Rembrandt', second year students, extending the 'detailed knowledge of art historical periods' acquired in three short terms, could devote themselves to American Art 1945–72, and in their third year study the representation of race in British art 1730–1860. The lacunae are larger than the fabric. In my young day the fabric was densely woven and there were no holes; then art history was the history of painting, sculpture, architecture and associated skills, from the birthpangs of the Italian Renaissance (with nods to ancient Athens, Rome and Byzantium) to the present day; it was the history of those who worked in these fields; it was the history of patronage from the Church, the state and individuals; it was also the history of nations, dynasties, the middle classes and the poor, the history of political ambitions and the conflicts of religion – it was, indeed, the history of history itself. We recognised art's connections with literature and music, theology and heresy, philosophy and theory. Art history was the key to connoisseurship, to our ability to distinguish the real from the fake and the painting that is wholly by Rubens (for example) from the painting that is partly by him or wholly by his students. Art history gave us a sense of period and nationality so that we could distinguish Italian painting from French, and a seventeenth-century painting from one earlier or later, and it taught us the importance of drawing as the first stage in the development of ideas, as document and record. Art history taught us to analyse and understand art, and gave us visual literacy far beyond the familiars of the *Mona Lisa*, the *Last Supper* and the *Night Watch*. It proved to be the most inclusive and wide-ranging of cultural disciplines, and that it was so was entirely due to Anthony's academic rigour in devising the syllabus, for exposing us to the grandees of every field within it (and occasionally outside it), for appointing Johannes Wilde to distil the mysteries of Michelangelo and Titian, Rubens and Rembrandt, Leonardo and Brueghel, and for teaching Mansart and Poussin himself. This was what Lasko and Zarnecki and their successors scorned.

*　　*　　*

Anthony aged, lost weight and became frail. By Michael Rubinstein he was unwillingly persuaded to write an apologia explaining, if nothing more, how he had become a Communist sympathiser and involved in espionage. He began it, but stickler for accuracy that he was, he too often found himself frustrated when he went to libraries or record offices to check his facts and, neither able to afford the luxury of taxis nor willing to risk the insults offered by their drivers, he wearied of the always time-consuming and often fruitless journeys that he had to make by bus, travel sick if he tried to read, conspicuous if he did not. One, in particular, to the National Newspaper Archive in Colindale, he found irksome, for there, after an hour's stop-start journey north through Kilburn and Cricklewood, the staff were ingeniously obstructive, balked his errands and wasted his time. He was, moreover, convinced that however innocent his research in such public offices, it was as noted and reported as it would have been in a totalitarian police state and might well, though wrongly, implicate in his skulduggery, men and women with whom his connections were entirely peripheral. There was another difficulty: though a practised writer with a stream of publications over half a century, divorced from the academic subjects that had been their constant, his writing, in terms of style, composition, wit, pace and narrative, became as deadly dull as any schoolboy's essay on how he spent a summer holiday. This, he said, was not how he wished to spend his dying days and, numbed by the chore, at some twenty-five thousand words he abandoned the uninspired memoir.

He should, of course, have burned or buried it, but it is the way of writers to hang on to the evidence of work and he could not commit the sacrifice. He allowed Michael Rubinstein and a handful of others to read it; they had thought that his written life might reflect his spoken warmth, wit, enthusiasm and evident humanity, but dismayed to find that his approach had been that of the tedious schedule, a supporting document rather than the life, they agreed that he should drop it. What had they expected of Anthony? Private man that he was, writing of his affections, relationships and sexual longings would have been impossible, and writing of his work as an art historian or for the Royal Collection would have seemed to him boastful, to his friends uncharacteristic, and to the general reader tedious. As for telling the truth, the whole truth and nothing but the truth – can any man do that and would his baying critics have believed him?

After Anthony's death, John Gaskin behaved as though the manuscript was in some sense a demon – hysterically he wanted it removed from the flat, but would neither touch it himself nor let anyone collect it; Anthony's brothers wanted nothing to do with it it – 'It's a desperate situation,' said Wilfred in a letter of April 1984. Dick could hardly take it to Moore's house, and I refused to take care of it, suspecting that if I did, the news would be leaked and life made hell again. John Golding eventually took charge of it (I would like to have been a fly on the wall that day) and deposited it in the British Library with an embargo that kept it from the public for a quarter of a century; this was not enough, and when the embargo ended in July 2009, there was a flurry of interest from the press, but, as Anthony had warned, it proved to be deadly dull and empty of revelation.

His seventy-fifth birthday in 1982 we celebrated in the usual

Italian restaurant with Joe McCrindle, but without John Gaskin, who was spending more and more time with his sister in the north, and there was a faint glimmer of pleasure in the event that John's presence would have dowsed. When he was in London, though physically recovered, he pretended that he was not, compelling Anthony to be the household slave – not his natural role and one irksome to a man aware of his frailty and anxious to complete the art historical work he had in hand. He had six months or so. On 24 March 1983 I spent most of the day with Anthony poring over photographs of landscape drawings by Poussin, his brother-in-law Gaspard, and by other hands long confused with them. In spite of publishing a general clarification of his ideas as recently as 1979[*] he was convinced that he needed to reconsider their attribution and adjust their order, and as these were matters not only of style and intellectual approach but the certainty of distinct but as yet not definitely identified hands, he needed, he said, another eye. We reached no publishable conclusion, but I had the consolation of a day with him that perfectly recalled the enthusiasm, the lively enquiry and the willingness to consider ideas conflicting with his own that had enlivened tutorials with him when I was his under-graduate student. Thirty-six hours later he was dead and all hell broke loose again. I flew to Cyprus to escape.

Miranda Carter has it that he died sitting at his desk, after breakfast, about to make a telephone call. John Gaskin told me that it was in crossing the room to answer a call that he died – it is an unimportant detail, but it might as well be right, and John saw it happen (Miss Carter was too late to interview him). It was the right death for him, quick and clean, with nothing of the long-drawn business of the hospital bed and its humiliations, nothing of the last-ditch interrogation that MI5 or MI6 might have tried. As I had long since asked Anthony to release me from acting as his executor – the *Sunday Times* had taken to employing me, largely to investigate

---

[*] Anthony Blunt, *The Drawings of Poussin*, Yale 1979.

art scandals, but I suspected that this was that paper's way of having me on board should any further revelations about Anthony's past occur – his death could easily have ended this chapter of my life, but it did not. John Gaskin was beyond all comforting, but it was for himself that he grieved, not Anthony. He could not be persuaded to leave the flat in pursuit of any of his old pleasures – not even for the equestrian competitions that were the only interest we had in common (though much more his than mine); he had no interest in exhibitions, art galleries, theatres, music or even novels – I saw no evidence that he could read. If asked if he had money enough while Anthony's affairs were settled, he always said that he had plenty and that there were many things to sell if he ran low – whether these things were stock accumulated in his Armour and Winston days, Eric Hebborn's forgeries or Anthony's few paintings and drawings, he did not let slip. Dick Spalding and I did our best for him until, late in 1987, he decided to leave London for Dundee to be near the remnants of his family – a great relief to us both, weary as we were of the relentlessly self-pitying and reproachful daily telephone calls and, worse, encounters in the now utterly depressing flat in Portsea Hall; he told neither of us of his intention and it was only from the abeyance of abuse, recrimination and reproach that we realised that he had severed what little was left of the relationship. There were months of silence until the telephone calls began again, still peevish, morose and even hostile – Scotland, it seemed, he hated as much as London; Dick too he treated to the same long calls and we compared notes. One humid evening in July 1988, after a particularly long and vituperative conversation in which, yet again, he threatened suicide unless I, in London, came promptly to Dundee to prevent it, I lost patience and told him to get on with it. Conscience-stricken, I called Dick, only to find that he had done much the same and we commiserated with each other. Three days later John rose early from his bed, dressed, walked to the railway line along the north bank of the Firth of Tay, on which there is at least one level crossing every mile, and stood in front of a train. I was told that there was very little of him to retrieve.

*　　*　　*

I refused to be interviewed by Miranda Carter for her book on Anthony. My grounds were that she was too young to know anything of the political atmosphere in England in the 1930s and the pan-European poverty that followed the Great Depression; what could she know, other than at second hand, of brutal Russian Communism then, of Fascism, Nazism and the Iron Guard, of the Spanish Civil War and the creeping aggrandisement of Germany? I thought too that as a woman she could know nothing of the compelling force of male homosexuality and might care nothing for the predicament that then obtained, the activity, even the mildest approach to it, illegal, society's cruelly punitive responses scandal, prison and disgrace. This was to be her first book – I knew of her only as a journalist, and I had had a bellyfull of those.

I was to regret the decision, for I could have remedied the small handful of minor points that are in error and her five hundred pages will probably remain in perpetuity those to which future historians must refer. I do not come out of it well, but then those who poured poison into her ear were neither present at the time nor picking up the pieces afterwards. With an amused contempt for homosexuals and knowing nothing of art history, Miss Carter conjured perfectly the sense of drift in Anthony's life at Cambridge as post-graduate and don, his intellectual brilliance evident but without particular focus, his career heading nowhere in the mid Thirties until he came under the influence of Fritz Saxl and Rudi Wittkower at the Warburg Institute. Aby Warburg had, in Germany, widened the boundaries of art history to embrace all cultural enquiries that might illuminate its mysteries; his largely Jewish staff, brilliant scholars all, had recently fled the Nazis and brought his extraordinary library to London, and it was as their pupil and employee that Blunt grasped the essentials of art history as a rigorous academic discipline. As with many of his pupils at the Courtauld Institute, of which he was appointed Director in 1946, art history became his life and purpose, his conversion swift, certain and irrevocable as he metamorphosed into the Ignatius Loyola of art history in Britain; within five years of his appointment he had turned the Institute from a finishing school for witless girls into a seminary with a worldwide reputation.

The pity is that his political life was not subject to such a transformation. In this too he drifted, uncertain, influenced by friends and lovers until, trapped by affections and unwise private loyalties, he became a Communist spy of sorts. It is difficult to believe that he enjoyed the dangers and absurdities of this as an intellectual game, or that so intelligent a man could not see that, compelled to depend on obviously unreliable friends, he was sowing the seeds of his own destruction. At heart he had no politics and never voted in any general election; he was touched by Britain's evident poverty in the Thirties, touched by the tragedies of the Spanish Civil War, touched by the inevitability of conflict with Germany, but it is to be doubted that he had any profound interest in the political reasons or remedies for any of them. How then could so scrupulously scholarly a man, so dry, precise, considered and unemotional in everything he wrote of art and architecture, be such a fool as to put his scholarship at risk for a political philosophy in which he had virtually no belief? And to this the answer is Guy Burgess, with whom he perhaps never went to bed, but who won from him undying loyalty – Burgess, at first handsome, charming, witty and homosexually amoral, at last a scruffy drunken slob with the halitosis of a dragon. The obvious question to ask is why was Guy a Communist? Had he not been, nor would Anthony.

Perhaps the conclusion to draw is that had Anthony first discovered the pleasurable disciplines of art history, he would never have enmeshed himself in the doubtful loyalties of Communism.

CHAPTER 9

The Aftermath of the Affair

Of the Blunt Affair there were many unexpected consequences, some trivial, some not. The gaggle of reporters at my gate remained until Christmas, half convinced that Anthony was somewhere in the house, keeping a twenty-four-hour watch; the very last of them, no more than a boy not clad for winter, late on a bitter night I hauled into my kitchen, fried eggs and bacon for him, walked him round the house to prove that Anthony was not there, made him telephone his editor and packed him off to Gloucester Road before the last train to the far East End sped through. Elsie Crombie, wife of Theodore Crombie, long-serving critic with *Apollo*, art historian and expert on Spanish art, took to telephoning every day, always ending with 'now let's give MI5 something worth hearing', at which she launched into extraordinary sexual fantasies, reinforcing my notion that elderly women are far more sexually unbuttoned than old men. She it was who, bored by Royal Academy Summer Exhibition Dinners, once took with her a tape recorder and a tape of farts compiled and sold by *Private Eye*, bribed a waiter to set it off under a table and sat back to enjoy the general discomfiture. Another *Private Eye* commercial venture, the Willy Warmer, she bought in quantity and gave to male guests at a dinner party according to imagined size, insulting some and pleasing others. Another old dame, one I did not know, invited me to a weekend in the country at the behest, she informed me, of Princess Margaret; not even Stephen Sondheim foresaw all the miseries possible in such a purgatorial occasion. The Princess arrived an hour before midnight for a ruined dinner scheduled for eight; by then the servants hired from the village had gone home to bed and the rest of us, some half dozen, absolutely plastered, had to buckle-to, carry and carve the

The author in 1967 – at the beginning of the book. *Below*: Claudio Corvaya in 1967

My mother in 1972,
the year in which we
both moved to
19 Eldon Road in
Kensington (facing)
with its vast studio
(below)

Top: Mentmore Towers with the marquees of Sotheby's sale, May 1977
Below: Eliot Hodgkin: *Mrs Riley's Milkweed*

The painting attributed to Georges de la Tour hanging in Paul Botte's kitchen in October 1958

Below: Henry Sutch (*left*) and Bill Martin (*right*) in the Big Room at Christie's

Rüdiger Joppien, Hampstead, 1971

Below: Joe McCrindle

Zoffany, Charles Macklin in *The Merchant of Venice. Below left*: De Wilde, Thomas
Collins in *The Merry Wives of Windsor. Below right*: De Wilde, Maria Theresa Bland,
Ursula Booth and John Bannister in *The Children in the Wood*

Anthony Blunt in Italy after his exposure
Below: Anthony Blunt shortly before his exposure

Antoine, Count Seilern, in the Sixties (passport photograph)

Below: Johannes Wilde in his Dulwich garden

Anthony d'Offay 9 and 23 Dering Street New Bond Street London W1 01-499 4695

3rd June, 1982

Terry Murphy Esq
175 Junction Road
London N19

RENOIR   Head of a girl   (sanguine)

Received from Anthony d'Offay Ltd the sum of
£20,000 (twenty thousand pounds) in cash

Terry Murphy

VSH 1696

26-37

Hill Samuel & Co Limited
19. ST. JAMES'S SQUARE, LONDON SW1   or Order

30-13-74

HILL SAMUEL & CO.
LIMITED

Pay L.W. Kortmann-Daxler Esq

Twenty two thousand pounds

£22,000.

ANTHONY D'OFFAY LTD

"809413" 30"1374: 02268253"

23rd August, 1982

C B Turner Esq
137c St George's Road
Lambeth
London SE1

and

Terry Murphy Esq
17b Junction Road
London N19

PURCHASE NOTE

Lawrence ATKINSON   Abstract Composition

£6,000

Acting on instructions of Mr. Norman Dinnie

I confirm that I am the vendor
of the above at the price shown
signed:

I confirm that I am the buyer
of the above at the price shown
signed:

26-37

-- be claimed by maiin

23 August 1982   30-13-74

Hill Samuel & Co.
19, ST JAMES'S SQUARE, LONDON SW1

Pay M.J. Murphy

£ 6000

PAID 26 AUG 1982
HILL SAMUEL & CO.
LIMITED

or Order

ANTHONY D'OFFAY LTD

955916 30-1374 0226 8253

000000600000

Andy Warhol, the photograph a gift

Below: David Hockney: Peter Langan, October 1969. Peter is in the kitchen of the original Odin's. His Löwenbrau, always drunk from a large brandy glass, stands in the right foreground

Above: Jill Allibone

Mary Debanne in a wild moment in Hyde Park

Above: Martin Shortis: the open plan office of the *Evening Standard*, 1990, the news desk in the foreground (*detail*)

Michael Leonard: portrait of the author as he might have looked as a Grand Tourist – one of the title shots later used in the television programme *Grand Tour*

Above: Fifty miles from
Santiago da Compostella
on what should have been
the final stage of the
pilgrimage

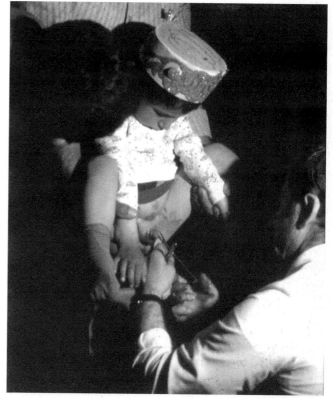

Circumcision in the wilds
of Cappadocia

The author now, photographed by Zsuzsi Roboz shortly before her death in 2012

baked meats of sacrifice; she then kept us up until four in the morning, kippering us with her cigarettes. Long after the crack of dawn, with not a sniff of coffee nor sign of a servant in the kitchen to clear the mess left from the night, I wandered into the village, called a friend and arranged for a late morning death-and-doomsday telephone message requiring my immediate return home. And a young woman with a Mini-Moke (the tiny Meccano-like jeep version of the Mini) and bristling with pubic hair (as I was to discover on the first day of 1980 warm enough for her to wear very brief crotch-clenching shorts) became my stalker.

The first disturbing incident was what seemed a determined effort by the police to connect me with the forgery of a major painting by a then forgotten leader of the School of Paris in the Fifties. Friedrich von Artus had sent it to me to sell in a London saleroom as no one in Germany cared tuppence for post-war French painting, and I had sent it to Bonham's, the only firm able to sell it before the end of the year. No one had any reason to suspect that it was not genuine; it was certainly of its supposed period (there is no convincing means of falsely ageing the reverse of a canvas with heavy jute content – only time does that), but as, after the sale, the painter himself declared it false, the sale had to be cancelled. The painter demanded a police enquiry. When two hefty detectives came unannounced to my house one evening, gave me the impression that they were members of Special Branch and drank my whisky, I felt it necessary to protect not only myself but Friedrich and Anthony, for I divined that they were fishing only because they hoped that Anthony, whose reputation had been menacingly smirched by association with Eric Hebborn (notorious forger, emotional seducer), might be involved. For the first time since the Affair began in September, I was scared – scared that I should unwittingly be the agent of some further erosion of his reputation. I lied, but the lie was so preposterous a dead end that the investigation withered and came to nothing.

The second incident took place in Kensington Gardens, early on a Saturday morning when the otherwise daily dog-walkers were few and the cyclists fewer. Apart from a distant figure at an angle to my right, I was alone, yet in all those acres he chose a path and walked it at such a pace that we must inevitably meet, and when we did he said, barely breaking his stride, 'I thought you should know that MI6 is still watching you' – and walked on. If a joke, it required planning according to precise knowledge of my dog-walking habit and perfect timing; if not a joke, what was the purpose? I had ceased to care that my telephone was being monitored (as journalists at the *Sunday Times* insisted), and had learned that my face was so widely familiar that I could not buy a loaf of bread in Harrods without winsome recognition by the boy behind the counter. Indeed, Harrods had to stop being a haunt for casual sodomy in the third floor lavatories, where it was from a Harrods boy in the men's department that I learned the trick of camouflaging the feet of the recipient in carrier bags so that any suspicious guardian of morals glancing under the door would see only the feet of a heavily-laden customer.

After being reported in a gossip column as 'Blunt's little friend lunching at The Ivy' (I had been making an insurance inventory of the beastly pictures there – for which my bill was not paid: they suggested that I 'eat it down', as David Hockney did at Odin's when Peter Langan bought a painting, but, in the event, there was never a table when I needed one), I had also to realise that whatever I did, no matter how innocent, might be used as a peg on which could be hung some snide anti-Anthony jibe and yet again the accusations 'spy' and 'traitor'. To risk a sexual folly would be particularly silly. 'What on earth can I do?' I asked Michael, my expert on outbreaks of syphilis among Russian sailors in Murmansk. 'Nothing here,' he said, 'and when abstinence becomes insupportable, go to the baths in Amsterdam.'

For the few years before AIDS became an ever-present threat, those baths were a constant of every European trip; whenever I did my duty earning a fee or seeing a major exhibition in Paris,

Frankfurt or Cologne, I then drove to Amsterdam, booked into a sleazy cheap hotel and took off for the nearby baths where one could spend both day and night, breaking off only for food and a few hours sleep, and continue the regime until sated. Oh to be in an orgy room again, inhibitions abandoned until all passion spent.

On a perhaps more serious note, the *Sunday Times* drew me into its web of further enquiry, but this was of some benefit to Anthony in that its investigative journalists Colin Simpson, Barrie Penrose and Simon Freeman, were all convinced that I knew much more than I did and, in betraying their confidences to Anthony, I was able to keep him informed of the directions of their research. These I could occasionally divert or even stall, steering them away from him and others. It also meant that I learned a great deal about Philby, Burgess and Maclean, Goronwy Rees and others – indeed, many others, for some of Anthony's old friends burdened me with names and notions, and retired officers of MI5 and MI6 fed me with information as well as lunch and dinner. With these it was difficult to tell whether they were confessing their own parts in various early aspects of Anthony's life, or ingeniously debriefing me to see if I knew anything that they did not – or so I thought until one of them gave me a bundle of ancient and faint carbon copies of what were obviously official reports written between 1930 and 1950 on worthies both Fascist and Communist suspected of sympathies, disloyalty or espionage. Many of their names I knew and I was left wondering how such institutions as the British Museum, the Victoria and Albert and London University could have been such hotbeds of political perfidy; some were still alive, some had family, some had overlapped with Anthony. I considered burning the parcel but instead lodged it with a much younger friend abroad, with instructions to send it to the British Library on my death; it may by then have some residual historic interest without doing harm to anyone.

Far the most important personal consequence of the Blunt Affair for me was the withdrawal of my American visa. By the end of

January 1980 I had received calls or letters from most of my American museum contacts suggesting that I should withdraw from my work as errand-boy, at least until the ballyhoo had died away; most blamed the prejudice of trustees and donors and the certain loss of funds and other patronage if my advice or activity was involved in any acquisition. I still had, however, a handful of significant American private collectors who had been sympathetic during the Affair, of whom some, including Joe McCrindle, were themselves the trustees of museums and well able to explain how things worked in their exalted circles – but these too, with the exception of Joe, I lost when, without a visa, I could no longer travel to New York and Washington. When my passport expired in 1983 I applied for a new visa; it was refused – but I had almost ceased to care, for by then it would have been difficult to revive my working contacts with museums as though there had been no hiatus, for curators die, retire or rise to greater galleries, and in many cases I knew that other dogsbodies had taken on my duties, and these I could not, with a clear conscience, seek to unseat; I had, moreover, begun to earn a frugal living as a scribbler.

That this was so was due entirely to Tina Brown, wife of Harold Evans, then editor of the *Sunday Times*. Early in January 1980 she, as fresh young editor compelling resurrection on the moribund *Tatler*, asked me to do a particularly Tatlerish thing – to give, at the magazine's expense, lunch to a dozen friends in my favourite restaurant, with a *Tatler* journalist recording our conversation. I had no favourite fashionable restaurant, nor had I fashionable friends, and in that grim winter, I learned that my professional friends were, at least for the time being, strongly inclined to shy away from me. I refused – but my note of refusal amused her enough to suggest that I might instead become *Tatler*'s art critic at £100 for a thousand words ten times a year. That this post as a critic was a contemptibly small acorn was made obvious at my first press view of an exhibition. This was at the old Tate Gallery (now Tate Britain) and was the Dali retrospective of May-

The Aftermath of the Affair

June 1980; with neither press card nor official invitation, I was not exactly welcomed and, though grudgingly admitted, the expensive catalogue normally given gratis to critics was refused on the grounds that *Tatler* was not an established journal. As well as with the milling mass of people whom I took to be critics (they were, and still are, only the Uncle Tom Cobleighs of the press), the gallery was crowded with radio and television crews and it was more difficult to see the exhibits than on a day when open to the public. I thought how odd it was to be almost certainly the only man in this assembly of hundreds who had hobnobbed with Dali himself over a period of years, and yet be an outsider. Only one man spoke to me – Angus Stewart who, though a man of magnificently Bohemian presence and later President of AICA (a useless international body of art critics incapable of criticism), seemed then to share my insignificance. To my chagrin, *Tatler* captioned my comments with the phrase 'blunt views on fine art'. There was no B for Blunt, but I thought the pun diminished me and for the first and only time in my life resented Anthony's shadow.

I remained *Tatler*'s art critic until June 1990, still then at £100 a column, but that mattered less than loyalty based on gratitude to the magazine that had given me my first toehold in the field. Tina Brown moved on to far higher things and Libby Purves, the most amiable of broadcasters on BBC radio, arrived in March 1983; she, however, was so scorned by all the pretty girls in *Tatler*'s offices that I took her to lunch at the nearby Westbury (where she insisted on nothing more than a tiny sandwich with which to toy), betrayed the treacherous doxies on whom she depended, and urged her – for *Tatler*'s sake, either to sack them or herself resign. The problem was that Libby, an ample frump, was in her way as wholly unsuitable to be the editor of a journal dedicated to celebrities and fashion, as I was as its art critic. I was not much thanked for what I said (and we have since not exchanged one single word), but in October, after only half-a-dozen issues, she departed and the office reverted to the gossipy frivolity that was *Tatler*'s *raison d'être*.

She was succeeded by Mark Boxer who made life more than a little difficult for me, almost forcing my resignation, but in 1983 work as a writer, mostly for short-lived or moribund art magazines, was very much hand-to-mouth and so poorly paid (largely at the rate of £30 for a thousand words) that I could not afford to surrender my steady £1,000 a year from *Tatler*. Unlike Tina Brown, who had asked of me only informed comment on the most important exhibition of the month, Mark wanted a more tittle-tattle approach with the focus on curators and directors and the artists themselves if still alive; when I did not give him what he wanted – gossip about the wretched speculative art dealers who attempted to turn Portobello Road into a hotbed of contemporary art, or flattering nonsense about artists with whom he had some acquaintance – he spiked (that is, rejected) my copy. I could have resigned; he could have sacked me and would have been perfectly right to do so. That he did not, I thought and think so still, lay some twenty years in our past, in 1963 or so when, as the creator and first editor of the first colour supplement to any British news-paper, the *Sunday Times*, he chose to publish the first of many behind-the-scenes articles on Christie's. As one of the experts there on paintings by old masters, then the most dramatic and important sector of the art market, I was appointed his guide. Tall and wonderfully beautiful, he did not rebuff the pass I made and amused dalliance may be the proper description for what followed, for he was of that not uncommon category of heterosexual men for whom experience with another man is, on his part, merely sexual, not homosexual, particularly if he does little more than let it happen. With his announcement that he was married and 'this must stop', stop it did. Even among the hundreds of sexual encounters that I had experienced, I had not forgotten ours; nor had he forgotten what may well have been a rare or even single adventure for so uxorious a man. Across his desk at *Tatler* neither of us uttered a hint of it, but the awkwardness of our first professional encounter was palpable, the *de-haut-en-bas* of it on his part calculatedly cold. I remembered; he remembered; it made him deeply uncomfortable and he wished me out. I did not go. After some sparring we established a *modus vivendi* that involved our never meeting and he left me in control of my reviews. On Mark's death in 1988 he was succeeded by Emma Soames who knew everyone ever likely to appear in *Tatler's* pages but was, as editor, an unloved termagant; overheard to remark that I thought her as sexually attractive as a saucepan of boiled socks, it was at last time for me to leave.

The *Sunday Times* I had deserted long before. Colin Simpson, its senior investigative journalist, was obssessed by the art market and, convinced that it was a nest of vipers (he was not mistaken), had in the mid Sixties exposed the 'Ring' – the mechanism that enabled a loose consortium of dealers to buy a work of art cheaply at auction (simply by not bidding against each other and, occasionally, by threat) and then auctioning it among themselves, one of them left in possession of it at a far higher price, the others all making money without the risk of ownership. Simpson then moved on to forgery, believing it to be rampant in the trade, even at its highest levels. In 1980 he lit upon a painting bought twenty years before from Wildenstein by the Metropolitan Museum, New York, *The Fortune Teller*, attributed to Georges de la Tour, a rare and enthralling seventeenth-century painter whose chronology and authenticity were in utter confusion and dispute (and are so still). Wildenstein was then and had long been the most formidable of French dealers and the painting, if genuine, should never have left France; that it had, suggested to Simpson that it must be a forgery and in this he was supported by Christopher Wright, a diligent young art historian who had contributed substantially to an authoritative monograph in 1974.[*] I had seen either it or an identical picture in September 1958, in the possession of a small and private Parisian dealer, Paul Botte, and had thought it not by La Tour but by an imitator, a

---

[*] Benedict Nicolson and Christopher Wright, *Georges de la Tour*, Phaidon 1974.

pasticheur, even a modern forger and, when consulted by Simpson, had told him so. I wish that I had not, partly because it brought me into conflict with Michael Kitson, whom I venerated as my tutor and who had been loyal to Anthony throughout the Affair and its immediate consequences, and partly because as it was a painting on which Anthony had commented at length as genuine,* there would inevitably be an accusation from some ill-informed source that he had been involved in passing it off – *Private Eye* on 7 November 1980 published *Fake's Progress* with a photograph of Anthony. Of two television programmes, one, American, was merely scandalous, the other, earnestly one-sided on the BBC, failed to prove the painting's authenticity; and Simpson's reports in the *Sunday Times*, as earnestly other-sided, could not conclusively prove it a forgery.

My problem was one of connoisseurship; no matter what the documentation suddenly produced, I simply could not make *The Fortune Teller* fit comfortably with what was known for certain (or even uncertainly) of La Tour's chronology and stylistic development. It is like, yet at the same time disturbingly unlike the other paintings with which it must be grouped; the so-called signature, ridiculously elaborate and prominent, is not a signature but an inscription (but when was it added?); and the scientific evidence provided by John Brealey (Anthony's adviser on how to clean a Poussin and by then working for the Metropolitan Museum) was selective, almost disingenuous. Stephen Rees-Jones, my sometime Professor of Technology at the Courtauld Institute, with whom I discussed Brealey's evidence in October 1980, observed that it was neither impartial nor reassuring and, when the controversy had rumbled on for a year, wrote to *The Times* in February 1982, confirming this view, criticising particularly the Metropolitan Museum's reliance on questionable tests of lead isotopes and

---

* Anthony Blunt, 'Georges de la Tour at the Orangerie', *Burlington Magazine*, August 1972, pp. 516–26.

linseed oil. My contribution was to argue that these isotopes give different readings according to the place of origin of the lead, and that only if the lead in *The Fortune Teller* and in La Tour's authentic paintings could be proved to have come from Lorraine or the Vosges, within carting distance of La Tour's workplace, could the dissenters be almost certainly mistaken. I still think this so, but in June 1982 a long (private) letter from Michael Kitson accused me of 'disingenuous twaddle', but ended with the conciliatory note that he would 'admit the possibility (though no more than that) that the picture, together with the two versions of *The Cheat*, is not by La Tour but by a clever pupil . . . ' Anthony had earlier (op. cit.) said, 'They do not fit anywhere in the main development . . . ' and, 'Generally speaking the borderline between originals and copies is quite clear, but in one or two cases some doubts may arise.'

Simpson was bold enough to go straight to Wildenstein and in spite of their Byzantine grandeur, cunning and reserve, they were at first sufficiently off-guard to reveal the name of their chief restorer for many years, long retired to Corsica and probably dead; at the mention of Paul Botte's painting they admitted to knowing of it – a copy, they said, one of several, and brought the interview to a close. If they knew of several copies of a painting wholly unknown until discovered during World War II, why did they not disclose this when selling the 'original'? The restorer, Emile Delobre, the favourite pupil of Gustave Moreau, was born in 1873, and is recorded as primarily a painter of copies after old masters, often of astonishing quality, worked for Wildenstein from 1910 until 1944 and, we were to discover, occasionally until his death in 1957. That he was dead was, to Simpson, of no account – his nephew, Albert Dion-Delobre, succeeded him at Wildenstein's and he too had retired to Corsica. Thither we flew on a small plane from Nice, by night and in a thunderstorm; not far short of the island the plane was struck by lightning and the left engine set on fire. Warned that we might be ditched, I took off my shoes and clothes. 'What the hell are you doing?' asked the man in the next seat (not Simpson), 'Getting ready for a long swim,' my reply. We were then told that we would reach the airport but, as the plane might burst into flames when we landed, we must descend the emergency chutes as swiftly as possible. We did, but into pelting rain, and clutching my bundle of clothes I sprinted barefoot to the terminal. Within ten minutes I was dry and dressed, but no one in authority would believe that I had been on the flight and I was put in custody for a couple of hours.

Albert Dion-Delobre told us that his uncle had painted *The Fortune Teller*, that the young man in it was Henri, Albert's son, and that he, Albert, had lightly cleaned the painting in 1958 in Wildenstein's premises in New York, that he had lightly retouched the paint surrounding the inscription to lend it greater strength, and that within the lace shawl of the gypsy pickpocket he had incorporated the word '*merde*' in capital letters so that he could shrug off any accusation of forgery, adding the extraordinary sentence: 'Unlike De Hory and Legros, we are not members of the gay freemasonry and have no one to protect us.' By chance, De Hory and Legros were to be the subject of an immediately following investigation, though not prompted by Dion-Delobre, who also told us that the canvas had been relined in New York by Loewy (a specialist firm) so that the original canvas was concealed. Was any scrap of this information true? Patrick O'Connor, an Irish painter, restorer, dealer and disgraced but amiable rogue, working in America, claimed to have seen Dion painting *The Fortune Teller* as a joke – but Patrick would board any bandwagon to revive his notoriety. Brealey promptly removed the *merde*, new paint between two coats of varnish, he told me – but this supported Dion-Delobre's account. Without a visa I could not go to New York and ask to see the technical evidence of the two layers of canvas and their age, nor see X-rays that might reveal changes in the composition, nor look scientifically at other evidence; those who could have gone, did not. Informed opinion ranged from the 'It is gloriously right', of John Brealey, to Christopher Wright's 'It is a squalid modern forgery', and there I think it stands, the dissenters in the minority. John Pope-Hennessy, high English panjandrum at the Metropolitan, damned all who questioned *The Fortune Teller* as upstarts and jackanapes and yet, simultaneously, in his *Study and Criticism of Italian Sculpture*, made a plea for connoisseurship – '. . . art history is a looser, more speculative science than some of its practitioners suppose, and the technique of connoisseurship must be inculcated and encouraged if art history is significantly to advance.' Hear, Hear: connoisseurship had been, above all, the premise of my misgivings in the case of the La Tour.

On the return journey, we flew to Nice to spend the night in a squalid back street hotel called the Ritz, where every man's fart was audible. Colin paid rather more than the sum required and in return was given a handsomely engraved receipt for ten times the figure. On the flight to London he passed me a sheet of paper – 'These are the expenses you will claim from the paper.' As they bore no resemblance to reality and I was attached to the *Sunday Times* by no more than a thread, I demurred. 'Don't rock the boat,' he said. 'You'll spoil it for the rest of us. No one passes through Nice without spending a fortune at the Ritz.' As Colin had paid all the bills, I gained a cool £347.65 in addition to the much smaller writer's fee that I was later paid.

*   *   *

'Unlike de Hory and Legros, we are not members of the gay freemasonry and have no one to protect us,' Dion Delobre had said; both were quite certainly queer and both may well have gained what advantage they could from it, but I doubt if they were as 'protected' as the Irish, Jewish, Armenian and Hungarian Mafias about which we occasionally dare to joke – indeed, I am inclined to say that their homosexuality made them vulnerable to the most dangerous exploitation by heterosexual rogues capable of murder. Elmyr de Hory, Hungarian by birth, Parisian by choice, a notorious pasticheur of Modigliani, Matisse and the Impressionists, 'the greatest art forger of our time' (a claim made for every briefly successful crook in the field), 'famous and legendary', had at seventy died in mysterious circumstances in 1976. Fernand Legros, some twenty-five years younger, his parents French, his birthplace Egypt, his passport eventually American, his base as an art dealer Paris, long Elmyr's Spalanzano or Svengali, had died in 1980 from throat cancer – from which no freemasonry or mafia could have protected him. I had known Legros in the early Sixties when he frequently dropped in on Christie's with a taxi full of paintings, straight from Heathrow, so immaculately dressed that he could not, himself, unload them, but required assistance from the commissionaire and all the staff of the reception desk. Among unimportant but good pictures by Daubigny, Harpignies and their ilk, worth Christie's while to sell but of small value, were always a couple by such second rank more modern painters as Derain, Vlaminck or Van Dongen, borrowing their honesty; these had diplomatically to be refused. It was a simple ruse, this genuineness of the true colouring reaction to the false, and when he by-passed me and asked straight for the chairman, it worked; it must have worked in other auction houses too. How these rogues came together, duped so many would-be connoisseurs, fell out and became the subjects of international police enquiry, is a tale first incoherently told in a wretched novelettish book by the American novelist Clifford Irving in 1970 when both subjects were still alive, later dissemblingly revised and brought up-to-date by one Kenrick Talbot* promoting himself as de Hory's kindly guardian and protector from himself.

De Hory's notoriety was enough for him to be much interviewed by newspapers and magazines, for Orson Welles to make a film of his life, *Question Mark*, and on his death (was it murder, was it suicide?) for the art market to show serious interest in his paintings. By then, scared by close shaves with the police, he had

---

* Kenrick Talbot, *Enigma!*, 1991.

become the genuine pasticheur rather than the forger, all his canvases flamboyantly inscribed on the reverse to assure buyers that they were the inventions of Elmyr himself and the police that there was no intention to pass them on as Fauve or Post-Impressionist. Christie's, at their secondary rooms in Kensington, had a remarkably successful auction, emptying the studio we were to understand; but how could it have been emptied when, for a year or two, so many more paintings followed in theirs and other London salerooms? Early in 1982, intrigued by the conviction that the forger was himself now being forged, I suggested to Colin Simpson that we might investigate, but he thought my notion too improbable and the sums of money involved (a few hundred pounds for each canvas, only) far too small. In April 1983, however, Simon Freeman, another investigative journalist attached to the *Sunday Times*, saw an advertisement in the *International Herald Tribune* offering for sale paintings by de Hory. I went to see the advertiser at his home near Regent's Park; he was Kenrick Talbot, claiming to have befriended de Hory from 1969 until his death, and to have bought some four thousand of his paintings in these seven years; some were hanging, many more were stacked in an upper room; a few were in oil paint, but most were in acrylic, a medium that de Hory loathed; and the canvases were all of Imperial measurements, not metric. Our guarded conversation was interrupted by the arrival of a gold Ford Cortina laden with many more – hastily dismissed, but not before I had noted its registration number. I left, convinced that all were forgeries and that I had seen the forger.

It was the beginning of a long and, at times, tedious pursuit with many ramifications, of which, in August 1983, I made a fourteen-page statement to the Fine Art Squad at Scotland Yard, depositing with them all my supporting evidence, never returned. It led first to Colin Turner – he of the car full of de Horys; he worked for Roberson's, a firm of artists' suppliers in Camden Town, had some pretty foul things to say of Kenrick Talbot and claimed that he was involved in de Hory's murder. From Turner it led to Mark Lewis, a tough little cockney living in Leytonstone, who claimed to be the illegitimate grandson of Wyndham Lewis and inheritor of a large number of his paintings and drawings that, for some time, he had been feeding onto the London art market; and to Dick Emmett, also in Leytonstone, a sweaty little tyke of sixty or so, who claimed to have bought paintings by Modigliani, Van Gogh, Renoir, Braque and others of the ilk from Talbot, their having been vetted by experts at Christie's, whom Talbot 'had in his pocket'. These daubs were appalling; they entirely lacked the occasional insight and sympathy that redeemed some of de Hory's pastiches and excused the innocents who bought them, and were instead brutally unintelligent in invention and inept in the handling of paint, the Cubist Braque an insult to both the painter and any viewer accustomed to looking at paintings of any period or mannerism. As for Mark Lewis's descent from the loins of the great Wyndham, this could only have been possible through random conjugation with a slut – far from improbable for a man who seemed to need a fiercely active but emotionally detached sex life, once so urgently that he fucked his landlady's daughter on the floor immediately within the front door of her house, only to be interrupted by the postman pushing letters through the letterbox to fall on his bared bum; that he would reward so casual a lover with a cache of drawings and paintings is, however, improbable, for none of his many known lovers and mistresses drawn from the artistic and intellectual circles in which he moved ever proved to be a source of lost or forgotten work.

In the course of several interviews Emmett involved not only Christie's but Sotheby's, Colnaghi's and the Courtauld Institute – all of whom he said had vouched for his wretched paintings; Colin Turner had restored them, he claimed, and had introduced him to Talbot. He modified his story so that his purchase of paintings was from Mark Lewis, introduced by Talbot, and his confusions and contradictions were so many that I concluded that nothing could be believed; the last straw was to be told that the paintings came from the collection of an old lady living in Winterton-on-Sea who happened to be Lewis's mother. Lewis, far the cleverer, maintained his simple story of descent. Both men, sensing danger in the enquiry, sought to divert my concentration; I was directed to Terry Murphy, a dealer in 'antiques' in the unlikely purlieus of Junction Road, Holloway, to an East End garage owner, George Clark, who owned some of Talbot's de Horys, thinking that he had invested in genuine paintings by Matisse et al, and to another garagiste, financially involved (but with whom I did not discover) who was, for a few days, physically the most frightening man I ever encountered; he was, however, supplanted by a demolition contractor in Bethnal Green who consented to a meeting in the open on a street corner of Cambridge Heath Road and threatened interment in the contents of his skips if I ever divulged his name. With such a Hercules this Antaeus could not compete.

For these rogues there was some compensation in Louis William Koolman-Darnley, of Rochester Terrace, Camden Town (now perhaps a good address but then a pretty slum), posing as a gentleman fallen on hard times, desperate to sell to Anthony d'Offay, the leading dealer in the field, his collection of works by Vorticists, Bloomsbury painters and toilers in the Omega Workshops. He was a garrulous old thing, a former music hall entertainer whose act had been a ballet of fountain jets that danced to coloured lights and the music of Swan Lake and the Sugar Plum Fairy. Never the top of the bill, this had not survived the war and he had then become 'an artist', and it was as an artist that he had first encountered Colin Turner at Roberson's. After a traffic accident in which his head and leg were injured, he had attempted to sue for loss of earnings; for this Turner, using Roberson's headed paper, had offered proof with letters withdrawing a non-existent contract for decorative paintings that, because of the injuries, could not be produced in time. With this deceit Koolman-Darnley was indebted to Turner and drawn into his plot.

Louis – I saw so much of him that we had to drop formality –

was to lend his name and person to a collection acquired in the Thirties, largely in exchange for cash and loans to other music-hall entertainers; these paintings, drawings and sculptures he kept in a wooden trunk, never opened, and having forgotten what it might contain, and at seventy-nine too frail to lift the lid, he had asked Turner to help. Turner had recognised many fine things and had turned immediately to d'Offay who, between the Augusts of 1981 and 1982, bought the following:

> *Henri Gaudier-Brzeska: an album of 68 drawings. £25,000, 28*
> *August 1981*
> *Jacob Epstein: an album of 56 drawings. £27,000,*
> *30 October 1981*
> *Ilya Gregorovich Tchachnik: Composition 1924. £12,000,*
> *20 May 1982*
> *An Omega Screen. £8,000 22 July 1982*

At much the same time d'Offay bought from Terry Murphy and Colin Turner acting on behalf of Koolman-Darnley:

> *Lawrence Atkinson: Abstract Composition. £6,000,*
> *23 August 1982*

and on their own account, independent of Koolman-Darnley:

> *Wyndham Lewis: a book of drawings. £11,000, 4 March 1982*

From Terry Murphy alone, he bought:

> *Renoir: Head of a Little Girl (red chalk). £20,000, 3 June 1982*

These are the completed transactions of which I have indisputable records; there may well have been others; certainly others were contemplated, and of some of these too I have records.

Very little of this money, some £5,500 only, reached Louis. Cheques for cash and cheques in his name were countersigned by Turner and diverted.

Had d'Offay had the sense, at the beginning of the negotiation with Turner, who in appearance, manner and speech was hardly a convincing emissary for a distinguished old gentleman with a great collection, to visit the old gentleman himself (for the very first Purchase Note makes it clear that Turner made no attempt to conceal him), he would have found Louis' bell to be one of half-a-dozen at the door, and the name-tag 'Louis William Koolman-Darnley, Artist' to have been indelibly embellished, in an un-educated hand, with a capital F – presumably expressing the esteem in which his neighbours held him. The improbability of finding treasure-trove in such a house was manifest, but it was not until early in September 1982 that d'Offay began to have misgivings; then he invited Louis to dinner at the Garrick and asked him to come to the gallery in Dering Street and comment on the things said to have come from his collection. He recognised none.

It was at this point that Louis discovered the extent to which he had been gulled by Turner; suspicions six months earlier had led to his threatening Turner with a demand for cash within 'forty-eight hours; then I ring Dering Street. You should be ashamed of yourself to so abuse the use of my name'. Though then bought off with a paltry sum, suspicion rankled and after the Garrick dinner Louis began to confuse reality with the conviction that he really had had a collection, that there really was a wooden trunk crammed with masterpieces on rolled canvas, albums, artefacts and sculptures – and in truth he did own a wooden trunk, but one far too small to contain what Turner had told d'Offay was to be the next phase of their bargaining. D'Offay, still unwilling to admit to himself that he had been duped, encouraged Louis to turn to his eminent solicitors, Kingsley, Napley and Co. who, canny enough to recognise that Louis might not be able to pay their bill, passed him on to Payne, Hicks, Beach and Co., who listed the works in question and, in the High Court of Justice, Queen's Bench Division, before the Honourable Mr Justice McCullough, on 17 September 1982, required Colin Turner to reveal the whereabouts of the following works of art and by no means to dispose of them:

a: An abstract sculpture of a bird, attributed to Jacob Epstein, 3 feet by 2 by 1½ feet.

b: An oil painting, *Kermesse*, by Wyndham Lewis, 9 by 9 feet.

c: An oil painting, *Plan of War*, by Wyndham Lewis, 5 by 8 feet.

d: A portrait of *Ezra Pound*, by Wyndham Lewis, 6 by 9 feet.

e: A book of drawings by Wyndham Lewis.

f: A pastel drawing attributed to Degas, 2 by 2 feet.

Thus, to Louis, these inventions, these forgeries that he had never owned or seen, had become his property and he wanted their full value, not another poxy five and half thousand quid; the reality was that he had been paid that sum for, from a distance, never directly, fronting the sting that defrauded d'Offay, and had taken no risk until, absurdly, he had involved the law. From the measurements of the canvases and the weight of the would-be Epstein sculpture any clear-minded lawyer would have realised that the trunk from which they came must be of wholly improbable proportions and the whole business a farrago of nonsense. Later, in July 1983, Louis said that d'Offay had more or less compelled him to take to the law because he 'feared that Turner might sell the paintings, not to d'Offay, but to foreign buyers, and this would be a great cultural loss to the nation'.

The one benefit of taking this course was that the solicitors' Outdoor Clerk, Simon Knowles, was extremely diligent in his attempt to serve to Colin Turner a copy of the Order and as a consequence two new actors joined the cast, a Miss Lawrenson, said to be Turner's girlfriend, and George Weissbort, a painter living in West Hampstead, said to be restoring the paintings by Wyndham Lewis. But Mark Lewis had also been said to be restoring them, in Leytonstone, in a workshop under a railway arch, and with d'Offay's wife driving, Louis and an employee of the gallery known to him only as Marie-Louise, had made a frantic search of every railway arch they could find in what might be defined as Leytonstone, because d'Offay 'had the wind up'.

They found neither Lewis nor the paintings. Then they turned to George Weissbort, but could not find them there.

I grew to like George, born in Belgium in 1928, resident in London from 1933, and a thoroughly English painter in the best traditions of the New English Art Club — still lives, portraits, landscapes all gently observed, the soft style always consistent in its unobtrusive brushwork and discreet tone. Apart from an unfinished Renoir on his easel when I first went to his house in a seedy West Hampstead terrace, I saw nothing suspicious. Turner, he said, was always asking his opinion of photographs, but never brought the paintings, and the only work that he had ever done for him was to begin cleaning a screen covered in rough cloth primed in white, on which were painted nude male figures prancing and dancing, but this, before he could do anything much to it, Anthony d'Offay had taken away in a great hurry. Was this the Omega screen said to have come from Louis' box?

The High Court move made by Louis forced Turner to find a solicitor, and to him the story was that he, Turner, had acquired all these treasures years before and that, having no confidence in his own appearance, he had enlisted Louis' help as a front to provide these works of art with 'an acceptable provenance'. For this, Louis was to be paid a commission; at approximately five per cent of the sums so far involved, £5,500 was a not unreasonable percentage. Most of this, however, was wiped out by the fees he had to pay his solicitor.

Of all this there was no consequence. D'Offay wanted no publicity and the pathetic boobies of the Fine Art Squad at Scotland Yard utterly failed to understand what was at stake even when it had been demystified for them. The only excuse for their inaction was that the affair had as many suckers and side-shoots as a briar rose and that by leaving them be, even more art market crooks might be discovered, even more grandees might be involved.

On 25 May 1983 Sotheby's had for sale two drawings in black chalk, Lots 103 and 104, catalogued as by Frederick Etchells, a minor but original Vorticist, his surviving work very rare, the estimates £4,000 to £7,000; these I had thought poor in quality in terms of drawing and hopelessly incoherent in terms of Vorticism or Cubism (to which they seemed closer), but it had not occurred to me that they were fakes until they were withdrawn from the sale on the advice of Sotheby's restorer, brought in to effect some minor repairs, only to observe that the paper was much later in date than the 1913 of the identifying inscriptions. Sotheby's had consulted Ronald Alley, of the Modern Collection at the Tate Gallery, who thought them genuine, and had then given the woman who wished to sell them an advance of £5,000. The woman was later identified as the Miss Lawrenson living with Colin Turner. At much the same time Christie's announced a forthcoming sale entirely of Vorticist paintings, drawings and watercolours, to be held on 30 June 1983, but this was cancelled, possibly because Sotheby's had had the decency to inform them of the Etchells catastrophe.

Christie's were naturally unwilling to discuss the matter with anyone and, without information or explanation, no one could comment and, without gossip, no harm was done. Francis Farmar, however, then an expert there, agreed to talk to me and showed me what he could. His description of the vendor fitted Mark Lewis perfectly, and the address in Winterton-on-Sea tallied with Emmett's story that Lewis's mother lived there. Further, he told me that the first approach with the collection had been made to Christie's secondary saleroom in Kensington by a Mr Mason, moon-faced and sweating, with a complicated tale about their being security for a loan made to Lewis and his need to recover it. This was hardly significant, but it indicates that even after I had begun to ask awkward questions in April – perhaps because of them – they had shunted a huge consignment of forgeries onto the open market. Christie's too had consulted Ronald Alley and after his inspection he had proclaimed himself 'perfectly happy' with it; as the expert dealer in the field and likely to be among the heaviest buyers, Anthony d'Offay too had been invited to examine the consignment, but, quoting Francis Farmar, 'He said nothing, and I mean nothing.' Mason was, of course, Emmett.

I asked particularly to be shown a painting attributed to Cuthbert Hamilton, of whom I knew as an original Vorticist, but of whose work I had never seen an example other than a drawing in the Tate. Enormous, it was virtually a bolt of canvas, the painted surface rolled face inward – something that should never be done; the raw side of the canvas did not look the seventy years that it should and, slowly unrolled on the floor, its painted side resembled nothing to be expected of a Vorticist intelligence, the subject a seated woman conceived in black outline and flat planes of pink, yellow, brown and dark green, entirely on the surface with not the slightest hint of Vorticist depth; worse, it stank of fresh paint, not of oil paint but of Alkyd, a synthetic resin introduced only in 1976, new and bright and plastic. There was no trace of the insect life that abounds and multiplies inside rolled canvases, not a wisp of the spiders' webs that are so difficult to detach. Dirt proved to be water-based black paint washed on and then washed off, leaving pigment in the interstices of the canvas, still soluble in spit, the always available cleaning agent. If, when Christie's feels less pained by this failure of connoisseurship, a researcher wishes to pursue the case, the whole collection can be found under the Stock Number DP 309.

Looking back through my 'Fake File' – a haphazard record begun with the exposure of Han van Meegeren when I was still a schoolboy – a Sotheby catalogue of 10 June 1981 came to hand, in which I had noted that Lot 149, *A Dazzle Ship at Sea* by Edward Wadsworth, sold for £11,000, was a fake – 'inconceivable . . . a pastiche . . . utterly flat . . . borrowings reversed . . . ' I said nothing at the time, for I had been insultingly abused for my opinion when, the year before, in a sale at Christie's on 22 February 1980 (a time when, as a consequence of the Blunt affair, I was much insulted without reason or excuse and wondered if opprobrium would ever end), I had doubted the authenticity of Lot 80, a

Vorticist Composition attributed to Wadsworth, bought for £110,000 by Baron Thyssen. Both were in oil, the Thyssen picture said by Richard Cork (eximious expert!) to be unique in this; neither had a secure provenance – they had taradiddle enough to seem a provenance but nothing that withstood examination, and the immediate untraceability of both vendors was gravely suspicious. In retrospect, I concluded that both paintings, though not by the same hand, had come from the same Lewis, Turner, Talbot background and Mark Lewis was later to claim that it was his – but then he also claimed that it was genuine.

*   *   *

Now we must turn to Modigliani. Investigation had moved far beyond the mass forgery of paintings by de Hory, a matter of little aesthetic importance and small sums of money – though the total of those sums ran well into six figures. Probing had uncovered forgeries in quantity of works by Wyndham Lewis and some of his fellow Vorticists, by Gaudier-Brzeska, Nevinson, Wadsworth and the Omega Workshop, and to these must be added odd attempts to produce work by Braque, Degas, Renoir et al. Christie's, Sotheby's, experts at the Tate and, particularly, Anthony d'Offay (though there may well have been other art dealers too), had been misled. To give them their due, some at the Tate had, very early, expressed their misgiving, but been overruled, as in the case of drawings by Modigliani, an artist whose name had been raised at the very beginning of the enquiry when I thought that the de Hory fraud was central to it; as this proved not to be the case and Modigliani played no part in the Vorticist fraud, the whispers that there was, in addition, a Modigliani fraud, had been set aside and almost forgotten, yet it was certainly the earlier by a year or two.

The whispers had been persistent, and on 6 July 1983, Richard Humphreys, a junior curator at the Tate, unwisely but honestly confirmed that the gallery had been given a drawing by Modigliani that was considered genuine until rumours of the Vorticist fraud reached Millbank, and it had then been handed to the police. Why, I wondered, had the Vorticist fraud thrown doubt on a Modigliani unless the dullards at the Tate knew of some connection? But my immediate response was to ask why the acquisition was not listed in the Tate's Yearbook for 1980–82: had something triggered suspicion and consigned the drawing to limbo until research proved the case one way or the other? Another young curator, on seeing a photograph of Colin Turner in the *Sunday Times* of 10 July 1983, recognised him and promptly told me a tale confirming that it was he, Turner, who had brought the Modigliani drawing to the Tate very early in 1981. He had come, without appointment, with a young woman giving her name as Miss Ryder, who was the owner of an album containing some thirty drawings by Modigliani. On being told that they were genuine and of some substantial value (impossible for the Tate to define) as well as of great art historical importance, she became highly emotional and made the dramatic gesture of tearing, without much care, one of the drawings from the album to present to the Tate as an expression of her great gratitude.

Miss Ryder was, of course, Miss Lawrenson, Turner's girlfriend, and the dramatic gesture coolly calculated, for it enabled him to ask for a photograph of the given sheet and its roughly torn edge, for this, matching the edge in the album, was proof of the drawing's presence in the Tate as a genuine Modigliani, thus authenticating all the remaining drawings when he passed them on. This he did by first ensuring that Joseph Lanthemann, an acknowledged expert on Modigliani,* knowing of the presentation to the Tate, wrote certificates of authenticity for every sheet in the album before it was disbound. Speaking neither French nor German, Turner's telephone conversations with Lanthemann were conducted by George Weissbort, who kept records. On 13 February 1981

---

* Joseph Lanthemann, *Modigliani 1884–1920 Catalogue Raisonné*, 3 vols., Condal, Barcelona 1970.

Lanthemann asked Turner to bring the drawings to him in Nice –
'Bring them under your arm – there may be difficulties about re-
export if you bring them in with all the proper documentation.'
He added, significantly, that as an official expert he could ask no
fee, but suggested selling them through the Zürich auctioneer
Walther Germann at Galerie Koller, with an introduction to the
sale catalogue stressing their art historical importance, to be written
by Lanthemann for a substantial fee. Alternatively they should be
sold through Giulio Urbinati of Galerie Le Point in Monte Carlo,
who would give him a commission for introducing Turner. On 10
March Turner told Lanthemann that he had not received his
certificates, nor had Germann, and that if they were not sent very
soon the Zürich sale, scheduled for May, would have to be delayed.
On 7 May Turner still had no certificates and Lanthemann refused
them unless given an understanding that he could catalogue every
sheet and write a prefatory essay that would be a lasting work of
scholarship.

The Zürich sale eventually took place on 28 October 1981, but
it was of only four drawings, Lots 59, 61, 62 and 67; a second sale,
on 7 November 1981, included two more, Lots 434 and 435. The
total reached was £45,000. Lanthemann had, presumably, given
up the struggle to secure publication of the collection as a work of
scholarship; it is doubtful that he received payment for certificates –
Weissbort opined that, his having received a letter from Lanthemann, Turner had the headed paper copied in London and wrote
the certificates himself; as Turner's was an illiterate hand and he had
no German, it seemed probable that Weissbort had been of some
assistance (I could never fathom their relationship, but was, and still
am, convinced of Weissbort's fundamental decency).

Most of the remaining drawings were sold to Galerie Le Point,
almost certainly the purchaser of those sold in Zürich, for some
from both sources were included in a major exhibition mounted
by the gallery in Barcelona and Madrid in 1983 – an exhibition
funded by the Spanish Government and including indubitably

authentic works from public galleries in Berne, Milan, Geneva, Düsseldorf and New York. As supervising expert, Lanthemann at last had the opportunity to write an introductory essay in the catalogue. Of the ninety-eight exhibits Urbinati listed his gallery as owning thirteen and having a further seven for sale; he let slip both that Lanthemann had guaranteed all these as genuine, and that he had for many years been dealing on the side and had contributed some drawings of his own that were for sale and others that belonged to clients and were for sale through his agency. When Colin Turner made a list of those for which he was responsible, it became clear that a third of the exhibits were fraudulent. This list and the copy of the Barcelona catalogue with which it tallied were among the papers that I passed to Scotland Yard.

Colin Turner was also responsible for fake paintings by Modigliani. A cache of these he claimed to have bought from the sister of Kenneth Clark, sometime Director of the National Gallery and, later, Lord Clark of *Civilisation*; K – as Clark's familars knew him – was, alas, an only child. 'Cache' is such a useful term – it can be applied to two or three or expanded to ten times that number if required by the stratagem's success. The first of these canvases so convinced Lanthemann in 1981 that he asked for the rest to be sent to him in Nice, where he showed them to Peter Wilson, retired head of Sotheby's, who might have supposed them to have come from a local collection; he did not; to Lanthemann's fury he damned them as forgeries. Turner, meanwhile, had sold £10,000 shares in them to Kenrick Talbot (he of the de Hory fraud) and J.L. Bendien, a businessman with a West End *pied-à-terre* (he lived in improbable suburban splendour in Crowhurst, Sussex) smart enough to convince other buyers that any paintings he might show them must be genuine. Lodged there, the paintings were security for his loan, which was for one month only at ten per cent, forcing Turner to act quickly. Klaus Perls, a New York art dealer who claimed to be 'the world's leading authority on Modigliani' (a title with which he often introduced himself to strangers), bought one painting for

£30,000, paid into an account held by Turner in a New York bank (Barclay's) in December 1981; the five that remained, Bendien kept and consigned to the London dealer Richard Nathanson who, Bendien complained, 'screwed' him for an enormous sum for insurance and then returned them as 'not kosher'. Asserting that there was yet more Modigliani material, Bendien then played me a tape on which Turner boasted of other paintings in the cache as well as seven large and three small drawings, not part of the album that had so excited Lanthemann.

Perls, before he realised the purpose of my enquiry, told me that he had sold his Turner-Modigliani to an American client and was absolutely sure that it was genuine. Bendien, blustering that he had been cheated by Turner and knew nothing of the ramifications of the business, released the five unsold 'not kosher' canvases to the police. Lanthemann died of cancer in April 1983, his reputation for scholarship in tatters, his great book worthless, his position as expert usurped by Osvaldo Patani, subsequently author of another substantial reference book.* When Patani reviewed the Barcelona-Madrid exhibition of June 1983 for the *Corriere della Sera* he claimed that of the two thousand or so works considered by Lanthemann (and others) to be genuine, at least fourteen hundred were fakes.

*   *   *

Of all this scrupulous investigative work there was no consequence. the *Sunday Times* published several reports over a period of months in the summer of 1983, always premature, ragged in argument, sensational in tone, and worse, inconclusive, entirely written by Colin Simpson while juggling this with other investigations and always slightly the worse for alcohol. They bore my name as second string, but from the very beginning I had argued for first finishing the research, and then, as straightforwardly as possible, presenting it in a single two-page article. Reconsidering it now, I

---

* Osvaldo Patani, *Amadeo Modigliani Catalago Generale*, Milan 1991–4.

see the difficulty. Dribbling the revelations had one advantage – that it stimulated a flow of information from largely disgruntled sources connected with Turner, from lesser employees of Christie's, Sotheby's and the Tate Gallery, and anonymous letters that mostly confirmed what we already knew, though one of them was the first indication that Bendien was involved. Important solicitors wrote convoluted and often silly letters to the editor, Harold Evans; these he passed to his features editor, Magnus Linklater, who, not much interested in art, took fright; he was also bored by the never-ending stream of information that he could not comprehend and, unable to see Colin Simpson's reports as usefully connected and inexorably constructing an important international case, he cut us short. Independently and unpaid, I tied as many knots as I could, wrote a day-by-day account of all that Simpson and I had done, submitted it to the Fine Art Squad at Scotland Yard on 23 August 1983, sorted my notes and evidence and filed it away in case, one day, it might be useful. It never was.

For reasons known only to themselves the Fine Art Squad, having all the information that we had uncovered and having themselves put considerable energy and resources into tracking down Colin Turner – even to having him in a police cell for some hours, releasing him on the grounds that the complaints made by Koolman–Darnley were a civil matter – lost interest. I felt at the time that the complexities of the affair defeated them and that, wholly unqualified in any technical sense, connoisseurship a word they could not even spell, they lacked the intellectual ability to present a clear case to the Director of Public Prosecutions, and the sceptic in me was inclined to aver that the distinguished legal minds in that great office were equally incapable and, perhaps as bored as Linklater and as befuddled as Simpson, were deeply uncertain of successful prosecution. Louis Koolman–Darnley, who was looking forward to cross-examination in the witness box as his unexpected final performance on a public stage, was convinced that money had changed hands, that either by Colin Turner who was, considering the figures of which we are certain, at least £150,000 in pocket, or by one of the dealers he had gulled, anxious to hold on to his reputation for reliability, the palm of Policeman Plod had been well greased. Poor Louis was bitter about the business, for even the paltry few thousands that Turner had given him were wiped out by the fees of the lawyer and the hearing in the High Court, and he was as penniless as ever.

We know that many of the drawings and paintings involved in this enquiry ended in the hands of the police, including the fifty-two Vorticist works that were to have been a whole sale at Christie's, but others did not and may still be in circulation, the drawings from the Modigliani album an indisputable example; but what of the four thousand paintings by de Hory, what of the fifty-four Epstein drawings, the sixty-nine by Gaudier-Brzeska, the unknown number by Wyndham Lewis and all the other things supposed to have emerged from Koolman-Darnley's magic box? Of these Ronald Alley, Keeper at the Tate, adviser to Anthony d'Offay, Christie's, Sotheby's and the Fine Art Squad made a laundering statement on 16 June 1983, worthy of a politician: 'It is a matter of great concern to everyone in the art market that forgers should now be taking advantage of current interest in these un-charted areas.' Note the weasel phrase 'these uncharted areas' – so uncharted that in April 1983, the very month in which this investigation began with the almost irrelevant Elmyr de Hory and Kenrick Talbot, Anthony d'Offay opened an exhibition of twenty-six drawings by Wyndham Lewis, supported by half-a-dozen notables claiming expertise. These waters, in my lifetime, have never been uncharted. The total asking price for d'Offay's drawings was £336,500; a discreet leak suggested that before the show opened, the British Museum had bought a twenty-seventh – for £42,500.

The difficulty for the future is that none of this material, whether it dates from the end or the beginning of the century, is sufficiently separated in age for most scientific tests to distinguish old original from modern fake, and only if the forger has been fool enough to use a recognisably modern paper or medium can we be certain on technical grounds; and the older they become, the less certain, technically, shall we be. Connoisseurship is then the only answer, and the chances are that forgeries of the 1980s will have an Eighties character, imperceptible when new but increasingly obvious with age – and that and intellectual misunderstanding by the forger will be his work's undoing. The great enemy of connoisseurship is, however, profit.

And what of Colin Turner, Mark Lewis, Kenrick Talbot and the rest? Where are they now? What have they forged since? Were they responsible for the neat little still lives that passed for Flegel and van Kessel in the old master sales of the later Eighties, for the paintings of birds so obviously not quite by Marmaduke Cradock? Were the gluts of whaling ships at sea, Montgolfier balloons, clipper ships off Boston and Shanghai, and other fashionable decorative trifles of the past thirty years or so, all theirs? Having blighted the market for late doodles by Lowry, will they turn to foul words on blank canvases by Tracey Emin and to the spots and spins of Damien Hirst? They cannot, surely, have been sitting on their hands since 1983.

When it became clear that there were to be no prosecutions, I asked the Fine Art Squad to return the evidence that I had accumulated, in case another use for it occurred. I was invited to collect it from Scotland Yard, followed by – as a reward – lunch and a visit to the Black Museum that is so notorious. Lunch began with drinks at the bar (a wretched ritual for me as alcohol and I do not work well together at any time of day and least at the halfway mark), and it was soon obvious that my visit was an excuse for a bit of a binge. At last in the dining room, where it seemed that hundreds of lordly senior officers were (every day, one must presume) able to eat at a most leisurely pace enough to feed an ordinary mortal for a week and drink far more, I was astonished to discover that Scotland Yard had its own French vineyard, and an abattoir too to judge by the steak that my hosts wished on me. For them, ruddy, perspiring and increasingly incoherent, it was such a merry occasion that lunch lasted until four, by which time the Black Museum was no longer accessible and I could not be shown either the amusements of sadism, torture and death that justify its name, nor the Modigliani, Vorticist and Omega Workshop forgeries expropriated over the past year or so – I had particularly hoped to see the rest of the sale announced by Christie's for 30 June 1983 in which the Cuthbert Hamilton was the extraordinary star. Sensing that the occasion was over, I reminded my hosts that I had come to lunch only to collect my evidence. 'You must come again,' they said, pressing two bottles of gift-wrapped Château Plod into my hands – but the second invitation never came, my hosts were moved on to higher things (for fear, it was said, that art might corrupt the incorruptible), the Fine Art Squad was reduced to one man and his dog, and the reputation of the art market and its marketeers as a phenomenon of impeccable expertise and absolute probity was perfectly maintained.

*   *   *

Late in the year Magnus Linklater called me to his office to investigate another rumour said to be about to rock the art world. Too trifling to interest Colin Simpson, to me too it seemed insubstantial and, after two days, proved to be so; Magnus nevertheless took my notes and worked them into a scrap of nonsense, published the following Sunday. I was furious – such rubbish did me no good and might well have done me harm in a world in which I had only the most precarious toehold. We had a row – I have always been rashly intemperate – and my link with the paper was severed. Once again I was without work, contacts or prospects, and more than a little desperate.

CHAPTER 10

The Evening Standard

It was the second time in the year that my pride – though I preferred to see it as scruple – had cut short a promising relationship with a newspaper. Towards the end of 1982 Stewart Steven, editor of the *Mail on Sunday*, had suggested that I become that paper's television critic at £200 a week – whoopee! Salvation and something approaching £10,000 a year. I wrote trial pieces for a month, not to be published but for Stewart to see whether I might fit his bill, and there was much 'splendid, my boy' (though he was six years my junior) as I reported to him with my pieces, much as a hesitant schoolboy with an essay for his English master. On 8 January 1983 my comments as the paper's new critic were, for the first time, published. 'Crucified' is the word in my diary, though some reference to the bed of Procrustes would have been more apposite, for my sentences were abbreviated, my paragraphs ripped apart, my punctuation reduced to the comma and full stop. What was printed could have been written by a boy of fifteen at a comprehensive school in Liverpool. To my anguished letter of resignation, delivered by hand that very day, Stewart's response was immediate and mollifying – 'Next Sunday I shall edit it myself and you shall read it before it goes to press – let's call it an agreed text.'

And so we did. He broke one sentence and split one paragraph, just to assert his position; to so little I could not object, but when it appeared in print, it had been much further deconstructed for idiots and I yelped and squawked again. Stewart explained that in his absence his sub-editors had 'got at it', and that this would not happen a third time; but it did and, resolute, I resigned. I know now, of course, but did not realise then, that all newspapers have a house style, that all writers suffer its imposition on their carefully honed texts and that the fee paid is the rarely substantial consolation for the damage done to the scribbler's reason, argument and language. How could I have been so dim-witted? I already knew from disappointing experience that the publishers of art books are not interested in art, nor in its history, but only in the profits to be made from books of scant distinction that fit their preconceptions and do not disrupt their uniformity. John Calmann, whose sister Marianne I had known for years, and whose father, Hans, was one of the most powerful of London dealers in old master drawings, had asked me as early as January 1973 if I would write a book for him on Hieronymus Bosch, the chronology of whose arcane paintings had intrigued me since my student days and to the sequence of which I thought I had the key (based to some extent on colour and the different figure scales that he employed). I should have realised that John wanted nothing more than another cheap picture book yet again repeating what every schoolboy knows and contributing nothing new to scholarship; had he wanted more, why should he come to me? I wrote a synopsis almost as long as the text he required, and when he called me to his office was treated to a performance of contempt and foul temper that far exceeded any I had experienced from Patrick Lindsay, my commanding officer at Christie's. He threw my synopsis on the floor and his whole telephone at me, the reach of the cord to its cradle mercifully short. On the basis of an edition of 10,000 he compared the costings of the book that I proposed with his, said that as I had 'no reputation as an art historian' mine was an impertinence, and mockingly suggested that I should not only write it without an advance, but pay him £1,000 for new photography and a further subsidy for its production – 'If we print a thousand, eight hundred will be remaindered.' Even if I agreed, he would consider publication only after his 'advisers' had considered it.

I have just re-read the synopsis only to realise how much I once knew and how intense and clear my looking was; were I today given it as the work of another art historian, I would enthusiastically commend it as a way out of the labyrinth; I also see that it might well have taken years to write and would have involved much travelling. Had John briefed me clearly instead of flatteringly, I could have compiled his picture-book within a week (such wearisomely inadequate things are the commonplace of art book scribblers and publishers), but he did not and his insulting tantrum made reversal and further overtures impossible.

Phaidon Press, in May 1979, did, except in one respect, brief me properly. They wanted a history of Victorian painting written round thirty full-page illustrations, with a wider introduction of five thousand words or so – a task scarcely more difficult than writing an essay as a student. Weeks of amusement lay in the preparatory elimination of the too familiar and the finding of the unfamiliar that would serve the purpose as well or better – and it was fun until I sent Phaidon a sample of the illustrations that I proposed together with the extended catalogue entries paired with them. I was asked to lunch – for which I had to drive to a pretentious restaurant in Oxford where the then current affectation was making pasta to order, of which the only benefit was much more time for conversation. In our case it was no benefit at all, for glum silence overwhelmed us even before the wretched linguini rolled from the mangle that produced it. Phaidon, I learned, had entered into an arrangement with Christie's to reproduce, without copyright fees, any painting that passed through an auction there, and my book must therefore be constructed round paintings that had been sold there in recent years. I could, off-hand, think of not one that could be described as a key work, and a visit to the *photothèque* in St James's revealed nothing that could be used to stretch the definition. This book too died the death, but a sensible writer would have taken Phaidon's paltry fee and scribbled them what they wanted – exactly what their stable of hacks invariably did.

After these disappointments I talked to Nikos Stangos whom I thought my friend – we were never close but when seriously penniless in the mid Sixties he had briefly lived under my roof and

I had given him money with an airy 'pay it back if and when you can'. As an editor at Thames and Hudson I thought he might encourage me with a commission, but I was of no interest – he could get as many books as he wanted from American professors on sabbaticals whose universities would offer subsidies for photography; me he would have to pay and that put me out of the running.

The next proposal for a book came from Lawrence King, an agent or fixer of some sort, very soon after I had cut short my attachment to the *Mail on Sunday*. It was for a history of art from cave painting to the present day, designed for first year students at American universities as both basic text book and *vade mecum*. There had been such a book for the past quarter century, but it was felt to be stale, stodgy and out-of-date – something fresher, brisker and not downright wrong was now required. As the last one had sold in tens of thousands over decades, the next was pretty well guaranteed to do the same – an income for life, so to speak (as I knew from a pair of ancient dog-walking women friends who had written an English Grammar fifty years before). I was only in part qualified and sample chapters were required; playing to my strengths, I wrote on Quattrocento Florence, Caravaggio and the Carracci, the Enlightenment and Impressionism. Perhaps, of the forty chapters proposed in my synopsis, I should have covered a wider spread, but at this early stage I did not want to reveal that I knew almost nothing about primitive pre-historic painting, nor of Japanese, Egyptian and African art, and that my grasp of the glories and grandeurs of Greek and Roman art was patchy and insecure.

It was not until 16 April 1984, almost a year later, that I had a response. The American publisher gave me lunch in a noisy Italian restaurant in Sicilian Avenue, the covered arcade that lies on the direct route from Holborn Underground station to the British Museum and resembles nothing to be found in Palermo or Catania. Lunch seems so often to have been the prelude to disappointment or disaster, and how should we account for this unholy tie of publishers to pasta? In mid April it was too cold to sit outside, but sit outside we did, talking against the echo of the crowd within and of the heavy traffic at both ends of the arcade. It was not for me to steer the conversation away from generalities, but when we had drunk our coffee and should be parting, I felt compelled to ask what he had thought of my draft chapters. The pause was so long that I laughed. 'Your silence tells me that they will not do,' I said, and still the pause continued. At last, abandoning the distance into which he had retreated, he leaned forward and uttered what seemed a carefully considered, even oracular, response: 'You will have to learn to write a less intelligent book.'

'You will have to write' would have offered hope; but to 'have to learn to write' offered no hope at all, for how can a man who is intelligent learn to abandon his intelligence?

This rejection mattered less than it might. I thought myself back on the treadmill of a thousand words for thirty quid for *Art and Artists*, a slowly dying little magazine in which one could at least be critical as long as this was never of the advertisers, or rather more (and very occasionally) for *World of Interiors*, for which, in its early years, one had always to be benign. Min Hogg, its founder-editor, sent me to Paris in the chill February of 1983 to write on an apartment of the night designed by Geoffrey Bennison, the cold formality of Style Rothschild made warm and comfortable by excluding the bleak north light. Geoffrey was a dab hand with such transformations; nothing looked new, rich things were used only if softened by age and use, value and importance were understated, rarity teased into knick-knackery and the knick-knack magicked into the curiosity; he conjured a sense of the nineteenth century with an inheritance from the eighteenth, lived-in and worn by generations of family, yet this marriage of Portobello Road and Bond Street (so to speak) was entirely new.

Geoffrey was also a dab hand at making buggers of men who had never thought of it. If his taste as a decorator was subtle and understated, his presentation of himself was the extreme reverse.

Plump, his gestures extravagant, his unremarkable ordinary speech lapsing into the bitchy repertoire of camp without embarrassment, his prize trick was to wear black fishnet stockings of the most flamboyant pattern under dowdy trousers, and when he thought he'd caught the attention of a suitable bloke – and blokes were his taste, the rougher and tougher the better – he'd draw the trouser leg higher and higher (never too quickly) until the bloke was in no doubt about what was being offered. In Paris this attracted no attention, for the ladyboys there were slimmer and prettier and younger and the blokes are rare, but at a large transport café on the fringe of London his better luck was notorious – he had only to catch an eye (or ear), reveal a stocking, tantalise and mince to the door to achieve a lightning stand-up fuck in the lavatory or, longer and safer, have it in the lorry driver's cab. This, the very bottom rung of the sexual ladder without the menace of attachment was all that he wanted.

This separation of the act of sex from the sentimental affections formed by homosexuals is a fairly common phenomenon; Geoffrey was, perhaps, an extreme example, but it was true too of Peter Claas, David Carritt and half a dozen art historians of more or less my generation, all of whom had affectionate relationships that were platonic; it was to some extent true of Anthony and, in my sexual opportunism, true of me. The most preposterous of my acquaintances was Tom Skeffington-Lodge – but then he was preposterous in everything by the time I first knew him, in the Sixties. He collected paintings by the then neglected Benjamin Williams Leader, winter landscapes rooted in mud draped in post-sunset gloom, always buying poor examples because they were even cheaper than the good. Born in 1905, his family wealthy (two thousand acres of west Yorkshire farmland), academic, liberal and actively Christian, his own high-minded and benevolent Christian Socialism was inspired by the plight of local miners. After a modestly heroic World War II in the Navy, mostly on Atlantic convoy duty (the most perilous of all), he was elected

Labour MP for Bedford but, far from the sort of original old Labour MP who would piss in the sink, his fussy upper-crust arrogance offended the party leaders Attlee, Morrison and Bevan and, never given the front bench seat that he thought his right, his political career was cut short at the next general election. Then he expected to be sent to the Lords as Baron Swillington of Yorkshire, a dormant barony to which he had some very slight claim and of which he never quite relinquished hope. If he is remembered at all it is only for Francis King's caricature of him as Dame Winifred Harcourt in his novel *A Domestic Animal* (1970); in the Dame he recognised himself and sued, winning the case and ruining Francis. A more spiteful defendant than Francis would have allowed the whole truth to be known – it might not have saved the case but it would have made Tom ridiculous; that the truth was already known to the Conservative Party was clear in 1969 when, in the course of another attempt to return to Parliament, he was dubbed 'the bed-and-breakfast candidate' by his rival, Julian Amery. Tom, by then a pot-bellied bag of bones with thinning hair and the speech of a churchwarden, was indeed the owner of a bed-and-breakfast house in Luton, where Vauxhall manufactured trucks and the drivers who collected and delivered were in need of beds, even prepared to share them if cheap enough; and when the Devil drove him, off Tom went to Luton to satisfy his sexual appetite.

*　　*　　*

On 30 April 1984 I had just returned from Kensington Gardens with the dogs when I had a telephone call from Bert Hardy, of whom I had never heard but later learned that he was 'a Fleet Street legend'. He asked, as though in command of the *Evening Standard*, 'Can you recommend anyone to be our art critic? We sacked Richard Cork three months ago – neither we nor the readers understood anything he wrote – and we've managed without until now but there is pressure from our readers to replace him.' I thought the question framed in such a way as to condition my response; it implied that they did not want me but thought that I might know someone who would do. My pause was for only a second or two but it felt an age, my mind racing, and then, contrary to the genteel social mores instilled by my mother – to be summed up as, 'Don't shake the tree, wait till the ripe plum falls' – I heard myself say, 'No. But I'd quite like the job myself.' To this the response was, 'We were hoping you'd say that; come to the office at midday.'

Why was it Bert Hardy who made the call? He was neither editor of the paper nor part of its team – though he was to become its Chairman in 1989 – and it was not he whom I saw a few hours later. The interview was with Louis Kirby and Roy Wright, the editor and his deputy. It took about two minutes: I was to write, not weekly, but only when there was a major exhibition in a major public place; I was not to write about poxy little shows in back street commercial galleries furthering the careers of unknown artists. I was to submit my texts to Roy, agree alterations and the final versions, and these would be printed; length was to be eight hundred words. Fretting that these were so few and sometimes fewer when advertisements took more space than planned, the consequent cuts in length quite arbitrary, I took to going to the office to read proofs and do my own cutting, for the usual procedure was to dock as much as necessary from the final paragraph, leaving an argument, even a sentence abruptly unfinished. This I have done ever since. When Roy raised an eyebrow at words beyond the range of Winston Churchill's recommended six hundred, I began to wonder whether I should use the commonplaces of the newspaper, but Roy sternly gave me advice that I treasure. I began a paragraph with 'Make no mistake . . . ' 'You are not a journalist,' he said, 'don't write like one,' and crossed it out. I owe a great deal to him. He let me have more words, argued that my increasingly long essays should not be crowded and reduced by advertisements and occasionally let mine be the only words on the page. He did not regard reviews as news and let me brood on exhibitions until my opinion had matured – and for this some institutions, particularly the Royal Academy and Dulwich, were grateful, happy to be the subject when visitor numbers had begun to flag. I was grateful too, for I believed that reviewing should be a considered process of seeing, thinking, writing, seeing again and then re-writing, never a creature of hastily formed (but ill-informed) opinion scribbled to a deadline. I was very much at ease and began to feel that I had become part of the paper.

Louis Kirby I never again encountered; his successor in 1986, John Leese, I did – a really decent man who asked me, if not riddles, wry questions that suggested an amused and sceptical eye on the art world, as though he felt compelled to acknowledge its existence but could not quite believe in anything it said or did. With his five years as editor the paper changed, became more various and less predictable; he supported well-argued difference and contradiction, and he liked words as much as I, liked the sight and sound of them and enjoyed the pinpoint accuracy of some as much as the lubricity of others. When cancer stalked and struck him, I asked Martin Shortis, then recently graduated from the Royal Academy Schools and an impressive draughtsman, to draw the paper's vast open plan office – a big drawing with the News Desk in the foreground, the Arts Desk and Londoner's Diary in the far corner, the perspective ingeniously curved to mask the necessary double viewpoint – to hang at the end of his bed in the Cromwell Hospital. A little recovered – enough to write a thank you and farewell – he took it home with him, but then he died. Even in death he did a charming thing – instead of flowers for his funeral he saw to it that I and others were sent growing roses for remembrance, roots to plant, cherish and enjoy. Mine still flourishes.

His successor was Paul Dacre, now High Panjandrum of the Mails and all they spawn – not a sympathetic boss, perhaps respected but not much loved. I was at once informed that I must never begin a paragraph, and preferably not a sentence, with the letter I. It was, and is, the custom of the paper to break up the mass of text with large and emphatic capitals; this is done only for the appearance of the page and signifies, not a new thread of argument, but nothing, nothing at all; this irrelevant whimsy of balance and composition is mere embellishment and as such an I is meagre and inadequate – an M or W is much preferred. How, I asked, shall I quote the first sentence of St John's Gospel – 'In the beginning was the Word . . . ?' 'You do not,' the answer.

He was editor for a year or so and we spoke only once. One of my contemporaries at school, not seen since then, appeared on my doorstep with a tale to tell, with which, as a minor diplomat in the Near East, he must not be identified. It was that the release of Terry Waite, foolish adviser to the Archbishop of Canterbury and then a hostage in captivity in Lebanon, had been offered to the British authorities, but in a state of raving lunacy. The offer had been refused, the British view apparently that to have him returned in that condition would rouse great public anger and make further diplomacy impossible; besides, the other hostages, still sane, were to remain in captivity. My schoolfriend – a mutual masturbating mate rather than a friend (a recollection that, while listening, I could not entirely banish from my mind) – thought the British agreement with the captors that all the hostages should stay in captivity until Terry Waite had recovered (on which matter they offered advice) appallingly inhumane and wished to leak it. 'Why to me?' I asked. 'Because you are only an art critic, you have nothing to do with foreign affairs, nor with the Near East (so much for all my Turkish travels), and you won't be the writer – nobody knows that we were at school together and nothing can be traced to me.'

I took him seriously, telephoned Dacre, asked to see him and within fifteen minutes was in his office. A minute or two into the tale, I halted, for something about his expression signalled weary familiarity with it. 'But you know this already?' It was more statement than question and his nod confirmed it. I made no note of anything he said – not much I think, 'D. Notice,' perhaps, and confused by the suddenness of deflation, went home with my tail between my legs, knowing that if the *Standard* could not use the story, no other paper could. I had no means of telling my informant of this outcome, for he had not defined the part of the Near East to which he was attached, and I was not best pleased with him for with half an ounce of sense he should have known that the matter was already common knowledge among editors. Months later, when Waite and the other hostages returned to England, we glimpsed him briefly as he left the plane and was then hustled away beyond the approaches of the press. Was this because he was still mad, I wondered?

When Stewart Steven succeeded Dacre in 1992 it was as though a menacing cloud had been removed. Jewish, and German by birth, Stefan Gustav Cohn (born 1935) was too young to be of the generation of European immigrants who, during and after World War II, so invigorated English culture and drastically changed the course of its development, but he was well aware of that influence and together he and I used occasionally to pay homage to Gustav Delbanco in his dotage – a sometime Cork Street art dealer (Roland, Browse and Delbanco, now Browse and Darby) who had in a small way been part of it. Old Gustav chuckled a lot, repeated familiar old stories, and slowly sank into the same urine-soaked senility as my mother; I gave up – one so stricken and so close is quite enough – but Stewart was made of stronger stuff; he needed to be, for his wife, Inka Sobien, a painter once imprisoned in a Russian gulag, was disabled by multiple sclerosis.

For me he was a good editor; he brought nothing from the *Mail on Sunday*, though it had been a failing paper diverted into resounding success entirely through his shrewd handling, but let the *Standard* be itself as a paper pitched at Londoners and Parliament, with an eye on Paris and New York. Never did he mention our disagreement over the television reviews ten years before, but he did bother to take an interest in what I wrote for him and often commented before it was in print (I had, on the other hand, arts editors who never read a word before my reviews appeared in the paper, and, perhaps, not even then). When, on 5 January 1994, thirty-five worthies of the art world, claiming to represent it (whatever it is), combined to write a letter to the *Evening Standard*'s editor, taking 'the greatest exception to Brian Sewell's writing', accusing me of homophobia and misogyny, insult and scurrility, and of a 'dire mix of sexual and class hypocrisy, posturing and prejudice', Stewart rubbed his hands together and turned their folly into a campaign for my support. Among the signatories were my erstwhile friend Nikos Stangos (what had I done to wound him? – never bear gifts to Greeks, I am inclined to say), Anthony's friend John Golding (by then not altogether a surprise), and Sandy Nairne (long the servile lackey of the Tate, the Arts Council or any other public body with which he could find employment, and now the unctuous Director of the National Portrait Gallery), who should have known better.

There was the most astonishing brouhaha. Nikos was fool enough to write another letter to the editor waspishly suggesting that I should write about cars instead of art, but the burden of correspondence and comment in a wide range of papers was in my support and Paul Johnson's essay in the *Spectator*, the cover headline 'God save Brian Sewell', just about summed up the public mood – never were there so many references to the Emperor's New Clothes. The most level-headed response was from Edward Lucie-Smith in *Art Review* under the headline *Out to Lynch*, cogently refuting the charges, recalling my enthusiasm for contemporary artists as various as Joseph Beuys, Michael Leonard and 'even Damian Hirst', and suggesting that, for the signatories, my real crime was that I ought to be one of their art world clique but had refused membership. Even so, I felt like a hunted animal and, on one television programme, confronted by a pair of shrill and vicious lesbians playing Diana to my Actaeon, I looked like one. I wondered how I should behave when next I encountered any of the signatories – as was inevitable. Norman Rosenthal, organiser of exhibitions at the Royal Academy, spat at me within its purlieus and twice, long after I had forgotten the row, used the excuse of a hostile review to thump me on the chest – but both these blows were after cardiac surgery and I was in no condition to hit back (one was hard enough to unravel a titanium stitch holding my ribs together). All three episodes were witnessed by members of the Academy's staff and I was thanked for my restraint – they did not know how much, had I been fit, I would have enjoyed a rough and tumble with that ill-mannered idiot. Almost to the day of his retirement he made a point of being present when I was in the Academy to prepare a review, circling like a rabid dog, murmuring, mumbling and even shouting to wreck my concentration – 'I know exactly what you're going to say . . . I could write your bloody reviews for you . . . you don't know anything . . . you've no right to be a critic . . . I don't know why we let you in . . . ' I had eventually to ask the staff never to let him know that I was in the building.

As for the other signatories, I developed the knack of not seeing them – except for Sarah Kent, the silly woman who was the despised critic of *Time Out* (I have a letter from its editor telling me just that); she had a fit of the vapours in the old Tate – 'I can't bear to be in the same room,' she cried, making no attempt to leave it; to save her dignity I turned on my heel and waited until she had moved on. A few apologised, saying that they had not seen the text of the letter but had been given its gist over the telephone; but this I doubted, for I had had warning of the letter from Leslie Waddington, the grandest of Cork Street dealers, who had been asked to sign one much more virulent but had told the writer that not only had he no wish to sign it but had warned her that it was actionable. I was grateful for his call but I wish that he had not mentioned libel, for the published text was considerably toned down; had the original been sent to the editor I would certainly have sued. Stewart damned the lot of them for fools: 'If they wanted me to get rid of you, writing that letter was idiocy – no editor could be seen to obey it.'

Stewart had much earlier, while still editor of the *Mail on Sunday*, made clear his attitude to the extremes of contemporary art when – perhaps as recompense for the miscarriage of my television criticism – he gave me the unusual commission to find for him a group of students still at art schools, good enough to earn their livings as professional painters. He recognised the common folly of enthusiastically predicting another Freud or Bacon at so immature a stage and set me a less hazardous and far more interesting task. 'I am not looking for the household names of the future,' he said, 'if we are lucky those will be a bonus, but they are too often the consequence of chance and hype rather than any quality. I want artists with whose work sensible people will want to live, rather than the mystifying sort always promoted by the Arts Council.'

I found a handful of promising artists, but it meant a slog through art schools as far afield as Manchester and Birmingham, Belfast and Newcastle (for some reason those in Scotland were left out), and their names and paintings were published in the paper's magazine, but, as Philip Solomon, a buccaneering art dealer much given to adventure, pointed out, newspapers last no longer than a day and if these youngsters were to be given a professional push worth having, their work should be exhibited in a London gallery – by which he meant the gallery that he had just opened in Bruton Place, then one of the arteries of the art market. At an extravagant lunch – at which I was as innocent as a child at a world chess tournament – I watched Stewart and Philip seek advantage in the deal, not because either needed it, but because it was custom deeply engrained in them. Stewart eventually agreed and Philip became an essential element in the exercise for all the years that the paper maintained its interest; when it withdrew after 1987, Stewart no longer seeing the project as energetic enough for his brisk dynamic *Mail*, Philip persevered and throughout the decades until his death in 2011, consistently supported young painters at the start of their careers.

We shared a love of dogs. He had three middling poodles to

which other occupants of the block of flats in which he lived decided to object; the fiercely argued compromise was that he could keep them but not replace them when they died. When the eldest gave up the ghost, in great distress he called me; I called a friend at the Mayhew Home for Animals and a young substitute was found; again and again we played the trick. At Philip's funeral there were no flowers, only donations to the Mayhew.

Stewart left the *Standard* in the autumn of 1995, his successor Max Hastings, who had for some weeks overlapped him as a lurking presence, observing in silence and determining our fates. His first morning as editor began what we called the week of the long knives, a series of interviews from which the paper's old soldiers, incompetents and skivers emerged ashen-faced to empty their desks and disappear into oblivion, a handful undeservedly. I, mere art critic and only a contributor, not an employee, was called in on Friday afternoon, the last scraping of the barrel. 'I'm not going to sack you,' he said, 'my mother would never forgive me.' 'Thank God for Anne Scott-James,' I murmured to myself, a critic I had admired since I was a boy. The best of editors, he brought his appointees with him and trusted them to make the paper what he wanted, to give it influence, to ensure that every member of Parliament read it and was frightened of its wrath, while he lunched and dined in lofty places with the loftiest in the land in the hunt for news, whispers, plots, intrigues and machinations, returning to Derry Street wagging his tail like a hound with a fat white truffle. Never in my years with the paper was it so sure-footed with news, anticipating the broadsheets of the following morning; never was I more certain that I had been right to refuse the blandishments of other papers. For this there were several reasons: to my bones I am a Londoner and this is the London *Evening Standard*; to my bones I am loyal, and this was the first paper to offer me the kind of employment I needed and for which I was perfectly qualified; and I knew that it was read by pretty well every member of Parliament, the Lords as well as Commons, all the denizens of Westminster and even Buckingham Palace, and that no morning paper had quite so concentrated and influential (and to be influenced) a readership.

Dominic Lawson, then editor of the *Sunday Telegraph*, suggested in the spring of 1996 that I might write an opinion column for him; this was permitted by my contract provided that the subject was not art and that I did not write as an art critic or art historian. An untamed political animal since the debates at school in the course of the post-war election of 1945 (I was then thirteen), I thought, as a man virtually disenfranchised by the voting system and who had only ever been able to vote for the least of evils since the Suez Affair of 1956, that I might enjoy this and agreed to a three-month trial. My very first piece was on a new method of abortion practised in the United States and destined here, in which the child is hauled out feet first and, while the head is still in the cervix, a suction-pump is inserted in the base of the skull to remove the brain, the legitimacy of this procedure a triumph of medical casuistry worthy of a medieval disputation. Max read it and on Monday morning commanded me to write no more, but I told him that I was committed for three months and could not go back on my word; moreover, I pointed out, I was not employed by the *Standard* but was merely a contributor with a contract that permitted me to write for other papers. This he did not know. Within minutes I was no longer a contributor, but on the staff as art critic and columnist, with a decent salary instead of casual payments, six weeks paid holiday, private medical insurance, an expenses allowance and the offer of a Vauxhall car. The Vauxhall I refused – I had nothing against the marque but had promised myself something out of the ordinary before I was too old to enjoy it and, short of finding a pre-war 25 with a coachbuilt body, Vauxhall could not fit that bill.

I told Dominic of my changed status and promised him his three months – time enough to find another writer. It was a useful experience both in finding every week a topic worth a thousand words of argument, and in dealing with the correspondence that it engendered. I had no idea how prejudiced, narrow-minded and mean-spirited the readers of the *Sunday Telegraph* could be – whatever I wrote about, they responded as though from the joyless, embittered, puritanical low church gloom of the later eighteenth century. These were people for whom I did not wish to write, whose rare support I did not trust, and I said my farewell to them in these terms:

'This is my final column for the *Sunday Review* – a weekly contribution that has given me great pleasure these few months past, though the correspondence engendered compels me to acknowledge that I have trodden on many toes. Let me, as a valediction, tread on more.

I am a natural Conservative, with the benefits and privilege of education, class and property, resentful of any government that interferes too much, belligerent towards a state that too often tells me that I must eat my Brussels sprouts and lumpy custard. My Conservatism is rooted in the conviction that all men are *not* equal, and that were we all given an equal chance, we would achieve very different ends and again be unequal within a generation – Christ's *Parable of the Talents* is as true of men now as it was in the day he told it, and if I were given Linford Christie's running shoes and jock-strap, I very much doubt if I would match him to the winning post. My Conservatism is rooted in philanthropy, in the conviction that none should starve on the streets, live, sleep or die there, that we all have responsibility for those less able than ourselves, and that a compassionate welfare state addressed to the needs and ills of the deprived is the mark of a well-ordered society. My Conservatism is rooted in the passionate belief that it is through education, cultural, Classical and Christian, that men learn the ancient virtues and philosophical abstractions – justice, probity, generosity, nobility, gravity, forgiveness, prudence, fortitude, self-sacrifice, honour and the Seven Corporal Works of Mercy – and that these, not the politics of envy, nor the politics of self-advantage, are the tenets that should inform society and government.'

Outsider II

To write on the same variety of social and political subjects for the *Evening Standard* was to discover a readership prepared to engage sympathetically with my occasionally maverick views on politics, society and sex. When I offended his friends and peers Max was vigorous in my defence – a letter rebutting a complaint from the Chief of Staff to the Archbishop of Canterbury, the hectoring George Carey, demonstrates how unreservedly: 'Brian Sewell is indeed intemperate . . . In recent months I have dealt with outraged correspondence about his column from assorted Zionists, art dealers, Scots, Jews and so on. If there is any section of society he has so far failed to take on, I am sure that he will soon remedy the deficiency. It is probably fair to say that dogs are the only people for whom he feels unqualified enthusiasm . . . I am sure the Archbishop is quite grown-up enough to take the view that if the likes of Brian Sewell are capable of stoking up fires too hot for him to bear, then he is likely to find the going very tough in the afterlife.'

Max was also very generous; aware that the column and an exhibition review amounted to my working eight days in every week, with no freedom at weekends, he'd suddenly announce that it was time I had a 'jolly' and send me off on an extended break to Paris, Berlin, Munich or some other centre of the arts. Irked by my lack of adventure, 'You can go anywhere you like, short of Hawaii,' he said, and was doubly disappointed when I went to Naples.

Up and down the hills of Naples and in and out its alleys I drove a Lancia Delta Integrale, a thrilling little car of almost razor-edged distinction, designed without compromise, and fell in love with it. At the time, I was writing an eccentric motoring column for the *Evening Standard*'s weekly magazine, and the Lancia was not only exceptional in itself, but in that it was fashionable when most of the cars of which I wrote were unfashionable, old and a disgrace to the industry – the Ford 10 of 1934, the Wolseley 12 of 1946, the ghastly Vauxhall Victor of 1957 and the Austin Metropolitan of the same period. In some, as a boy, I had been driven – by schoolmasters, priests and, particularly by Hodgetts (he had, as far as I knew, only this surname), a bluff friend of my stepfather who took me hill-climbing (a now forgotten sport) up Shelsley Walsh in Worcestershire and other muddy slopes in old ACs, Allards, Dellows, Singers and HRGs. Others I had driven, begged, borrowed and owned; and others still I found advertised, told the owner that I wished to write about his car, gave him lunch (my introduction to the worst of wayside greasy spoons), and then test-drove a model that not in a thousand years would I ever have wished to own – indeed I could have compiled a book on the worst cars ever made in England. This I greatly enjoyed as an escape from the art world and a reversion to boyhood, but Max indirectly deprived me of it by adopting a high moral stance over some minor misdemeanour committed by the magazine's editor, mood-changing in nature, replacing him with a woman who, without informing me, dropped what she dismissed as 'boys' toys'. I delivered my column and was greeted with a disdainful, 'Oh, I don't want that,' as though it were pornography. I complained, to Max, for the column had twice won a prize for motoring journalism, not because I expected him to overrule her, but because I wanted to go on writing about cars and needed his permission; without hesitation he gave it, but no replacement offer came.

We knew that Max had no wish to be editor for life, that he had an academic ambition to become an historian and that he would leave more or less when he did in 2002, but we shut our eyes and minds to it and were unhappy when he went. His successor was Veronica Wadley, intellectually (if that is the word for it) shaped by the *Daily Mail*. Like Max she brought her own team with her, and out went Max's infinitely more subtle, honest and intelligent lieutenants, among them my column editor, Bernice Davison, and my arts editor, Annabel Freyberg, both of whom I trusted and, indeed, adored. Bernice lasted a few months, but Annabel was replaced immediately and without even a day's overlap with Veronica, who knew nothing of her or her capabilities yet had, without warning her, weeks earlier appointed to her post Norman Lebrecht, former music critic of the *Daily Telegraph*. Him she was fool enough to elevate to the position of her right-hand man with power to decide not only how the paper covered all the arts, his immediate bailiwick – though of mine he knew absolutely nothing – but with influence over the whole paper. Never was a favourite so puffed-up with amour-propre, so arrogant and so thick-skinned; never was a man so loathed by those with whom he worked and sought to oversee. For the first time in my life I was told what I should write and what view I should hold. Veronica told me that I should be loyal to him, but to this my response was that loyalty had to be earned and was not to be bestowed at whim or order. After his extensive revision of a review we had so blazing a row that I said, 'If you want me out, then you must tell me to my face.' He lasted a year or so and then, like the Cheshire Cat (though his was the smile of Iago), he began to fade.

There was trouble with my column too. It had always expressed my opinion, not the editor's and not the paper's, but in the newly-imposed traditions of the *Daily Mail* this simply would not do and I was expected to become Veronica's instrument. At first this was a matter of style – Veronica read everything in proof and we had a brush or two about the length of paragraphs and sentences – 'Do you realise,' she said one day, holding a proof between finger and thumb as though she had just retrieved it from the privy, 'your first paragraph is five inches long?' She walked off without another word when I replied, 'The argument is five inches long and cannot be broken.' Prompted by a column critical of Israel that she, for once, had failed to check – 'You've lost me forty thousand readers in north London,' she cried across the open office – she eventually told me that she had left me in peace long enough and that she now intended to control the column. I must tell her in advance the subject and the view I took on it, and that only if she agreed to both should I write the piece. To counter any evasion on my part she gave me all the telephone numbers at which she might be found out of hours and at weekends, and even those of her secretary and deputy. That I often had no view and that this was usually formed in the thinking and writing, often requiring radical revision as I progressed, she was unable to comprehend.

We jogged along not too uneasily, my position strengthened by my being given the Orwell Prize in April 2002, until a formidable row over her wish to illustrate a column with an irrelevant photograph that had taken her fancy; this required my re-writing a paragraph to make it relevant and I refused; she proposed to have another scribbler re-cast the piece and that too I refused. That brought about the end of the column. I deeply regretted (and regret) its loss, for I much preferred its variety to what had become the dread sameness of the art world, and had I been compelled to abandon one or the other, would have chosen to keep the Tuesday column, as it had been known. In an interview with Roy Greenslade in the *Guardian* in June 2004, Veronica attributed her decision to snuff out the column to her concern for my health – 'I felt responsible about Brian working too hard,' she said, and went on to labour the point with my age, my pacemaker, my not-the-best-of-health and the assertion that reviewing art exhibitions took a lot out of me. I was sickened by this disingenuous deceit – her sacking me was nothing less than a foolish demonstration of her power.

So thought others on the *Standard*. No one liked her; worse, no one respected her. Unctuous at one moment, shrewish another, no one trusted her. Her entry into the open-plan office immediately caused a general hunching of shoulders and ducking behind computer screens. Bill Hagerty, another *Guardian* writer, commented that, interested only in the paper's features and 'unable to differentiate between the readership of the *Mail* and the more sophisticated *Standard*', her editing was the subject of scathing derision. My observation was that she was hopeless at managing her writers, editors and necessary lackeys, whether male or female, that she was in thrall to her favourites – notably Will Self and Tim Lott, neither of whom troubled himself to give her of his best – and that she occasionally behaved like a fishwife in the general office, a man her usual victim. But there she was, in her power suit, eroding the readership by tens of thousands year on year, profit turned to haemorrhaging loss, Paul Dacre, the paper's over-arching panjan-drum, and Lord Rothermere, its owner (though rumoured to have been heard throughout the building with his cry: 'It's the product that's wrong'), both so blind to her misrule that when her quin-quennium was over, they foolishly reappointed her for another. Poor Veronica, incapable of realising how incapable she was, held the post until January 2009, when Alexander Lebedev bought three-quarters of the ruined paper for a pound. Then she was immediately out.

And so in a sense was I. As an economy measure I was discarded from the staff with compensation enough to buy a Ford Mondeo and the invitation to return as a contributing critic at a quarter of what had been my salary. I could have had a huff and walked away but felt a tug of loyalty to readers who, for a quarter of a century, had so often expressed their support for views that had earned me the art world's enmity, and I asked myself what I would do with a life that did not entail the daily discipline of art criticism. Cultivate my garden? Having heartily and unforgivingly despised Norman Lebrecht for unseating Annabel Freyberg without a thought of the consequences for her, to which other paper or journal could I go (supposing that one might want me) without doing exactly that to another art critic? As to not one was the evident answer, I swallowed my pride (though not entirely my reproach and resentment) and behaved as though nothing had changed. But it had.

The new editor was Geordie Greig, seduced away from *Tatler*; affable, even amiable, under his deft and Tatlerish touch the paper began to recover its circulation, and with the abracadabra of giving it away it now has the largest readership in all the years of its existence. I doubt, however, that it has the slightest influence in the House of Commons or the Mayor's Parlour, for too much of its editorial matter is by lightweight writers of no broad, deep or long experience and whose opinions are worth no more than those of any twitterer – though in this they may be perfectly in tune with the shallow interests of today's society. I plod on as seriously as I ever did, conceding nothing to the despots and nabobs of the art world, mildly irked by occasional hints that I should be more respectful to them. When Norman Rosenthal, of whom the Royal Academy had at last rid itself, wrote to the *Standard* complaining that my review of the Academy's Hockney exhibition was ' . . . not only mendacious and venomous but reaches new depths of jealousy . . . ' and more of this kind, Geordie allowed it to be printed. I wrote him a note:

24.i.2012

Dear Geordie – 'Mendacious.' The other insults crowded into his letter by Norman Rosenthal (published yesterday in the ES) are just bad tempered nonsense, but mendacious is a nasty word, dangerous too. Why did you allow it? Removing it would not one whit have reduced Norman's malice, but letting it stand seems an odd disloyalty to me. I am not best pleased.

Yours ever,   Brian

This he ignored. Many who loathed Rosenthal – including Royal Academicians – urged me to sue him, but this Geordie had scuppered by printing the letter, lending it his editorial weight; the *Standard's* letters editor had argued for removing the word, but had been overridden. I sent another note:

26.i.2012

Dear Geordie – 'Mendacious.' The accusation is defamatory and requires public withdrawal and apology from Rosenthal. You, however, in publishing it, have put me in an impossible position. I must ask, too, why the *Evening Standard*'s lawyers did not prevent the publication of the word. I feel that I cannot let it pass. What is to be done?

Yours ever,   Brian

Outsider II

And yet another:

7.ii.2012

Dear Geordie – 'Mendacious.' The wound suppurates. I have heard nothing from you of your proposed contact with the irksome Rosenthal, but perhaps you inspired the observation by Matthew Bell in the *Independent on Sunday* on 29 January.

I am intrigued by the idea of suing the *Evening Standard* – is there a precedent for the defamation of a contributor by his employer and a consequent suit?

Yours ever,   Brian

Only with this did Geordie take action. An exchange of emails with Rosenthal resulted in his agreement to 'withdraw' the word 'mendacious' – a pointless exercise, for though the word was published in print his withdrawal was not and floats somewhere in the ether where no one knows of it. To me there was no apology.

As I write, Geordie has left the *Evening Standard* to become the editor of the *Mail on Sunday*, a rung on the ladder that he may well climb to become the Dacre of his day. The appointment of Sarah Sands as his successor has just been confirmed on twitter: is such a matter really so trifling as to be worth no more than an informal tweet?

CHAPTER 11

The Venomous Critic

In my first term as a student at the Courtauld Institute (in 1954 and at the conclusion of my National Service), I was instructed that method was all, that the eye counted for nothing, that abject belief in tutors – one in particular, Dr John White of *The Birth and Rebirth of Pictorial Space*, scarcely older than his students – was an article of faith, and scepticism a mortal sin. We were expected to hold in awe all works of art, no matter how wretched, no matter how much endowed with false importance by the accident of survival. That kind of worthless awe, however, did not last more than a few weeks before a student revolution put an end to it and, graduating to the feet of Johannes Wilde, we became aware of an entirely different authority – the authority of the eye; here was an old saint who knew his dry documents in every detail, and yet in his tutorials, as opposed to those of lesser men, we were aware of a still questing sensibility and a still lively emotional response to paint and images – he was to Michelangelo and Titian what Klemperer was to Beethoven and Mozart, the guardian Sarastro who, from the antechamber known as Knowledge, opened the door to Wisdom and encouraged us to look beyond. His friend Antoine Seilern opened other doors and so did Denis Mahon, their passionate enthusiasm for possession utterly infectious, their knowledge of art history at least as well founded as that of our tutors, yet informed by connoisseurship and an indefinable excitement that was far from academic.

These were the doors that I sought to open with my criticism, for critics in general I held in contempt. Years before, in January 1958, at the Royal Academy's Winter Exhibition (as they were then called), The Age of Louis XIV, on which I had worked with

Michel Laclotte and Anthony Blunt, I had encountered a posse of them from Paris, caricatural figures in camel hair coats draped open over their shoulders, perfume and body odour blending as on an unbathed tart; they twittered, raucous as magpies, complaining of the choice of works, the word *affreux* (frightful) echoing through the galleries, their enmity for the distinguished fellow Frenchman who was the exhibition's genius, blatant, their disdain for me, his dogsbody, palpable. They were strutting windbags, gascons, fanfarons, their opinions worthless.

The English critics whose number I joined were far less well dressed, with not a malacca cane between them, but just as unpleasant. I thought at first that I might make friends but was soon disabused; instead I learned that the world of critics was small, exclusive and greedy, morally without scruple, and damned if it was going to let a new man in. The art world thirty years ago was a cosy coterie greedy for patronage, and no place for the independent spirit. Patronage may seem an odd word in this context, but the jam on a critic's gingerbread was then provided by, for example, various arms and dependencies of the Arts Council asking him to play some part in the organisation and cataloguing of exhibitions, paying him handsomely for doing so – but only if they had his uncritical support. Art dealers too might ask him to write an introduction to a one-man show, for which the fee was a few hundred pounds or perhaps one of the exhibits, but the critic was required to suspend his critical faculties and gush enthusiastic bilge (this is still the case). An editor might commission a contribution to a magazine, but only if the scribbler toed the editorial line – Peter Fuller, late and still much lamented (a hideous car crash for which he was in no part responsible put an end to him), as editor of *Modern Painters* always put me through my paces on an issue, and if my views did not conform with his, said 'Thanks very much' and gave the work to someone else. The BBC, source of more patronage than any other body, was particularly vindictive if criticised; my harsh words on the intellectual level of its fawning programmes on the visual arts – little more than advertising – and the largely execrable generalists who dominated them, immediately ensured my total exclusion from all its programmes (this is so still). I was far too maverick and subversive to be welcome in such bosom nookeries.

Other institutions were as spiteful; the Arts Council and the Hayward Gallery, though they invariably denied it, dropped me from their press lists as a response to savage comments and never invited me to any of the international junkets that, long ago, were in their gift (these blandishments have since fallen away to nothing). Not, after mocking its sometime chairman, the preposterous and endlessly quoting Lord Morris of Castle Morris (a Welsh academic), did I receive so much as a press release from the now mercifully defunct Museum and Galleries Commission. The Royal Academy occasionally let me know that I had incurred that body's august displeasure, and in November 1994 informed the committee of one of its supporting bodies that I was permanently blackballed and not to be invited to take part in a debate. The coin of patronage had, and still has, the image of censorship on its reverse.

I am one of the brave brotherhood of those who have been publicly insulted by Norman Rosenthal. By a Bond Street dealer who thought his stock and reputation impugned I have been beaten about the head and shoulders with a wet umbrella – clammily unpleasant but, unfurled, an ineffective weapon. I have been punched in the right eye by a young painter, the blow so heavy that it disrupted sight for several weeks and the bruise spread over my cheek and neck before it faded, pummelled by a lesbian clad from top to toe in black leather (for me an occasion of almost helpless laughter), and jostled from their exhibition by video artists who shut down their contraptions and turned off the lights as soon as I entered their room in the Camden Arts Centre. These small events, the screams of feminists and the low booing of billiards players in the Chelsea Arts Club, are expressions of rage easier to tolerate than the closing of ranks by those who run the art establishment, whose defensive refrain 'He's only an art critic' they believe excuses them from taking notice of anything I write or say. Even Nicholas Serota once felt it proper to terminate a discussion with 'I'm a museum director and you're only an art critic' when he thought he'd lost an argument. To compliant critics, however, serving their purposes, these panjandrums are quite prepared to drop to the low kowtow.

In the Eighties (but less so in the tight-fisted Nineties) it was scarcely necessary for a critic to have a kitchen or keep a cellar, for the Academy, the Barbican and countless commercial galleries plied him with food and drink at lunchtime press previews (the Barbican's sandwiches were marvellously substantial with a perfect note of squidginess to make a mould of the roof of the mouth); and at evening private views he could gorge on canapés. Bernard Denvir, a critic whose importance I failed to recognise at the time (it was obscured, perhaps, by his self-importance), took his wife to every possible press and private view and, finding so little use for his kitchen, converted it into a second bathroom. At the Royal Academy's *Painting in Naples* exhibition in the autumn of 1982, there was a major logistical mishap: the Italian Tourist Board, in its innocence, invited to lunch, not the critics but the press, apparently unaware that there is nothing to choose in bad manners between a herd of journalists and a horde of locusts; when the critics arrived neither food nor drink was to be had and littering the floors and propped against the walls of the Academy's elegant private rooms were a hundred swollen bodies of sated hacks, for all the world like the plague-stricken Naples of Luca Giordano. Among critics, those who took greatest advantage of such hospitality were not the regular contributors to major newspapers, but the even worse paid wretches writing for small circulation magazines and local rags, or who were merely members of the International Association of Art Critics and never wrote anything at all; I once met one of these in Bond Street – 'You're going in the wrong direction' was her greeting. 'There's food at Wildenstein's.'

The Venomous Critic

When the Tate Gallery mounted its Hockney Retrospective in 1988 I was asked by a dealer specialising in his work what it would cost him for me *not* to review it. Five years earlier I might have found this deeply shocking, but by then John George, editor of *Art and Artists*, the puny little magazine that had offered me most work, had long since declared that: 'There is no such thing as an honest critic,' following it with: 'Art criticism is drivel, unmitigated drivel' – but his magazine depended on it and the advertising revenue it generated, and he could not stop the rot. His associate editor, Edward Lucie-Smith, one of the busiest critics of the time, speechifying at an exhibition in honour of his fiftieth birthday, confessed: 'I once thought of having principles – then I decided that I was too old for them.' In this Edward neatly encapsulated the status of the critic – rather than principled and poor, the critic must be, if he is to succeed, an essential part of a symbiosis with the market place, curators, the Arts Council and all others who use the arts for self-aggrandisement – and if this means being intellectually dishonest and despised, so be it. Edward eventually, through the medium of photography, became an artist of sorts himself; John George, honest soul, resigned from *Art and Artists* and became a postman to support his wayward ambition to write a doctoral thesis on Czechoslovakian contributions to philosophy; and when their desuetudinous magazine then fell into the hands of Bernard Denvir, it promptly died.

Art criticism in England thirty years ago was thus at a low ebb, corrupt, fawning, swamped in meaningless jargon, distorted by political correctitudes, the flattery of curators and their institutions its only purpose. I thought it would stay so, and to some extent it has, but, against the odds, there are now perhaps half-a-dozen critics to whom no obligations matter more than intellectual probity and who tell the truth; critical jargon, the political correctitudes and intellectual dishonesty have become the bailiwick of the curator in the field of contemporary art – the very man who should enlighten, now obscures, anxiously addressing his jabberwocky, not to the far wider audience that now visits exhibitions, but to other curators and their ilk. Catalogues of contemporary art are now incomprehensible.

Between critics and the curators of old master exhibitions there is a different gulf – its name is Superiority and it is maintained by curators less than half my age and hardly a whit of my experience. To one of these at Tate Britain, after ten minutes of being pressed to listen to what he had to say about Charles Ginner (a contemporary of Sickert, the subject of his exhibition), I posed the question, 'Where do you think I have been this past half century?' He did not understand; I had to tell him that I had been looking at pictures, among them many by Ginner, and that I probably knew more about the man than he did. To his, 'Oh I'm so sorry, I had no idea . . . ' I had to counter that in his bibliography he listed an exhibition catalogue that I had written in 1985, but obviously had not read it, for though everything he had told me, and much more, was in that catalogue, he had given me no credit. Nor did he know that I had been largely responsible for the selection and cataloguing of pictures in the *New English Art Club Centenary Exhibition* of 1986 – a trifling achievement, I admit, but one that fitted precisely with his field. The point is, I suppose, that at a certain age one drops below the horizon and young men at the beginning of their careers hardly know of one's existence – for years I have wondered why, when I have been around for so long, no one ever asks me anything: I am probably the only person living who knew and listened to the recollections of Pierre Coulette, Duveen's forger for forty years, or witnessed Bomberg shoo away from his doorstep an importunate dealer, or watched the shrewish widow of Frank Dobson burn his erotic drawings and smash his small terracotta sculptures of sexual conjugation. When I am gone no one will know of these small things.

Apart from my misgiving about the authenticity of Dürer's *St Jerome* in the National Gallery, recorded in the Annual Report of 1996–97, no art historical observation I have ever made has been acknowledged; was not one of them of any interest or pertinence? I have asked questions that any responsible scholar or critic might ask, but now no longer do so, for they are never answered. What sort of questions? No curator now openly admits to failure of any kind in the presentation of an exhibition – at least, not to a critic. Let us consider hypothetically an exhibition devoted to the history of Cubism from which Picasso's great *Demoiselles d'Avignon* is absent. This is a seminal work; without it the exhibition is the Bible without the Book of Genesis. The critic who knows something of Cubism and the fundamental importance of this picture, has the right to know the reason for its absence. Is it in such fragile condition that it is unfit to travel? Is it so highly valued that no insurer will accept the risk? Is it subject to a loan restriction – not outside America, say, or to be lent not more than once in a quinquennium? Is it that the authorities of MOMA have no faith in the temperature and humidity conditions of the borrowing museum? Is it that they have no respect for the scholarship of the exhibition's curators and believe them to be frivolous? Is it that they are planning an exhibition of their own on the same theme?

I have asked such questions and have been adamantly refused answers as though I am some kind of enemy, though the enquiries were made in an intended defence of the curators. I have asked questions about the *inclusion* of pictures that seemed unworthy of exposure in exhibitions (as was the case in the National Gallery's 2003 Titian exhibition), and again been refused an answer. The questions were nevertheless legitimate and again asked in an intended defence, for if the critic knows that the first choice of a curator, the sublime picture in the Prado, was refused, that his second choice, the adequate picture in Palermo, was promised to another exhibition, and that there remained to him as his only choice the overcleaned and heavily repainted wreck in São Paolo if he were to make his point, then the critic understands the presence of the restorer's ruin, even if he himself would have dropped the point rather than lower the overall quality of the exhibits.

Outsider II

To some extent I understand why curators may wish to be protected from people calling themselves critics, for far too many claiming to be of that ilk are nothing of the kind, but mere journalists incapable of understanding connoisseurship and interested only in sensation that can be better divulged, whipped up and managed for an institution's benefit by its press officers, whose duty it is to proclaim every exhibition the biggest and the best, a blockbuster, beano and bonanza (who can forget old Titian's 'first ever one-man show' at the National Gallery?). Press officers are not employed to tell the truth, but to control information, turn it into propaganda and compose lengthy press releases that both act as bait for idiot journalists and relieve them of all responsibility for what they write – or say, for the worst examples of regurgitation are invariably performed by those who masquerade as critics on radio and television.

I quite understand, too, curatorial contempt for the legion of so-called freelance critics who enjoy no regular employment and write nothing but, as members of AICA, attend every press view in hope (now vain) of the refreshment that was once the generous commonplace of these events. But there remain a dozen or so of us who deserve to be treated as the equals of curators, at least in our ability to make art intelligible to those who hasten from the Clapham Omnibus into the National Gallery, and some critics even have knowledge and experience that curators should exploit.

For my own part, I no longer expect a curatorial response to any small contribution I make to the sum of knowledge – indeed, so lofty are curators now that I doubt if they care tuppence what the critics say; when a new curator is appointed in a national gallery or museum, no attempt is made to introduce him – he is just suddenly there, another minor deity beyond our reach.

I now ask only two things of galleries. The first, often granted, rarely offered, is to be let into exhibitions days before the cattle market of the press view so that I do not find myself obstructed by journalists who cannot tell a Titian from a Tracey Emin, nor excluded from rooms in which television presenters are at work, for these tin gods have absolute sway over access and presence and make as much noise and nuisance as they will. The second, rarely granted, is to be able to read the catalogue a week or two before the exhibition opens. It is beyond my comprehension that catalogues are often not available until hours before the opening of exhibitions that have been perhaps as many as five years in preparation. Catalogues are now of biblical proportions and page length, cost a fortune, weigh a ton and contain a dozen essays in which a dozen scholars expound a dozen views – and yet the responsible critic is given no opportunity to read them before he must put pen to paper to meet the deadline of his editor.

In my three decades as a critic, the visual arts have become news as never before and my old remedy for these dilemmas – to write a considered review two or three weeks into the life of an exhibition, the catalogue diligently read, my arguments for or against it and the show punctiliously checked – is no longer possible. The pace has so quickened that without the cooperation of the exhibiting institutions, art criticism must inevitably be shallower and less well informed – a self-fulfilling prophecy, as it were, that justifies the curatorial conclusion that critics are contemptible and need be given by their press officers only such information as the curators think fit (the blind leading the blind). Matters are not helped when in newspapers and magazines, television and radio, critics are replaced by novelists, biographers, hacks and celebrities who write and speak for fees quite undeserved, parading at best the uninformed opinions of the amateur, at worst their downright and misleading ignorance. Matters are not helped when institutions exploit the press for maximum publicity: long ago, Serota knew exactly what would happen when he hung a dead horse in the entrance of the old Tate, and exactly the response to the Emin bed, just as the Royal Academy exploited the Myra Hindley portrait at the Sensation show. One may argue that the press expressed genuine outrage and was right to do so, or that in these cases it was neatly suckered by these institutions into doing precisely what was wanted and expected of it; the proper response, impossible to achieve, is to ignore such manipulation. The press did not learn the lesson then and is still manipulated now.

These are melancholy ruminations. Have I achieved anything other than a certain notoriety for speaking my mind, tact and dissembling eschewed? I know that in the world of journalism art critics are at the bottom of the heap, rarely read even by their editors. I know that in the world of contemporary art, critics are expected to be unreservedly the compliant minions of White Cube, Victoria Miro and all other merchants in the field, the lickspittles of the Arts Council and the toadies of the various Tates. I know that even the world of ancestral art prefers arse-licking to honest argument. In the face of all this, however, I still believe that art criticism should be passionately engaged with art itself, that the critic should be morally and intellectually honest, and should bring to bear, not an often ill-informed opinion, but the knowledge and experience that are the grounds of judgement. The critic must treat his readers as his equal when he discusses complex ideas and layers of meaning in a work of art; he must never pretend to see what cannot be seen – for that way lies Hans Andersen's emperor with his new clothes; and he must not lazily and dutifully praise every lunatic phenomenon ever produced by any man who has dubbed himself an artist. This last is precisely what is wrong with so many critics – that for fear of being in error, for fear of offending those who have influence, and for fear of vexing those who have the power of patronage over his work, the critic indeed nods dutifully and attempts no judgement of quality, invention or achievement.

Picasso one week, Mondrian the next, from the sublimity of Leonardo to the banality of Hockney, from the dense opaque impasto of Freud to the descriptive precision of Zoffany – thus does the art critic perform his intellectual leaps and bounds, thus does he discover the inadequacy of language. A day to see an exhibition and think; a day to read the catalogue and think; a day to write and think; a day to rewrite and crystallise my thoughts – would that I had a month.

With the National Gallery's astonishing exhibition Leonardo: Painter at the Court of Milan, of November 2011 – astonishing because none of us dared dream that such an accumulation of his masterpieces could ever be achieved – I had two days over a weekend to write a review, informed by only an hour in the exhibition on the Friday evening, influenced by sixty years of received authority and my own random seeing, thinking and opining. But that was sixty years of seeing Leonardo's paintings scattered all over Europe, separated not only by distance but by occasion, not gathered under one London roof with those available in Britain – and one of the purposes of such a gathering must be to see if it provokes a change of mind. The other purpose is, of course, to please the crowds happy to stand in awe of a genius known even in his own day as 'the most outstanding painter . . . his works quite perfect', and known in ours as 'the most universal genius' or, more romantically, in the words of Michael Levey, Director of the National Gallery 1974–1986, as 'supernaturally beautiful in youth and supernaturally wise in old age'. Even critics, I among them, did precisely that, overwhelmed to be in the presence of the master's masterpieces, and only slowly (if at all) did we realise that this was an unprecedented opportunity for scepticism.

With so little time to write I put aside misgivings (other than my certainty that the *Salvator Mundi*, newly discovered, is so much a wreck smudged and fudged in its repair that it must be discarded as a mere curiosity; and would Leonardo, so inventive in every other painting, have been so enslaved by traditional iconography in this?), and wrote an enthusiastic review that, though observant, was not critical. As an introduction to the court of the Sforza family, to the industrial (and therefore international) city of Milan at the end of the Quattrocento, and to the reasons that compelled Leonardo, the most Florentine of painters, to desert Florence for so seemingly alien a culture, the review has some merit and I am not embarrassed by it, but the more I saw of the exhibition, the more discrepant seemed the paintings, and the more I changed my mind about their chronological order and their authenticity. By the time the exhibition closed I was convinced that *The Madonna of the Yarn-winder* is a workshop production in which Leonardo played a part only as inventor of the composition, that the *Madonna Litta*, from St Petersburg, must be excluded from the canon; that with it, though for different reasons, must go the *Portrait of a Musician* and, most controversially (for she was used as the exhibition's poster on every wall in London), the *Lady with an Ermine*, Cecilia Gallerani, from Krakow. These four paintings, long attributed to Leonardo, are by four different painters, none of them the master.

The Madonna from Leningrad was lent on condition that its authenticity was not questioned, and the catalogue entry (written by its Russian curator) repeats the assertion that it is 'the Hermitage's most valuable treasure', dismissing as illogical any suggestion that Leonardo had little, if any, hand in it. The painting would not have come to London without the National Gallery's agreement to this condition and that would have been a great loss, stifling debate, but of this the visiting public was not made aware and will, supported by the catalogue, always recall it as an authentic Leonardo.

I had accepted without reservation the authenticity of the *Lady with an Ermine*, which I had seen only once before, under uneasy circumstances while the Russians were still dominating Poland. Seeing it in the company of other paintings by Leonardo a niggling doubt took root. I could not find a sequence into which it comfortably fits – it is in too many respects different. Then a zoologist informed me that the ermine is not an ermine, but an albino marten, a much larger animal, and if this is so, then the argument that it is a punning reference to the girl's surname in that the Greek for ermine sounds like the beginning of Gallerani, no longer holds; nor do the supposed symbolisms of virginity and fecundity embodied in that animal. If the painting is not by Leonardo, the master of proportion, then the assertive disproportion of the hand is perhaps explained.

The Venomous Critic

We have almost exterminated the marten, but it was once widespread in Europe and in demand as a household pet; if caught as a pup it was easily domesticated and from Roman times kept as an expert ratcatcher; unlike all members of the ferret family, including the ermine, it has no smell noticeable to the human nose and leaves no odour clinging to the hands and clothes — that a wealthy girl should have so embraced a ferret is beyond the bounds of possibility; that the marten was an albino would have greatly increased its value. In removing the ermine we remove the clutter of a hundred years of misinterpretation, and with it, possibly, the attribution to Leonardo and all the associated assumptions; we must start again. This is why we must have exhibitions. This is why we must have critics capable of judgement, not in hapless thrall to the reputations of paintings, painters or art historians, nor influenced by monetary value. The purpose of an exhibition is to expose its subject for better or worse, and the purpose of the critic is to question received opinion and worry what he sees as a terrier does a rat. To look, think and look again leads to critical seeing; seeing leads to truth; truth must be the prime objective of both the exhibition and the critic.

In the course of looking at Leonardo so intensely I have concluded that he had a hefty influence on Caravaggio who, as an apprentice in Milan, must have absorbed into his memory every gesture and grouping of Christ and the Apostles in *The Last Supper*.

*   *   *

It is a solitary business, this looking at pictures with concentration so intense as to be exhausting, even painful, and it must be done alone sans interruptions. Roger Fry, father of English art criticism, commended trance-like hanging about for fifteen minutes waiting for spiritual harmony to couple the critic to the work of art; I, on the other hand, gaze at it summoning everything I know or have thought about the artist and the work, and reconsider him and it in the light of the exhibition, its curatorial purposes and its display, for giving a work of art new neighbours can transform and reveal more immediately than any words.

Is this a great Picasso, I ask, or a piece of casual cookery? Is this Mondrian the beginning or the conclusion of a train of thought? Is this attribution to Leonardo to be sustained? What has happened to the genius that Hockney seemed to display in early middle age? I ask, and seek the answers. I make notes only of an elegant phrase if it floats into my mind – the process is otherwise only of the gaze. It is not contemplation; it is a savage analysis, a cruel dismantling of the thing seen, and memory is both summoned and seared by it. It is far more the rigorous academic discipline of the art historian and the informed intuition of the connoisseur, than the opinion of the common critic and the jargon of the curator.

Have I reached the sad end of a once promising career? Shall I hie me to a monastery? Shall I buy a coat of camel hair and a bottle of something expensively malodorous by Calvin Klein and start again? Or shall I plod on wearily, as the ploughman in the elegy, certain that I have been ploughing sand, frustration my horse, futility my ploughshare?

CHAPTER 12

Mother

It was on 20 August 1982 that my mother suffered what she recorded in her diary as her 'little fright'. But for a few days she had lived in my house for a decade, her quarters entirely separate from mine – though mine, as she had to pass through them, were not nearly separate enough from hers. Her sitting room was on the first floor facing the pretty painted terrace on the south side of Eldon Road, larger than any room of mine, her bedroom above it, balconied. My quarters were below and, of course, in the extraordinary north-facing studio that occupied every inch of what had been the garden, its coved ceiling twice the height of any room – uncharitably cold in winter, but so expensive to heat that I could never afford to keep its temperature much above freezing point. We lived our lives separately, I thought, but her diaries so often record that I had an unknown visitor for the night that she must have had the hearing of a wolf or spent hours hanging over the banisters. In theory it was a sensible arrangement – I could keep a watchful but unobtrusive eye on her in terms of diet, physical fitness and general wellbeing, and she, if I was away, could deal with any emergency that might occur; she enjoyed answering my telephone and kept useful records of calls, not only of the who and when of them, but of her derogatory and contemptuous opinions of the callers. It was in this way that she became something of a confidante for both Anthony Blunt and John Gaskin, hearing from each about the other, things that neither would ever have told me; celebrating her seventy-ninth birthday during the crisis of 1979, she proved a staunch ally and a dab hand at putting down with dry severity any journalist whom she considered intrusive and impertinent.

There were minor eccentricities to tolerate and minor squabbles to repair. She had a rooted objection to large cars parked in small front gardens with so long an overhang that she had to step into the gutter, and was sharp with any driver bold enough to swing across her path. The young manager of Waitrose in Gloucester Road (the original first shop of the firm) took me aside one day to tell me that with her insistence on paying the correct sum to the very penny, she caused queues to form at the check-out desks, and would I perhaps do her shopping for her. I thought at first that this might be, as it were, a euphemism for shoplifting (common enough among old ladies), but it came about through her capacity for running addition as she put things in her basket – but she always read the price above the goods instead of below so that, although her calculation was impeccable it was invariably wrong, and whether her figure was more or less than the sum required, she insisted on paying it. The manager opined that, swings and roundabouts, Waitrose probably gained as much as it lost and he had instructed the girls always to take whatever she proffered, but she was so sharp that she always saw the discrepancy between her arithmetic and the figure on the till and was inclined to argue; worse, he said, 'It buggers the accounts and stock-taking.'

As old as the century, she had worn very well and could have been mistaken for sixty, still erect in spite of the beginnings of a painful spinal affliction that was eventually to bend her into the form of a question mark. There was probably no connection between this compression of the spine and the 'little fright', but the one immediately followed the other. She had come to lunch, as she frequently did when I had a delicious left-over from a kitchen supper with friends, and it was at precisely two, when I had taken things to the scullery, that I heard a short faint whimper that was not a dog's. I was just in time to catch her as she began to slide between her chair and the table and transfer her, unconscious, to the settee in the window. Her doctor diagnosed a minor stroke and between us we got her upstairs and into bed, peace and quiet the recommended medicine.

Within three days she was up and about again, seemingly so unaffected by the episode that, with the agreement of her doctor, within the week I set off for eastern Turkey with Michael Waugh. I had not left her alone – Margaret Evans, a friend from Castle Hedingham, came to keep her company until my return. There was, however, another little fright before the end of the year, and then another and another until I lost count of them. The pattern was constant – a sudden loss of consciousness and a full recovery after a few days of rest; but it was never a full recovery – it was always a small percentage short and, added together, these small percentages began to amount to a significant change, less in her physical abilities than in her state of mind. This, at first, I did not realise; by the winter of 1984 when I again went to Turkey for some weeks, interested to see it in midwinter, and Margaret again came to stay with her, my mother was a very different woman. On my return I found Margaret dressed to leave at once, her cases packed, desperate to get out of the house. On our way to Liverpool Street for her train to Colchester, she told me how appallingly my mother had behaved and that she would never again agree to stay with her.

My mother had indeed changed; my longish absence had perhaps been something of a tipping-point, for though she looked the same, little was left of sweetness in her nature and she had become reproachful, shrewish and demanding, her moods veering within the same few minutes of conversation from whimpering self-pity to tantrums of rage and accusations of theft, cruelty and neglect. Her spine began to curve, even to corkscrew and I now know, but did not then, that she must have been in severe and constant pain, both chronic and acute – and if I have any recriminations to make against myself for my treatment of her for more than the decade until her death, it is that I failed to recognise the degree of pain that she endured. Injections every few months were at first a help, but as years wore on these ceased to ease her pain and her doctor gave up. When she fell and broke her right wrist the hospital X-rayed both it and her spine; the wrist could be mended but the spine was beyond any remedy. For three months she forced herself to write with her left hand and with her wrist repaired declared herself ambidextrous – however foul her temper had become, she had not lost her determination. With another fall she broke her hip and was again in hospital, but in one in which the nursing care was not care at all and, as no one bothered to feed her, I took to visits that coincided with the absurdly early times of lunch and dinner; one day she had fallen out of bed and I found her badly bruised about the face, as though from a heavy blow. Her recovery was very slow and when eventually she was sent home she was intellectually in a sadly diminished state; even so, she made me swear that never again would I allow her to be carried off to hospital.

I moved her bedroom down a floor so that it was immediately above mine and, if she fell out of bed, I would hear the thump and respond; the floor beside the bed I covered with thick padding and sheepskins so that if I failed to hear she would not be too uncomfortable and cold. She could no longer dress herself, could walk only with a Zimmer frame and in hospital had learned to be incontinent. She needed, every day, a morning bath, a fresh nightdress and dressing gown, and fresh linen on her bed; these she sometimes needed twice a day – and I needed help. Help – rarely the same nurse for more than five days – came from an agency specialising in such matters for which the day fee doubled for the night and both doubled again for Saturdays, Sundays and public holidays; to have daily attendance and deal with the nights myself, the sum totted up in the first year to £26,000, wiping out far more than my gross earnings, and on this sum the government, rubbing salt in the wound, demanded VAT. There was no other form of help – no claim to be made against the income tax I could not pay (and the consequent persecution), no grant of any kind for which I could apply, no service available from any public authority: I cursed my ownership of a house in Eldon Road and wished myself at the north end of Ladbroke Grove – with an address in that slum the local authority would have fallen over itself to help me.

Then Ingrid appeared. A widow struggling to pay her son's fees at Marlborough, she had asked our common doctor if he had any patients whom she might, for money, assist, and he had suggested my mother. She saved my sanity. With not a hint of squeamishness and the sort of practical capability that refuses to recognise the impossible, Ingrid appeared at eight every morning and in two hours accomplished everything that had taken the professional nurses a day, and then went off to do the same for another old lady. In a whirlwind of cooperation my mother was bathed, changed and breakfasted, while I put her soiled clothes and linen in the washing machine and hung them in the boiler room to dry. I then had perhaps three hours in which to see an exhibition before returning to see my mother to the loo and give her lunch, and then another four in which to think, research and write. That I wrote at all was entirely due to Ingrid, for at the time she came into my life I was in despair. Even she, however, could not prevent an accusation that I had abused my mother.

Frustrated with her restriction not only to the house but to one floor within it, my mother frequently expressed her rage in tantrums, never to Ingrid, always to me, the worst and most frequent of which occurred in the evening. Every night I prepared her dinner on a tray as pretty and colourful as I could make it, always in a dish rather than a plate so that it was easier for her to eat with only a fork. It was always at the moment of delivery that she picked a quarrel and, no matter how much I tried to deflate it, pursued it to the pitch at which she felt justified in lifting the tray as high from her knees as she could and throwing it on the floor. If nothing smashed I could let the dogs clear away the food while I recovered the crocks and cutlery, but with a breakage I had to do the whole job myself. I then had to prepare more food and try again. I took to drinking Madeira, at least half a bottle every evening, to lend me, not tolerance but resignation.

It was after such an episode that I finished a whole bottle before going upstairs to settle my mother for the night. On her way to the bathroom she seemed to be lifting her Zimmer frame unusually high, slowing her progress and throwing her dangerously far back in her narrow arc of balance. I suggested that she should lean forward a little and lift the frame much less. 'Oh you,' she said, screwing up her face in enmity, 'you know everything,' and in lifting her frame even higher, fell backwards, full length, striking the back of her head on the glass door of her sitting room. The glass shattered and blood poured from a long slash in her scalp. She lay, conscious but scared and still, among shards like sword blades. I had somehow, simultaneously, to stem the flow, call an ambulance and shut the excited dogs away.

The ambulance men were disconcerted when I refused to travel to hospital with them and my mother, saying that I would follow later (as I did), but that I must first clear away the glass and blood and settle the dogs; they told someone at the hospital that I stank of alcohol and opined that I cared more for the dogs than my mother and might have pushed her. Nurses then identified bruises on her arms as caused by shaking (they were caused by Ingrid's helping her in and out of her bath and by my levering her from the deep armchair in which she sat all day), and the police and social workers were informed. Eight hours later these appeared on my doorstep. Nothing came of it but never have I felt so unfairly menaced.

In all this there was only one moment of humour, so wry as to be black – a letter demanding her attendance to do jury service. Bitterly I responded:

The Jury Officer, Southwark
24.vii.1992

Sir – Something must be amiss with your computer. My mother, Jessica Sewell (as you address her, sans Miss, Mrs or even the irksome Ms) is well beyond her ninetieth year, paralysed by strokes, almost blind, hard of hearing, incontinent and incapable of rational judgement (though not irrational).

You are welcome to have her in your court, but you must send an ambulance and nurses; you must feed her by hand and put her on the potty; and you must learn to ignore her random yelps and exclamations.

Do let me know if you intend to insist on her attendance.

Yours faithfully,

Brian Sewell

To this there was no answer.

And so the wearying business continued, yet with the help of friends and Ingrid (the most unfailing friend of all) I managed from time to time to escape again to Turkey (and write the book), and break new ground in Algeria, Tunisia and Pakistan. It was indeed my journey to Pakistan in October 1994 that settled the matter of my mother. I had by then exhausted the charity of friends – they would willingly live in the house and care for the dogs, but not for my mother – but one of them knew someone who had some trusteeship connection with a nursing home and persuaded its manager to take her for two weeks or so. Off she went to South Kensington and I to Rawalpindi, Peshawar and the tribal territories into which Pakistan fades on her north-western Frontier with Afghanistan, idly hoping to find some trace of Alexander's furthest point in his great trek to the east. There, at altitudes of ten thousand feet and more I experienced several bouts of a perturbing and disabling nausea that I attributed to the altitude, but on returning to London another bout hit harder and became a full-blown heart attack. Force majeure, my mother remained in the nursing home and years of disabling cardiac trouble followed for me.

When, after some weeks in hospital, I went to see her, she had retreated into a world of nebulous recollection far away in time and did not recognise me. 'I cannot understand,' she said with absolute clarity, 'why my mother does not come to see me.' As her mother had died in 1934, the slip in time exactly sixty years, I did not quite know how to answer but chose not to remind her of the death and posed a question of my own: 'Who do you think I am?' 'I have no idea,' she answered with some petulance. On another visit, when I found her curled up, leaning back, feet on a footstool, eyes shut, her fingers rapidly running about the keys of an invisible piano, I pulled up another stool and sat at her knees wondering if it was Chopin or Debussy that she could hear until, after some minutes, I put a hand on her left knee. I was looking at her face and I'd swear that her eyes stayed tightly shut when she said, 'I've told you before. Never interrupt me when I'm practising.' She had told me before, when I was tiny, but then her fine cello was her instrument, and she did not own a piano until she went to live in Hedingham, by then in her mid fifties and I in my mid twenties.

After some months she fell into rapid decline. The Portuguese and Filipinos who nursed her were kind, gentle and affectionate in spite of her infantile provocations. Her physical strength fell away and even anger was beyond her. Almost unable to see or hear, the quality of her life was wretched – a never-ending round of rousing, bathing, changing, feeding, mopping and falling out of bed, deprived of conversation, books and music; and yet I am convinced that as those things that had made her life enjoyable slipped away from her, she became adjusted to their loss. She accustomed herself to each downward step in her condition and holding on to life became an end in itself, a test of endurance and stamina, and in the end, of instinct. For so many years she lived a life that I could scarcely bear to watch and tend, and yet what little there was of it was hers and she was driven by some ancient force to keep it.

On 1 June 1995 I had a call to say that she was dying. I spent the day and night with her and she did not depart; nor did she on the two following days; early in the morning of 4 June, at six or so, the nurse said that her heart seemed a little stronger – 'She'll not go yet,' she said. 'Why don't you go home and have a few hours sleep. I'll call you if there's a change.' The dogs were so wildly pleased to see me that I took them to Kensington Gardens before I thought of bed and we were there when the nurse tried to recall me, there when my mother died. How like her, I thought, to cheat me even of this small duty of respect. How sad, I thought, that she died without benefit of clergy, without the last rites of the Catholic (or any) Church.

I did not love her then. The clever, witty, funny, loving mother of my childhood, the shrewd big sister of my early manhood and the companionable woman at the opera and Royal Academy, had all been succeeded by a spiteful old harridan whose fervent wish had been to outlive me – as she very nearly did. Had she died at eighty, I could have forgiven her spying watchfulness, her loathing of my homosexuality, her disappointment in me, her reproach for my ingratitude – 'You will never know what I have sacrificed for you' almost a refrain – for then so many better memories of her at Whitstable, in the National Gallery, in Paris and of her extraordinary tenderness with my deceitful stepfather when he was dying, outbalanced them; but in great age she became an erratic tyrant, for thirteen years the ungrateful termagant around whose needs my life revolved, destroying me.

I did not weep. For two days I did not register her death but took to my bed and slept. Only then did I set about the bureaucratic business of the death certificate, the funeral and will. There was no will. In hunting for it I found all sorts of papers that proved her long association with Philip Heseltine and Peter Warlock, the split personality who had fathered me, and other lovers too, and I wondered where these had been in my peripatetic childhood when we seemed to own nothing but a suitcase, a cello and a violin. Without a will there were no instructions for her funeral but I had some recollection of her impatience with old friends who had wished to be buried rather than cremated. Arrangements were therefore made for cremation at Mortlake, the service to be conducted by a Catholic priest – but I had forgotten that Catholicism and cremation are not bedfellows. A day before the event the undertaker telephoned to ask if a Church of England cleric would do and I agreed — after all, my mother had often slipped into the little church at the end of Eldon Road to take Holy Communion, acknowledging no distinction between one Mass and another. Some misgiving prompted me to read the Order for the Burial of the Dead in the Book of Common Prayer in the Restoration English of 1662, and I took it with me to Mortlake in case the priest preferred a version in the ugly modern English to which so many churches are now wedded. It was just as well I did, for the cleric was not a proper priest but some kind of non-denominational stand-by for emergencies — deacon might be a decent term for him — who had never seen or read the Order of 1662 and found it beyond his comprehension.

The hearse and one black car drew up outside my house. Colin Darracott, the staunch friend who had done so much to keep me on an even keel when my mother had been impossible to manage, and who had eventually drawn from her the identity of my true father, was the only other mourner. To my distaste a man in a top hat led this cortège at a swaggering pace to the end of the road, then leaped into the passenger seat of the hearse without its pausing, and off we swept to Mortlake. I looked down at my feet and saw that I had forgotten to put on my shoes — socks I had not worn since the heart attack.

We were met by the deacon carrying a book. I took it from him, saw at a glance that it was exactly as I feared, and gave him mine, the various passages marked with coloured tabs identifying which he should read and which were the responses, the long chapter from Corinthians (I have never cared much for St Paul) cut very short at ' . . . . so in Christ shall all be made alive'. We had the one prayer book between the three of us; the deacon read as far as ' . . . whosoever liveth and believeth in me shall never die . . . ' (the first paragraph), stumbled over it and stopped, complaining that he had never had to read such language. With 'I will read it then', I took it from him, for long ago it had been for some years my intention to become a priest – an intention unseated by steadily increasing unbelief, the history of art as a demanding discipline, and by the eventually overwhelming menace of my homosexuality. For a moment, my unbelief suspended, it seemed to me that with the grace of God, for me to assume this priestly duty for my mother was entirely suitable; but with 'I know that my Redeemer liveth . . . ' there came a catch in my throat, the tears began to well, and that was that – God was not prepared to sanction my impertinence and silenced me. Somehow Colin and the deacon found their way through the rest of it while I sat hunched in a pew, sobbing. Sobbing for whom? – for my mother as she was at ninety-five, whose humiliated servant I had been for thirteen years and for whom I had at times developed a despairing hatred? Or was it for myself, at last free of this dark emotion but so stricken by a failing heart that I could not renew the life I had led before the 'little fright'?

*   *   *

Throughout these thirteen years of slavery there had been the constant and generous comfort of another woman, the daily companionship every morning of Mary Debbane, a near neighbour in Southwell Gardens, five years my senior. We used to walk our dogs together, in deep midwinter before dawn in the damp mists, in high summer in the cool clear light before the heat set in. We talked without reserve or barrier. We compared our burdens – hers a husband of whom she always spoke as 'the horizontal one', deprived of his voice by cancer and suffering clinical depression, mine a mother bitterly resentful of the senility that in her lucid moments she knew to be destroying her. As Mary had spent the immediately post-war years of her young womanhood in Paris and Alexandria, she knew a thing or two about the perverse realities of life and we talked much of sex and its tribulations – and again and again I was surprised by the amused and perceptive frankness with which women of an age beyond three score and ten can confront and tolerate the wayward sexuality of men (we wretched creatures have secrets from each other, but not them). Joe, her husband, increasingly demanded the services of prostitutes and, as he could not make himself understood on the telephone, it was she who had to book these visitors and explain that it was fellatio that he required. 'Why don't you do it for him?' one had asked. 'It will save you a lot of money.' She found the women by collecting their cards from the telephone box in Gloucester Road and was surprised to find that Young Swedish Model, Helga new from Berlin and big-busted Veronica from Venezuela were often the same woman.

We talked of euthanasia and how she wished it, not for her husband, but eventually for herself. I thought of it in the context of my mother, but she, I had observed, clung the more strenuously to life with every reduction in its quality and was very much the other side of Mary's coin. In the event the death of the 'horizontal one' came almost suddenly and with not much fuss; a dozen of us supported Mary as she saw him off with a service at the very high Anglican church across the road in Southwell Gardens – not quite the Greek Orthodox ceremony required by his absent family, but with enough in the way of bells, incense and fluttering altar boys to convince the angels that we wished him well. I looked about me but could see no strange woman with fellating lips mourning the loss of a regular client.

For Mary the death of her husband proved not to be the expected release into the bosom of old friends and the renewal of pleasures enjoyed before his illness, but was instead the loss of the dutiful purpose of her life. The effect was profound; it was as though she had lost her reason for being. Her energy diminished further and faster with the death of Charlie, her dog. Suddenly she had no compelling reason to leave the house and thenceforth almost never did. The sherry, cigarettes and coffee that were her sustenance were brought by the Toy Boy, the Ponytail, Merlin's father, Michael the Plumber, the medieval-seeming Elizabeth of

Woldingham, the Princess and Hortense – I never knew her sobriquet for me, but herself she called my Doting Elderly. Like the Lady of Shalott, she lived by proxy, the telephone her mirror. She talked more and more of death; she did not fear death itself, only the indignities that she had seen precede it. She persistently pursued information on euthanasia; she asked her doctor for advice and was refused; though professing disbelief in God and any possibility of afterlife, she discussed it with the parish priest and the nuns of a neighbouring convent, all of whom gave her the proper conventual response; none of the rest of us knew how to help and yet, in the end, her departure was accomplished with astonishing aplomb.

On a Friday afternoon her hairdresser paid his weekly visit and was alarmed to find her jaundiced. She bade him do her hair and call the doctor only when he had finished. Within hours she was both elegantly coifed and lying in a hospital bed, the colour of mustard and, dressed in dark pink, an inspiration to any passing artist of German Expressionist tendencies. Cancer of the pancreas had obstructed her bile duct, the doctors said; it is incurable, but a by-pass operation might give her two more months, they said; without it she would be dead within days, they said. Feeling no pain, she refused the operation and settled down to die, but, disconcertingly, began to look as though she were recovering. She was calmly matter-of-fact about it, her only sign of uncertainty her whispered 'don't let me die alone'. On the following Wednesday she ate yoghurt without once fumbling the spoon and behaved so sparklingly that death seemed quite remote. Tonight, I thought, is not the night for me to stay.

But it was. Near midnight she complained, for the first time, of pain and was given morphine; an hour later she asked for more; and in another hour she was dead. I was not with her. Nor was any other of her friends. Did we let her down, or did she snatch the opportunity to engineer her death with a white lie or two? Did she really feel pain so suddenly? Am I in error in fancying that she contrived death in the quiet dignity she craved and of which the promise of euthanasia would have been a comforting reassurance? If in some sense she managed it with a small and exquisite deceit that left no one shouldering the blame, then I am more in awe of her than ever.

Dylan Thomas would have had Mary 'rage against the dying of the light', but that was not her style. I knew her to be capable of rage – rage against cruelty to animals, against the gross inhumanity of men, and against belief in a god whose supreme indifference to his creation was so often and so magnificently proved by natural disasters – but I had never seen her rage for her own benefit. The only thing she asked of life in her last years was that she should choose the moment to relinquish it in a quiet and comfortable death of the kind once described by an old Etonian as 'slipping away into the next room'. When the now forgotten 'Doctor Assisted Dying Bill' of 1997 failed, Parliament, fearing too little bathwater and too many babies, denied this dignity to those who, unquestionably lucid and articulate, are capable of expressing an unequivocal and determined choice.

* * *

How long shall I remember Mary, born in 1926, the year of the General Strike and Eisenstein's *Battleship Potemkin*, her death one of the closest, most telling and most touching of departures from my life? She was my confidante, a sharer in the small adventures of an urban life, a voice of common sense, and her memory survives in recollections prompted by bottles of Tio Pepe on an Oddbins' shelf, in sniffing the smoke of a Gitane and the whiff of coffee roasting, in the placard informing us that Sainsbury's have a special offer on champagne. I have eaten the tiny tin of caviar that, too late, I bought to share with her, though for years, sitting in my fridge, it acted as her monument; and I no longer reach for the telephone every morning – as I did for years – in mutual reassurance that we were still alive; these small things tell me that my memory of her is fading. Is there, after seventeen years, daily recall of my mother? I was determined that there should not be, but I hear her voice in mine, there are too many paintings everywhere with which she is inescapably associated, and on the rare occasions when I see a real Daimler with a fluted radiator, fluid flywheel and epicyclic gearbox, I think of her crashing my 4.5 litre Sportsman through the iron railings of Richmond Park with six dogs on the back seat. And I have inherited her spine.

CHAPTER 13

Heart Attacks

The date of my first heart attack is not noted in my diary – nor is much else in late October 1994. It came early in the day: I had walked the dogs and had a shower and was sitting in a white towelling dressing gown sipping coffee and attempting to write, but feeling slightly out-of-sorts in a way that could be attributed to jet lag, for I had returned from Pakistan only the previous day. Out-of-sorts turned to nausea and I took to my bed; there, to nausea a dull constricting pain in my chest and a different pain in my left arm were added; I was alarmed enough to telephone my doctor. At just after nine he was already seeing other patients and would call back between noon and one. 'I might be dead by then,' I said, 'I think I'm having a heart attack.' Allowed to disturb him, his response to my symptoms was that I was indeed having a heart attack, that he would both call an ambulance and come himself, 'and if the ambulance gets there first, go with it'.

Alone in the house, I thought it sensible to open the front door while I still could, but when I got out of bed my feet were dead and my legs gave way. On hands and knees I crawled to the door, opened it an inch or two and retreated to the hall, closing the glass inner doors behind me; I then lay exhausted on the floor where I could at once be seen. One thought excluded all others, even anxiety and hope; it was that no one should die while experiencing such pain, for it was of a quality that obliterated all composure and the quiet business of the commendation of the soul. Many years have passed since I abandoned the beliefs and observances of Christianity, and yet I cherish the notion of dying easily and with my wits about me, hands folded as in a medieval effigy, my dogs about me on my bed, farewells done, sins remembered and confessed, affairs in order, and the ritual comfort of prayers murmured in Latin as in the fading light my consciousness departs. Mop and Titian surged about me in silence until the ambulance men arrived and then put on such a show of raised hackles, growling and snarling that they would not come in. 'Call off your dogs' they shouted through the glass, but by then a stricture had developed in my throat and I could not speak. My dogs, I thought, are putting on such a brave defence not realising that they may be killing me. A passing policeman solved the problem; recognising that Mop was the leading dog, he took off his tunic and, holding it wide open, wrapped it round her head and shoulders and, pushing against her thrust, tossed her backwards down the stairs to the kitchen; when Titian meekly followed, he shut the door on them.

I remember nothing else until we reached the hospital, the then spanking new Chelsea and Westminster with its absurd collection of contemporary art. There I had the clearest vision, not of the conventional tunnels and lights of the near-death experience, but of my brain leaving its skull; it hovered just out of reach of my right hand and then slowly drifted away towards a door; 'For God's sake bring back my brain,' I shouted – at least I think I did – and again lost consciousness.

For a long week I lay in bed attached to instruments. People brought food but left it out of reach and, eating nothing but some peas that I could just touch with my fingertips, I lost half a stone in weight. The curatrix of the hospital's pointless paintings (sick or well, no one stops to look at them, but to decry them is politically incorrect), one of the art world's signatories to the notorious letter demanding my dismissal from the *Standard*, earned a shoddy shilling or two informing the gossip columnists. I wanted only to sleep but friends came, with the best intentions, to sap my energy. When the cardiologists decided that they needed only to open the arteries with a balloon (an angioplasty) rather than to operate – a procedure that they could not offer for some weeks and for which I might wait at home – I was released. A nurse I had not seen before came with instructions not to eat red meat, chocolate or oysters, not to drink coffee, not to have sex. 'What precisely do you mean with not to have sex?' 'Well, you know . . . ' she replied. 'No I don't – sex comes in many guises. Am I allowed to masturbate?' To this she made the sort of whimper-cum-splutter that a maiden aunt might make and scuttled off puffing with affront.

I left the hospital in the clothes in which I had arrived – underpants and the white dressing gown, unshod, unshaven and with not a penny in my pocket. The first three taxi drivers would have nothing to do with me but the fourth recognised me as a writer for the *Standard*, took me home, saw me through the door and would not take payment. I went to bed and very warily, almost enquiringly, I masturbated. Why should this puerile and much mocked activity seem so important to a man in his sixties? I do not know: I know only that it was an indication that, in spite of the heart attack, my body was not in other aspects malfunctioning, that I was still a man and had not become a vegetable. Why is it not to be mentioned in polite society, unless by a stand-up comic whose audience will, at the mere mention of it, fall about with laughter? As a subject of serious discussion it is taboo; is this because it is far more common among adult men than we admit or suppose? As all my married friends confess to it but keep it from their supposedly disapproving wives, it is still a secret pleasure in which they must not be too absorbed for fear of the wife at the bathroom door with her, 'Darling, what are you doing in there?' Wives can demand privacy without rousing suspicion, but men cannot. Is masturbation the real reason for the garden shed?

When the widening of my arteries took place it was not quite the calm and insignificant procedure promised – 'You will feel nothing,' they said, 'just watch the screen above you and see it all.' The *Dies Irae* from Verdi's *Requiem* echoed through the operating theatre – not the most comforting of music in these circumstances – and I subsided into a private twilight gloom; but then I felt something deeply unpleasant and the violent shaking of surgical shock began, with nurses and my cardiologist leaning heavily on me to prevent me from falling from the table. Only when the anaesthetist deepened my twilight to unconsciousness could they continue. The heart is reached by way of an artery in the groin and the incision must clot closed when all is done; I emerged from my drowsing to find the most handsome of young doctors – head boy and captain of the first XV rolled into one – pressing hard on the small wound and shut my eyes again to prevent any reaction, not quite as successfully as I had hoped. 'You're enjoying this,' he said with a grin.

The angioplasty did not last and within a year I had another heart attack. Had Colin not been in the house to hear the thump of my collapse, I might well have died; it was eight in the morning and as the nearest ambulance was trapped in traffic, he lugged me out to his car and drove me to the hospital. I was only faintly aware of things as the doctors did what was necessary, but quite clearly heard a young man ask, 'Why are we doing all this? This man is sixty-five and whatever we do he won't have much quality of life when he recovers. Why don't we let him go?' 'Mr Sewell may be inert and not responding,' said an older voice, 'but he's not dead yet and I suspect that he can hear. What you've just said will not encourage him.' I saw that young doctor some months later and reminded him. Now that I am eighty I am grateful that his superior bade him continue whatever it was that he was doing to me.

The surgical response was, eventually, a quadruple bypass; at some point I was enough awake to feel frozen with cold and with an almighty effort summoned the words to ask why – or so I thought – but heard no answer and lapsed back into comfortable unconsciousness. The impression of that chill remained with me and later I asked again, 'Why was I so cold?' 'Because you were; you were in a bath of ice; we were lowering your temperature. Were you conscious? – we thought we heard you mumble something.'

Everything hurt. My ribcage had been ripped open and stitched together with titanium wire; every muscle, tendon and ligament along the spine had been uprooted, stretched or crunched; every pulse in my skull and neck was beating loud as a lead drummer in Led Zeppelin, the noise intolerable, the metal structure of the very bed on which I lay seeming to reverberate in time with them. In the recovery room I would have welcomed death to end such torments, but I had things to do – such absurdly unnecessary things as seeing a painting at Sotheby's and going to the opera. It was these that drove me to recover.

I did both. The opera was Sophia Larson's debut in *Turandot* at the ENO. I had not heard her before, nor have I heard her since – a mystery, for I found her the most dramatically convincing singer in the role, her fine rich soprano perfectly suited to a production that, for the first time in my experience, made sense of an improbable and rather silly plot; her natural body language too lent it conviction. The later of my two small ambitions, and far the less stressful, I have no doubt that it contributed to my recovery; not for one moment did I sense the discomforts of the Coliseum's seats. Discharged on the fifth day after the bypass, on the seventh I tottered on a stick into Sotheby's to see, perhaps for the last time, Orazio Gentileschi's *Finding of Moses*, to be sold on 6 December 1995, lot 61A, a masterpiece irrecoverable if bought by a foreign museum. Painted by Orazio while at the court of Charles I and hung in the Queen's House, Greenwich, it encapsulates a sublime moment in the history of British art and patronage, and I believe its distinctly unclassical landscape to have been inspired by the Thames. I gorged on every brushstroke. As I turned away, 'My God, you look ill,' said an Italian dealer I had known for thirty years, a friend of Claudio. To my 'Oh I've just had a heart bypass' his response was, 'That was a mistake – it was not your heart that needed to be bypassed, but your tongue.' I wished that I had that sort of command of any language but could only murmur the insulting: 'Vaffanculo.'

On my way home, over-confident, I stopped at the V&A on some foolish errand now forgotten and, on leaving, was stopped by a guard and accused of shop-lifting my substantial and glossy catalogue of the Gentileschi sale. I refused to accompany him – 'You've made an accusation in public. You will apologise in public. Fetch the manager of the bookshop.' This he could not do without leaving me, so took my arm. I furiously forbade him. And then the manager appeared, took one look at the catalogue and apologised. I was shaking and thought I might faint when I tottered down the steps to the street but, unsummoned, a taxi driver stopped and took me home – it was another reason to respect the intelligence and responsibility of London cabbies, and not the last. Years later, when somehow the leads of my first pacemaker broke and I had a blackout in Pimlico Road, it was again a taxi driver who picked me up, literally carrying me, and took me to the *Evening Standard*; the Brompton Hospital would have been a better destination, but he had assumed me to be drunk after too good a lunch.

Blackouts were frequent after the bypass, sometimes with just enough warning to find myself a tree in Kensington Gardens or a sheltering gatepost, and I learned not to stand on the kerbs of pavements or on a platform's edge. I became a guinea pig for Dr Richard Sutton's tilt-table, an instrument of torture to which one was tied prone and then, deeply relaxed, tilted into the vertical to induce a faint, the nauseating consequence of a drop in blood pressure. There were, too, all the usual effects of swollen ankles, fingers drained of blood and other circulatory problems, and there were days when my blood pressure was so low that I dared not leave the safety of the house. The bypass quite certainly saved my life, but it also changed it – I could no longer ski or play tennis, the regular annual breaks in the pattern of my life, never again could I scramble about in mountains or walk twenty miles every day for a week, and I found myself breathless – with anxiety, I suppose – when driving even short distances, yet I had been a driver who enjoyed the skill, planning and endurance involved in covering eight hundred miles in a long day. My life changed radically from irregularly active to regularly so sedentary that even walking the dogs any serious distance was out of the question. The point was rammed home to me when, on a trip to Venice with friends from the V&A, we went to Possagno to see Canova's museum and I could not walk up the long slow slope to the great church above the village, but sat at the bottom and miserably watched my companions meander into the unattainable distance half a kilometre away.

For a while I became something of a zealot about matters of the heart. We should all, I preached, know enough to recognise the warning signs, foolishly believing that had this been my case I might not have had the attacks nor needed the disabling surgery – for that is what it was, disabling. Now I am not so sure that I would have believed the preliminary messages from my body and nor am I sure that I would have acted on them – one must have the heart attack to know how much it hurts.

A slow change I would have borne more easily and without the anger and resentment. I had always been reliably fit, my stamina exceptional, but the sudden removal of my toys, as it were, occasioned nagging rancour that I could no longer do what I had done so easily. At the same time, to others I became more indulgent and less critical, not towards the art and artists of my work, but to the failings of more ordinary people, and I no longer particularly cared if things went wrong. I became, I think, an oddly softer, kinder and more generous-minded man after the heart attacks – except where television is concerned.

CHAPTER 14

Television

It was the Blunt Affair that first brought me into contact with television, its minions and exponents, all pushy, abrasive, arrogant, self-admiring and under no circumstances to be trusted. They look you straight in the eye and stab you in the back; they wheedle and cajole to lay their hands on your material, but once they have it, toss you aside; they pretend, if not friendship, amiability, but if it suits them, they mock and mimic, deride and ridicule; and in their editing they subvert, distort, corrupt and lie. There was a time when I thought that television in the hands of the educated could be the greatest force for education beyond the ancient groves of academe, for cultural breadth and critical debate, for connoisseurship in the arts and for the background that one can no longer gain from school, but it is now in the hands of the barbarian for whom the notion of cultural background is quite incomprehensible. Television is now devoted to the amusement of the masses, often by the masses, and if the arts appear at all they are as often as not in the hands of presenters who know nothing of them, who speak of Leonardo da Vinci with a girlish gush of ignorance, or of Damien Hirst with the pubertal adulation of the fourth former with a crush on the head boy.

It was never my intention or ambition to perform on television and that it came about was due entirely to a small company that made modest travelogues for Channel 4 – half-hour programmes that offered honest insights on foreign cities and their environs presented by people who were informed, interested and able to command only a low fee. I was offered Vienna in midwinter and it was there, in the Kunsthistorisches Museum, the exchequer limited to the close examination of only one of the dozen or so paintings

239

by Pieter Brueghel, that, looking through the camera lens, I experienced a revelation. The selected painting was, not surprisingly, his bleak *Winter* of 1565 from his set of the *Four Seasons*, but my choice was the infinitely more complex *Christ Carrying the Cross*, for through the monocular camera – eliminating the wide peripheral vision of a pair of human eyes – the almost undiscoverable figure of Christ (though he is dead centre in the composition) and every detail on the road to Calvary could be isolated and examined in ways otherwise not possible; it was as though I had found a hundred other Brueghels within the broad sweep of movement from the distance on the left to the very different distance on the right. If only, I thought, I had been able to do this for the ten years that I was teaching prisoners in Brixton.

It was an innocent and inexpensive little programme: there was no money for a box at the opera, or even a back seat in the Gods, but we pretended by walking up the steps to the door with wealthier visitors; nor was there money for the Mozart Mass sung in the Cathedral for the benefit of presidents and princes, so we huddled outside in the wind-driven snowflakes and listened to the broadcast – 'Ora pro nobis,' I murmured to myself. We searched for Mozart's burial place – as unmarked as Moore's at Corunna (not a drum was heard, not a funeral note), bought *Stollen* from a stall in the Christmas Market and ate *Torte* at Herr Sacher's very expensive café. It was the first of four seasons for me as well as Brueghel.

In spring we went to Bavaria and followed in the footsteps of mad queer Ludwig and I was, I'd swear, haunted by him, for something uncomfortable and strange – the sense of possession – took hold of me when left alone in the throne room of Neuschwanstein; I had just looked from a window onto a view fit for Altdorfer to paint and a pall of melancholy engulfed me – I had felt it once before, in Heracleia-under-Latmos, in the sanctuary of Endymion, a beautiful youth loved by Zeus, Hera and Selene.*

* See *South from Ephesus*, p. 60.

When we reached Starnberg I sought the site of his drowning in the lake, marked by a great timber cross, and waded out to it to weave about it a wreath of wild flowers; it stands waist deep – not nearly deep enough to drown so tall and strong a man unless held down by murderers.

In summer we went to Istanbul and I sat outside the Harem slicing cucumbers, as men did for centuries to prevent the Sultan's many wives from pleasuring themselves, and stood in awe of emeralds and early Chinese porcelain; we sailed the Bosporus and imagined a Turkish army bursting through the doors of Hagia Sophia, a young celebrant clutching the Host to his bosom and miraculously stepping into a solid wall as though through a door, so that Catholics believe that somewhere in that building rests the body of Christ subverting its conversion into mosque and museum. And in the autumn off we went to Pakistan and I came home in a rage against the abject poverty of the poor and the blatant cruelty to animals – my memory is scarred by the tethered pelican outside the chemist's shop, pinioned and filthy, by puppies dying in the gutter, by a donkey fallen under such a load that its legs splayed and it could get no purchase, three men kicking it, and so on and so on. Give the production team their due, they let me say what I wished, and all hell broke loose. It may have been that outspoken programme that scuppered my chances of ever working for the BBC – far too uncontrollable, unequivocal and unsparing for that, in the arts, patronising, complacent, mealy-mouthed, cliché-ridden institution and its top-heavy bureaucracy.

In the summer of 1993 I was asked to make – or so I thought – a programme for *J'accuse*, an interesting series in which the reputations of the great were impugned. I chose Leonardo da Vinci as my victim and wrote a carefully constructed script based on recognised sources and the too few surviving works. I realise now that in my inexperience I may well have mistaken the term 'present' for 'make' – a presenter merely fronts a programme conceived, researched, produced and directed by other minds, to which he

contributes nothing other than his smiling face (my smile had long
since atrophied) and is responsible not even for his words. I was put
into the hands of an unfriendly and uncomprehending Australian
director, an ex-ballet dancer grown too muscular and burdened
with feminist tendencies; she knew nothing of Leonardo and was
intent on bringing into the programme as many as she could of her
Australian friends and corybants – one of these last a very pretty
youth to play Leonardo in frustrated tantrum; and to these she
added Sarah Kent of *Time Out* and half-a-dozen others of the
monstrous regiment masquerading as art critics and historians, not
one of them of any reputation. The squabbles amused onlooking
gossip columnists primed by Kent but the ultimately unscholarly
and shoddy programme was to me a wretched disappointment, a
perfect example of a good idea made shabby by a formula. Someone
should have taken me on one side and explained that I was not
making the programme, that what I thought was of neither interest
nor consequence, and that if making was what I wanted, then I
must get a degree in media studies and conform to the dire pattern
of pitching a programme well below the intellectual ability of the
audience, including every classic cliché and banality in its con-
struction, bowing to every possible political correctitude of race
and gender. 'You,' someone should have said, 'are only the
presenter. Yours may be the face on the screen, but in the hierarchy
of those who make programmes you are the shit at the bottom of
the heap. You will do as you are told.' Had that position been
made clear to me I would have resigned and the dreadful directrice
could have made the programme entirely from the slop of her
imagination.

Nine years passed before another offer came. It was from Kim
Peat, then the commissioning editor of programmes on art and
religion for Channel 5. Throughout this period Martin Durkin of
Wag TV had repeatedly made approaches, flattering but without
substance, and nothing had ever reached beyond the 'Hey – I've
had an idea . . . ' stage. This time there was not even an idea, just

the suggestion of lunch with Kim in Rules, a restaurant where ageing schoolboys perspire over steak and kidney pudding in July. Nothing of interest was said until, Kim having paid the bill, we were outside on the pavement performing the rituals of parting, when she said, 'How do you feel about the Pilgrimage to Compostella?' 'Oh that would be wonderful – I've done the Spanish half – I'd love to finish it. This time next year, I suppose?' 'No. If you want to do it you're off in four days' time.' It did not occur to me until much later that a more desirable candidate for presenter must have fallen by the wayside.

As the great feast of St James is on 25 July we flew to Compostella and did the pilgrimage backwards and without any kind of the intellectual or emotional preparation that I knew I needed. Nearly forty years had passed since my last exposure to Catholicism in all its ritual splendour and, privileged to be in the cathedral – access to which was denied to thousands of genuine pilgrims on the morning of the feast – I was overwhelmed, I think with grief. What I felt so powerfully was not exultation, ecstasy or rapture; it was pain, misery and guilt, my Catholic inheritance in reproach for my abandoning it. I was trapped with evidence of every belief that reason and my homosexuality had compelled me to relinquish. I could hardly draw breath and could not speak. I wept. I could not perform for the camera. For what seemed an age I could not even watch but stood, shaking, my back to this great Mass, my brow against the wall. First Aid attendants came but could not help and I could not explain. I do not know what the crew made of my behaviour, useless to them: I gave them no spontaneous commentary on the service, none of the excited looks expected, none of the bogus involvement in which presenters specialise.

As the deceitful exercise of the pilgrimage itself continued, I realised that I was profoundly affected by the faith of others, of all who had truly made the pilgrimage. French students told me of their final ritual after the cathedral celebrations and before their journey home – it was to go to the nearby coast, strip naked, burn the clothes in which they had walked so far, and swim; thus newly bathed and clothed the return hike could begin. I thought it a beautiful idea and much more than a symbolic practice, and the embrace of the warm sea on my nakedness as I swam out of sight into the Bay of Biscay seemed entirely spiritual. So too were my farewell kisses for three boys one morning in Burgos, two walking back to Germany, one to Switzerland, their boots worn very thin and second-hand, who told me of another custom – the exchange of boots; any pilgrim rich enough to buy new boots must leave his discards tied to a tree where they can be seen, for there is always another pilgrim on the road whose boots are in even worse condition. My young director, a man of occasionally prurient interests, instructed me to ask them if they masturbated on the pilgrimage, but when I refused, falteringly asked them himself – the word is common to both languages. I recall only my own appalled confusion, not their answers. My three kisses on our parting were those of ceremony, an old man much given to the sins of the flesh recognising in the young something devout and righteous that he too once had. And in Lourdes, that Benidorm, that Blackpool, that Disneyland of Catholicism, two comfortably adult women from the north of England rammed home the irrelevance of quotidian human behaviour and appetites with their absolute conviction that a miracle was possible for their companion, an old woman in a wheelchair, that if God chose to use them as the instrument of his intervention in her ills, he was not likely to be obstructed by the flaw of a random sin or two.

Why were we in Lourdes? It is on no route to Compostella and as a shrine post-dates the pilgrimage by far more than a thousand years. We were there because this was television, and as the researcher employed by our television company could see no distinction between one pilgrimage and another, any pilgrimage would do. We even went to Sacré-Coeur in Paris – the monstrous white elephant of Montmartre consecrated only in 1919, because some fool of a graduate from a polytechnic university thought it a place of ancient pilgrimage. Time and again I wailed, 'Why are we here?' in some wretched church once visited by Napoleon III or the Grand Duchess of Bessarabia when I knew that only an hour away there was a greater station or hazard on the road to Compostella. It was on this journey that I learned how inflexible television is and that however flawed the research, once a schedule has been constructed on it, no change can be made. I learned that it is complacently content with its devices, tricks and mannerisms, with visual clichés that are utterly irrelevant, that it will spend hours on a traffic roundabout setting up a shot that for its effect depends wholly on the absence of traffic, and that I might be compelled to cross a bridge in Blois a dozen times because it was suddenly shadowed by a cloud or a clattering Deux Chevaux came from behind and blocked the camera's view; there isn't a cameraman in its employ who cannot be distracted by the utterly irrelevant.

In churches, chapels and cathedrals I was appalled by the crew's downright disrespect for worshippers and unsuspecting clergy – the only way I could put an end to their clambering over altar rails to arrange their lights, microphones and camera angles was to walk out and refuse to return; as for pleading the significance of the Reserved Host, I might as well have attempted to explain a logarithm to a Hottentot. The director, having dug deeply into the how and what of my homosexuality, mistook my misery for sexual deprivation and, no doubt at vast expense, procured a blond American to join the crew and service me. There was no servicing. I would not have it. I was insulted by this trivialising of my spiritual turmoil. Loren was, nevertheless, companionable and we escaped from the others for dinner, which otherwise I would have chosen to eat alone or not at all; we shared an interest in music, and in other circumstances I might well have been drawn to take him to my bed, but the thought that he had been procured for me made that impossible.

When the ordeal was over I told the director that I would never attempt another programme of this kind – or perhaps of any kind –

that it had been intellectually insufferable to work to another man's research knowing it to be puerile, inadequate and in gross error, and that I thought the whole business so trapped in the aspic of custom as to be immutable – as indeed it is. No director is capable of making a programme that involves travel without making it a travelogue. For me the best thing about the pilgrimage had been my days distanced from the crew because I was on a horse, a sweet-natured mare who took in her stride all the noisy pagan celebrations in the streets of Compostella.

The programme, *The Naked Pilgrim*, won the Sanford St Martin Prize for religious broadcasting. If only you knew, I thought as Cardinal Cormac Murphy-O'Connor presented it. Some viewers shared my Catholic miseries; others enjoyed the show; the most extraordinary response came from a woman in Highgate:

22.vii.2003

Dear Mr Sewell – I have just seen you on television in *The Naked Pilgrim*.

You are so inspiring.

You know everything about art.

You are a god.

May I kiss your penis?

Yours sincerely,

Ianthe Pole

'Nice bum' said an elderly woman in Kensington High Street. Martin Durkin, whose idea the programme had been, was delighted with it and began campaigning for another.

*   *   *

For two years or so I resisted Martin's meagre blandishments and then, at last, promised that the 'Written and presented by . . .' assertion of *The Naked Pilgrim*'s titles would be entirely true in any new case, suggested the Grand Tour, a subject that with a television programme in mind I had explored in a tour of my own

in 1989. Uncluttered by the obligations of companionship this had
been a concentratedly intense experience, built on and connecting
all my earlier travels in Italy. Eliminating all the post-Classical and
pre-Renaissance places, buildings and paintings in which the Grand
Tourist showed no interest, I concentrated on the ancient Roman
and the High Renaissance, and in a different frame of mind, on the
Baroque and Neo-Classical that were the modern and contemporary
art and architecture of their day – Turin, for example, the Italian
equivalent of Bath as rebuilt in the eighteenth century. I proposed
a programme to the BBC but, having neither agent nor other
interested party to effect an introduction, received not even an
acknowledgement of my synopsis, nor even its return. With no
particular objective in mind I had continued to collect material,
read diaries and journals, make notes and collect souvenirs; with all
this in hand, I was well prepared.

My synopsis for Martin was not only of the places on the Tour –
from the Alps to all the glories of Piedmont, Lombardy, Tuscany
and Umbria, to Rome, Naples and Paestum, and thence to Padua,
Venice, Vicenza and Mantua – but of the mundane logistics of
travel in the eighteenth century, the damp sheets of it, the piss
and shit of it, the fucking and the syphilis. I prepared notes on
accommodation, carriages, food, clothes, medicine, sex and every
other aspect of the young Grand Tourist's life, including even
death and burial, and in this lay my undoing, for Martin saw in
some such things the possibility of incorporating travelogue. In the
travelogue the presenter must, if he sees one, mount a dromedary,
drink a fermented mixture of the milk of moose and the spittle of
seal, and eat with evident relish the smoked testicles of his host's
enemies; thus I, on the Grand Tour, within the grounds of
Stupinigi, hunt wild boar, pretend to buy dapper clothes from a
fashionable Milanese store, within sniffing distance of the exhausts
of Modena take the wheel of a Ferrari too rare and precious to be
allowed to take the road, and in Rome I must have my portrait
painted by the hapless Batoni of today. With every one of these

irrelevances I proved uncomfortable and eventually uncooperative, for the hours spent on them were hours not spent on great monuments and works of art; they were not what I had expected to cover, not scholarship, not history – they were the trifles of a travelogue and I, I thought, was making a serious programme about education, connoisseurship and the origin of such cultural institutions as the Vatican and British Museums in the century of the Enlightenment. I was mistaken: Martin had instructed his team to make a travelogue and, just as on the pilgrimage they had set their camera on me as I emptied my bladder behind a tree, so they set it again when I had to stumble from the car in Naples to vomit in the street. In Florence, in the Protestant Cemetery, they took elaborate pains to surprise me with the graves of Sewells said to be the bastard sons of William IV, conveniently adopted by a friend. 'Why show me these?' I asked. 'Because we wanted to tell you that you may be related to the Queen.' 'Don't be bloody silly – Sewell is my stepfather's name.' Their researcher back in Islington, whose research in every point of conflict they preferred to mine, had exhumed this useless information and we wasted a whole day on it; yet in Rome, the high point and very purpose of the Grand Tour, I discovered that we had no permit to film in the Vatican and were to omit the overwhelmingly influential antique sculptures of Laocoön and the Apollo Belvedere, Michelangelo's illusionist ceiling of the Sistine Chapel, and Raphael's frescoes of *The School of Athens* and *The Fire in the Borgo*. I imagined what I would, as a critic, say of these omissions, what conclusions I would draw of the man whose name followed the 'Written and presented by . . . ' and was cold with rage.

The Grand Tour was an incompetent failure that ran wildly over time and over budget. It need have done neither. Had Martin made clear that it was to be a travelogue I could have chosen to collaborate in the hope of only a little embarrassment, or – more probably – to resign. Alternatively, had we adhered to my scrupulous scholarship and employed a cameraman who knew how to explore a work of art instead of wasting time on innumerable driving shots ('the audience needs to know how you got here'), men on bicycles, cats on walls, white lines in the road and other banalities, the programme could have been taut, dense and well paced. It had odd moments that informed, a few that were quite beautiful and many that amused, but it was not what it could and should have been. 'Let's break the mould, let's abandon the clichés,' I had said to the director before we set off for Venice (this programme too was made in reverse), and he had enthusiastically agreed, but when it came to the point the travelogue remained intact and I was the broken mould.

I have made no television since. In 2010 I was asked by Tabitha Jackson, commissioning editor of Channel 4, to submit a list of proposals. It was as follows:

An Art Quiz inserting knowledge and instruction between ribaldry and fun.

Francis Bacon: a serious assessment based on the handful of survivors who knew him (of whom I am one), removing him from the current generation of art historians who impose their own interpretations rather than his.

Solitary paintings: great works of art that are isolated from others – Grünewald's Isenheim Altar, Van Eyck's Ghent Altar, Piero della Francesca's Resurrection in Borgo San Sepolcro or his frescoes of the True Cross in Arezzo, Stanley Spencer's Chapel at Burghclere, Roger van der Weyden's Last Judgement in Beaune, the swathe of great altars that stretches across Central Europe from Colmar to Krakow, and so on . . .

The Northern Grand Tour: Paris, Brussels, Amsterdam, Berlin, Dresden, Vienna, the minor German courts, Strasburg and Geneva, following the footsteps of James Boswell and others of his time.

Mad Ludwig of Bavaria – fantasy castles, palaces and Wagner.

The most influential pictures ever painted: Michelangelo's Sistine Chapel, Raphael's frescoes in the Vatican, Leonardo's Last Supper, Caravaggio's Conversion of Matthew, Kandinsky's moves into abstraction before the First World War, Picasso's Guernica, and so on.

Outsider II

The symbolisms of Faith, Food and Sex in art.

The Definition of Terms: an attempt to give viewers a sure grasp of such lubricious and often meaningless portmanteau terms as Baroque and Rococo, Classical, Romanesque and Neo-Classical, and the several Gothics and Renaissances.

To this last Tabitha's specific and only response was a snorted 'and certainly not that', yet of them all it would have been my choice, for it and the influential pictures have the bones of academic severity in them. Aware of the inevitability of travelogue in art programmes I offered three in which travel was integral, but none intrigued her. I can only attribute this to ignorance and incuriosity – the enemies that years before I had encountered from the BBC when Tom Lubbock and I proposed a programme on the eighteenth-century art historian and connoisseur Johann Joachim Winckelmann; not even homosexuality, murder and its ghastly penalty could persuade that commissioning editor that Winckelmann was interesting – 'Never heard of him,' he said, and that was that. The only other recent contact with the panjandrums of television was made by one of them suggesting that I should pair with Noel Fielding, lunatic comedian and cult eccentric, to make programmes on the visual arts. I refused, point blank – that way another murder lay.

The field is thus held by Andrew Graham-Dixon with casual enthusiasm, and by Waldemar Januszczak who has the physical charms of a North Korean despot and a command of French that compels him to pronounce Seurat as Sewer Rat. Eheu, eheu . . .

CHAPTER 15

Loose Ends

Thus quite certainly at the very end of a once promising career, all other avenues closed, there was nothing left to do but reconcile myself to my role as a Cassandra bewailing the end of the ancestral arts that have served mankind so well since his beginning. An old dame dressed as gypsy fortune teller, reading my adolescent palm at a church fête in one of the sunny summers soon after the close of World War II, observed that if I survived the break in my life line at sixty or so, I might live to be a hundred. Was it a coincidence that my first heart attack struck at sixty-four? The life line after its pronounced break is very long and curls almost to the back of my hand before it fades (I note with amusement that the line of Venus cuts very deep and ends abruptly – were the hazards of HIV and AIDS imprinted there?); but do I, at eighty, wish to spend another twenty years crying into the wind unheard, unheard?

When my palm was read my death was to me an impossibility and the disappearance of my future unimaginable – Damien Hirst's *Physical Impossibility of Death in the Mind of Someone Living* is true only of and for the young. After the heart attacks, the surgery, the loss of physical activity, the nauseous slides into unconsciousness with every sudden drop in blood pressure, the idea of death became a preoccupation reinforced by that of Jill in February 1998. Hers was quite unforeseen – five days of mystifying illness and she was gone, and she was the younger of us, if only by nine months; and with her eminence as an expert on Victorian architecture she had made so much more of her life than I of mine. My immediate contemporary at the Courtauld Institute, my near neighbour, my most persistent borrower of books (always returned – a rare thing in borrowers), my companion on three significant journeys and many insignificant, her death was the first to strike home my own fragility. The emotional effects of the death of Elsie Crombie in 1992, as old as my mother and almost as intensely close (and another neighbour), I had managed with some control, but for this there were the practical reasons of so many things to do in seeing to her wishes beyond the business of her will.

She was a passionate espouser of animal causes, a rescuer of dogs, an able pianist, a friend of Brendel, the discreetly rich patroness of young musicians. As the wife of Theodore, gentle, scholarly and respected contributor to *Apollo*, she and he were very much of the Establishment, but with this her outspokenness and eccentricity often did not fit. She loathed smokers and, at great expense, had commissioned a contraption resembling a diver's costume, the helmet an enormous globe of glass equipped with whatever technology was needed to enable her to breathe, hear and be heard; it caused such a stir that she was dropped from almost every guest list, exactly as she wished. In pursuing her war against fur coats she was expelled from Harrods too. There an elegant woman in a fur coat, disturbed by a light touch on hip or thigh, would look down in alarm expecting a pickpocket, only to find frail Elsie in her wheelchair stroking the fur. 'Oh how beautiful it is,' Elsie might murmur, 'how silky. Extraordinary that they can make such reproductions now.' The trap thus set, the woman invariably responded with, 'Reproduction? No, no – of course not. This is real . . . ' At this Elsie withdrew her hand as though from ordure, screamed to all in earshot, 'It's real, her fur coat's real,' and turning directly to the woman wailed, 'How could you? How could you?' ending in a high-pitched caterwaul.

Chaos was the invariable consequence. Fur-coated customers fled, deals were not done, crowds gathered about the mayhem, security men were called and Elsie was expelled – but she had made her point and, holder of an account in the bewildered shop, returned to make it again and again. I once witnessed it and it was wonderful. She left her emeralds to the cause. In her memory, without the wheelchair and the wailing, I sometimes ask of strangers, 'Is that a *real* fur?' Quietly and coldly done, it is marvellously dismaying to the wearer.

Harry Blacker, her near contemporary, was the Ancient Mariner of art exhibitions on the days reserved for critics, for he stoppeth one of three and often more, but though he firmly held one's arm he was never a greybeard loon. I first encountered him at an exhibition in my very early days as *Tatler's* man – he grasped my arm, bent my ear and told me a Yiddish joke, and that was the pattern, armature and flesh of our friendship. He had an instinctive eye for quality in paintings and the courage to say what he thought, which kept him low in the hierarchy of critics – the *North London Advertiser* is no match for the *Sunday Times* in curriculum vitae or obituary. He drew neat little cartoons signed 'Nero' that gently mocked the Jewish society that was so much the staple of his life and delivered little homilies, of which one has governed my reaction to beggars ever since. On Hungerford Bridge after some wretched show at the Hayward Gallery we came upon a young beggar, haggard, ill-kempt, the sockets of his eyes black with fatigue, and I emptied my pockets into his hand; later, when it transpired that the waif was an *Evening Standard* reporter investigating a claim that London beggars are Croesus-rich, Harry consoled me with the tale of a rabbi who, rebuked by one of his flock for giving money to a beggar with 'Don't you know he's a millionaire? replied, 'No, I do not, and if he is, let it be on his conscience, not on mine.'

Harry, born in Whitechapel in 1910, the son of Russian immigrants, with no education after fourteen, was something of a saint, and those of us who did not brush him off grieve less for his death (for that at eighty-nine may have been a mercy), than for ourselves, our loss. I took to missing press views, knowing that he'd not be there – an odd memorial, but my memory is all that I can offer him of immortality.

Preoccupation with one's death has odd little consequences; I bought no new clothes or shoes, convinced that I had no time to wear them out; knowing that I would never play them again I sold my violin and cello, but bought books without a thought of never reading them; I enjoyed a surfeit of opera and thought so much of buying a great car to remind me of the intimacy of machine and man that I had enjoyed when young, that I did not buy one, unable to make the choice; I funded three post-graduates in their pursuit of higher degrees; and four years after the first heart attack, still physically exhausted, I sold the house in which I had lived for thirty years or so. Tall and narrow, the first of a terrace built in 1840, typical of Kensington when it was still a modest urban village, its staircase steep, its condition neglected since modernised in 1929, the roof a constant anxiety, the basement occasionally inclined to flood, it was, my doctor observed, no place for a man with my cardiac condition. 'Find a flat,' he said, 'live on one floor. Make life easy for yourself.' Flats and dogs, however, do not fit well together. 'Get rid of the dogs,' said my doctor, as though they were useless ornaments to my life. A low-built house with a garden seemed to me a more practical solution, but such a house is very rare in Kensington and I was compelled to exchange all the comfortable familiarities of the borough in which I was born and still felt a villager, for the suburban unfamiliarities of Wimbledon, where I feel as much marooned as Robinson Crusoe. It is not that Wimbledon is a foreign country, for as a child it was a place to go on summer impulse on a Green Line bus from Kensington High Street, to lie in the long grass, have tea and return to Kensington as though the afternoon had been spent in *The Wind in the Willows*; and as soon as the war ended and I could have a dog, for the first and all subsequent dogs, seventeen of them, it has represented the wild alternative to Kensington Gardens, the long walk, the swim, the romp in the snow, a place of badgers, rabbits and foxes, herons, swans and wildfowl – but I know now that it is no place for townies.

The move to Wimbledon ended what had been an oddly contented period after the death of my mother. I had been warned not to live alone and young Valerian Freyberg came to keep me company while I searched for alternatives to Eldon Road. He brought me the pleasure of brotherhood – or what I imagined it to be. I lived my life, he lived his as a young political animal in the House of Lords (the amusements of Hansard were delivered every day) and we shared what we could in leisure and domestic matters – I will never forget the particular joy of hearing with him at the Albert Hall the concert performances of Wagner's *Ring* while Covent Garden was closed for refurbishment – for him his first exposure to it, though not to the Hall. He had a friend, the painter Szuszi Roboz, who had a box there, and after producing a portrait of me that disturbingly discerns something of my soul, she took to nourishing my musical life too. To own a box when the Proms are in season must be one of the richest aesthetic pleasures of London life and she, a survivor of years of hiding and deprivation when Admiral Horthy was in command of Hungary and of 1944 when he fell to the Nazis, perhaps found in it some small recompense. As a pupil of Annigoni, she was a survivor in another sense. A year or two ago I refused a concert if so-and-so was to be a fellow-guest. He was. 'Then are you free on such-and-such a date?' she asked without a pause. I was, and accepted her invitation knowing nothing of the programme but expecting it to be an evening of Schubert or Richard Strauss. It was not; it was an exquisite punish-ment knowingly inflicted – entirely of Sondheim unrelieved, I would rather have had a tooth drawn. There can be no more such punishments; for some days in July this year, tiny, delicate, fawn-like, Szuszi lay like a medieval effigy in surrender to the cancer that was draining away her life, and on the month's ninth day she died.

The nation does not know it but Valerian was a significant campaigner for free entry to museums and galleries (as too was I), acting as a conduit of information and asking questions that a member of the House of Lords might ask but a high museum official, prevented by his position as a civil servant of sorts, might not. It was an important campaign that has greatly increased the number of visitors (though not entirely without unforeseen dis-benefits), but in the beginning it was not wholly supported by the then new Labour government – indeed, so much was it doubted by so many Labour men that the cynic in me is amused to see that its vociferous opponents have forgotten their original position and have taken to claiming it as their own achievement, while those who were really working for it, including one particular museum director, have never been acknowledged.

I took Valerian to one of John Vere Brown's birthday parties and halfway there, my feet suddenly cold, I confessed that John, an old and close friend from whom I had no secrets, was not only homosexual but what many might describe as a foul-mouthed old queen – moreover, most of his guests were likely to be so too; but my suggestion that we skip the party and go home, he refused. An hour later I found him in the garden holding court with absolute aplomb as though these were the most natural of circumstances and, thinking of myself at his age (when I would have run a mile from such company), I wondered how it was that one so young had quite such poise. There were tiresome rumours that we were lovers, spread by the high panjandrum of one of the country's great museums disappointed that Valerian had shown no interest in his daughter, his behaviour quite disgraceful but common enough among heterosexuals, so many of whom deem the platonic friend-ship an impossibility for homosexuals. It is not; the friendship of a homosexual for a heterosexual, uncluttered by a hint of sexual interest, can be intense, generous and loyal – and last a lifetime.

There were two John Browns, the painter and the photographer, and bound in one body they destroyed each other; much of his work as a photographer is in the National Portrait Gallery, but his paintings, hundreds of them, are to be found only in the homes of friends. My friendship with him reached back to an encounter in 1959 in the shadow of Delacroix in the Tate Gallery, to Dartmoor a year later among the standing stones of Grey Wethers, bleak against grey skies, and later still to the desolate flat lands of the north

Loose Ends

Kent coast in winter in icy greys and whites. In these and other windswept wastes I learned from him that colour is to be perceived in even the dullest light and that what to a mere townsman's eye must seem barren, cheerless, desolate and cold, can be persuaded by a painter into fields of warm brown and red and orpiment.

Early on a bright Sunday morning in May 2000, the eve of his seventy-fifth birthday, John and I had a merry conversation about this and that, as old friends do, until I cut it short with, 'We must stop gossiping or we shall have nothing to say tomorrow at your party.' The truth was that I wanted to go out with the dogs and get on with the day, and I hoped that impatience had not put an edge into my voice. Back from the Common I found a message that John had in mid word broken off a subsequent conversation, and that alarmed neighbours had found him dead in bed amid the wreckage of his modest breakfast. 'You must write an obituary,' said Max Hastings (John had photographed his mother).

It was then I realised how little I knew of John Vere Brown, JVB to me, Beige to others and John Very Brown to those friends who knew of this error made by some unfortunate girl in Harrods when John had an account there. I knew none of the staples of the conventional obituary, nothing of his father, nothing of school and very little of his life and work as a photographer of portraits and the theatre. I knew only his negligible parallel life as a painter, and his inheritances from his mother – the noble profile of a Roman emperor, the pitch of her voice, her tendency to strangle it with mews and hesitations and blurt startling political incorrectitudes no matter what the time or place or company. Her substantial house near Primrose Hill he sold and, one by one, he bought a dozen others, always losing money when impatiently he left them, for in almost every case his passion for removing walls and ceilings had induced collapse. The last house he owned was a stone barn in Derbyshire in which I, with Alan Bates and his brother, spent days stuffing the gaps between the stones with papier-mâché to keep out the wind; made of newspaper the papier was a perfect match for grey stones, but most of it was promptly eaten by the local mice. John died in poverty. At his funeral Alan Bates read *Lycidas*, Milton's elegy on the death of a friend of great promise.

I owe John other friendships – with Yonty Solomon, a gifted pianist, his near neighbour on Primrose Hill, an intellectual and aesthetic exchange, and a brief sexual fling with Samuel Menashe, the American poet, before his poetry was published by Gollancz. At that stage he wished to be known only by his surname and even his lovers had to address him thus – but like the Nusch of Nusch Éluard (another poet's wife) it was oddly sensual in pillow talk. He wrote a poem for me, impulsively pressing into my hand a lined sheet torn from a notebook as we walked through Cornwall Gardens –

> Running water, shining bright,
> Running water, shining bright

– and took amiss my foolish quip 'Oh Menashe, it is too long,' made before I knew that gnomic brevity was then the hallmark of his work.

John Brown's was not quite the first of the long close friendships that embellished my post-student life; of these the earliest was a John of another colour, John White, a clerk in the offices of Christie's when I joined the firm, eighteen in 1958 and pretty enough to stir the loins of any man with eyes to see, waiting to wed his childhood sweetheart – which he did, the marriage swiftly maturing beyond its once sweet simplicity. In the years between its end and the beginning of another, he lived with me and assorted tempestuous mistresses and we fell into the custom of an occasional oyster feast, reinforced after we had both had heart attacks, by the instruction of my cardiologist – 'If you must eat oysters, be gluttonous: two dozen twice a year will do you no harm, one every day will clog your arteries.' But in 2006 John, by then retired and living in far Herefordshire, began to die of cancer. He spoke cheerfully of coming to London before the end of April, after which, because there is no 'r' in the month, oysters are traditionally forbidden until September – 'Something to look forward to,' he said when April came and went. So too did September. I went with another contemporary from Christie's, Ray Perman, to see him. We took him to dinner in Abergavenny and lunch in Hay-on-Wye, but we had to lift him into the car; there were no oysters, and other food he could only poke and prod. When we left for London I hardly dared hold him in our customary hug, his ribs too apparent to my fingertips. 'I'm still coming,' he said, 'we've got to have those oysters.' Over his shoulder I caught but could not hold the sad eyes of his wife.

For the next six weeks or so we spoke almost every day, but oysters dropped out of our farewells. At our final conversation he seemed rather stronger and more confident; shades of *La Traviata*, I thought, and sure enough, early the following morning his daughter telephoned, and that was that. Had John held on for five more months our friendship would have lasted half a century, yet I, his oldest surviving friend, refused to give the valediction at his funeral – and just as well, for at it I was choked with tears. But I should have had the courage to stand before that congregation and speak of his steadfast friendship, I should have honoured with merry recollection the most honest, loyal and guileless man I ever knew.

What then of oysters? John left me money with which to continue our feasts and Ray Perman seemed the obvious companion. He had joined Christie's at seventeen or so as a 'boy' in the catalogue subscription office. Born in Lambeth in 1942, he has lost neither his south London accent nor his instinctive cheek and, in spite of becoming perhaps the most important business engineer that Christie's ever had, in both London and New York, the most shrewd and effective reformer of its hapless ways, is still, for me, a 'boy' – a boy who as a boy was so knowing that he can never have been innocent. In the fashionable tight trousers and bum-freezer jackets of the early Sixties he knew precisely the effect that he had on men (useful in the art trade), but it was with one Susie in the office, playing whore on a pile of carpets in the basement, that for ten shillings he lost his real virginity. What began for me as a tease in which neither of us was serious, has been a firm friendship for more than fifty years, and only in one small thing, the oyster feast, has Ray failed me – he has an allergy.

The last friendship formed in the late fifties was with Carlos van Hasselt, then an assistant keeper at the Fitzwilliam Museum in charge of drawings and watercolours, whom I met in Paris in 1958 at the Congress of Art Historians. A *bon vivant*, he was already stout, knew everyone who mattered both professionally and socially, and was known by them, and for years I revered him as a young uncle, discovering only very late in our friendship that he was two years my senior and not the two and twenty that I had assumed. In 1961 he was appointed curator-in-chief of the Fondation Custodia, the formidable collection of Dutch paintings, drawings and archival material formed by Frits Lugt, prodigious scholar and connoisseur (then in his late Seventies), housed in the Palais Turgot in Paris, which, combined with the Institut Néerlandais, was to be a major outstation of Dutch culture.* His apartment there became a home from home for many young men employed by Christie's and Sotheby's, as well as young curators from all over Europe and America.

Most of my memories of Carlos, apart from those of his generosity, are associated with his scholarship, his eye and his fund of gossip, but an exception is the sudden ability of this portly man to run, this man who would always take a taxi to travel half a mile. It was in May 1968. The perfect example of a man in a mid-life crisis and sick of working in the art market, I was in Paris idly renewing work on Rubens for the doctoral thesis that I still half hoped might get me into academe. It was a fine Saturday after-noon and in a restaurant on the Boulevard Saint Michel I had just

---

* For both Lugt and Carlos see J. F. Heijbroek, *Frits Lugt, Living for Art*, Fondation Custodia 2012.

had lunch with Carlos who was, for the moment, my mentor in all things to do with Rubens. Idling over coffee we became aware of something that disturbed our ease – a murmur from the street, no more. We should have stayed where we were but curiosity drew us out into a gathering turmoil – and then we heard the sirens, so loud that they must have been switched on by the police to announce their presence rather than their coming; then we found all side streets obstructed by their vans and we and a thousand others were trapped in the Boulevard.

With truncheons raised for the immediate blow, armed policemen launched themselves into the crowd. Incredulous, I stood my ground – this was Paris and de Gaulle, not some corrupt tribal tyrant, was on the throne. Carlos, however, seeing cracked heads, blood streaming and fallen bodies trampled, shouted 'Run' and grabbed my arm. Even at such a time it is astonishing to see a man who has acquired such dignity of position and the portliness of middle age, suddenly break into a sprint, but sprint he did, this way and that, with me in tow. At one point we were pursued, but Carlos knew where he was going and the *flics* did not – even so, not until we'd crossed the Quai des Augustins and ducked down to the footpath by the Seine, did he slacken.

Later I knew that I had witnessed one of the notorious student riots for which 1968 is most remembered. Alone, I saw the beginnings of another in the Place de la Concorde, and again I ran, for in the face of such blind brutality obviously enjoyed by those inflicting it, the sane man can do nothing and should fade away. Reports of these *événements* echoed round the world, not least in Britain where, within a month, students in a dozen universities, in colleges and even art schools, had confronted their authorities with sit-ins and demonstrations, but with far less intellectual authority for what they did.

By chance Kenneth Clark, Lord of *Civilisation*, was in Paris too in May 1968, towards the end of filming material for that celebrated television series, and it may be that the student riots there influenced his pessimistic conclusions, not only about the hopelessly damaging fragmentation of art, but of society through the demanded abolition of its institutions. He was right to compose a valedictory elegy for the vanishing past of the fine arts, but where society is concerned, it is not unreasonable to come to a contrary view and argue that when French students lent their intellectual weight to the inarticulate protests of the proletariat, they achieved what could have been, but for the police, a wholly bloodless revolution; the most sustained strike in French history gave both students and workers what they wanted, and sent de Gaulle to cultivate his garden.

Carlos retired in 1994; at sixty-five, though troubled by a worsening cardiac condition and the sort of weight that is so firm to the touch that one knows it will never diminish, he was not ready for retirement and, continuing as habit the duties of the past three decades, he travelled all Europe to see exhibitions of which he sent me criticisms on postcards in his small neat hand. Increasingly he felt, as I do, forgotten and ignored by curators much younger and less experienced than himself, and the changes that they wrought in their museums and galleries made them unfamiliar and unfriendly – one of the cruel truths of his profession is that once a curator has retired from his post, the successor generation brushes him aside, the accumulated wisdom born of long experience of no interest to the young. After six years of this disenchantment he suffered a paralysing stroke; the further five years vouchsafed him, speechless and incapable of responding to the gossip that had always been his only frivolous relief, were a terrible torment for so generously gregarious a man.

Of such ancient platonic relationships there is only one more of which I must write – it is with Rüdiger Joppien. In the autumn of 1968 we were both researching in the English rooms of the Witt Library of the Courtauld Institute in its original premises in Portman Square – not a library but a collection of photographs; we worked on opposite sides of the vast common table, he in absolute concentration, his face half concealed by the fall of his hair, and the hair the rare dark auburn that the English of my mother's generation always described as Titian red, though it was never to be found in the tresses of any Venetian Venus – indeed only in the sacks of henna sold in the souks of the East does this rich and wonderful colour exist. For several days we worked without so much as a friendly nod or the beginning of a smile, and not once did he look up until, at last, puzzled that I could get from him not the slightest form of acknowledgement, I willed him to look at me and when, suddenly, he did, it was to reveal a face that I felt I had seen a thousand times idealised by Pre-Raphaelites and Nazarenes.

What then? My diary is uninformative, but we became friends over Philippe James de Loutherbourg, the subject of his doctoral thesis and of an exhibition that he was to mount in Kenwood House in 1973.

I wove him into my professional friendships, particularly with Gert Schiff, the great authority on Fuseli, but ours was always to be a friendship constructed and maintained on the warp and weft of journeys, presences, absences, telephone calls and letters. I was often in Germany in its early days and when I could I stayed with Rüdiger in Cologne, where he changed addresses with astonishing frequency – one attic is for its freezing chill seared into my memory; later, after his marriage, in the apartment where he and Kathrin were joined by Charlotte, Johanna and a suicidal rabbit, conditions grew steadily more comfortable.

With Rüdiger it seems that no subject is excluded from his interest, ranging from the Panoramas popular in England in the eighteenth century to the voyages of Captain Cook and Joseph Banks and the artists who travelled with them, from the metalwork of Christopher Dresser to the glass of Dale Chihuly, from the doubtful authenticity of the latest Raphael at the National Gallery to the confusion of drawings by Franz and Ferdinand Kobell. This has meant, of course, that Rüdiger is not where he should be – that is in the first rank of historians of English art in the age of the Enlightenment and imperial expansion. For me this is a matter of great sadness, but not surprise, for in English art scholarship we have no place for the universal man; we must specialise; we must know a very small subject in very great depth, constantly publish trivial findings, and in this one field be considered expert. Rüdiger is too universal.

*   *   *

As an old man must, for in such memories he offers an oblique view of himself, I have written of a few old friends; there is a handful more – Baby Helen, a significant player in the first half of my life who, as hapless onlooker from the shores of Massachusetts, has devotedly and perhaps despairingly (so many have been my follies) watched its second, and Wendy Baron, the most important of all Sickert's women,* has been a constant since our student days – but most friends have come and gone, the friendships exhausted when too often we had nothing left to say other than 'Do you remember . . . ?' and stirring dead embers was how we spent our evenings.

I should, perhaps, have written of the few artists I have en-countered, as any mercenary critic might – Sewell on Bacon, Freud, Hockney or any other notable I could persuade to paint my portrait or engage in conversation – but I have kept my distance and my freedom as a critic. These three I knew in varying degrees long before I took to criticism and it never occurred to me that every word they uttered should be preserved by some devoted amanuensis. Hockney was first of this triumvirate and I was wise enough to buy one of his drab early townscapes and fool enough to refuse a more recognisable daub, *Help*, of 1962, when it was still wet, for £200 (probably now worth as much as my house). It is of

---

* See Wendy Baron, *Sickert Paintings and Drawings*, Yale 2006, the most towering of her many monuments to the old boy.

no significance that I did not much care for Lucian Freud and thought him cold and calculating, though I may know a little more than most of his dispute with Anthony d'Offay. That Francis Bacon, nearish neighbour, occasionally enlisted me as errand boy, woke me at dawn to play chauffeur to his still somnolent drunken lover, John Edwards, and ferry him to Long Melford for breakfast with his family, is hardly a contribution to the history of art, though that Francis deliberately cultivated the fart by drinking foul vegetable juices every morning, usually in Harrods' juice bar, possibly is. Should I dramatise my slightly frenzied acquaintance with Ruskin Spear in his later years into a claim that it was he who, overlapping with Francis Bacon at the Royal College, taught him how to paint? – the claim was certainly made. From an afternoon alone with Henry Moore at Perry Green, had it happened in my days as a critic rather than in 1978, before that transformation, a book could easily have been born, for in 1992, after a gap of fourteen years, I offered the Planning Inspectorate of the day a defence of Hoglands as he left it at his death in 1986, against its revision and development by the Henry Moore Foundation, as passionate as though I had eaten the great man's biscuits only the day before. The tale of my late friendship with Derek Hill, though I had known him since the early Sixties, I told in a foreword to Bruce Arnold's biography,* a formal note of affection and respect from which I felt compelled to exclude his obsessive, giggling and not particularly enlightening reminiscences of mutual masturbation when a boy.

When Michael Reynolds, founder of the annual Discerning Eye exhibitions, died in 2008, his deathbed admonition to a mutual friend was 'Tell Brian to protect my reputation' – a heavy burden for a man who knew how fragile that reputation was and had nothing to support it other than his recollection of sitting, or rather sagging, for his portrait a month after his quadruple bypass, a portrait for which we both ran out of time and energy, a failure.

* Bruce Arnold, *Derek Hill*, Quartet, 2010.

We were both outsiders and, a painter to his bones, his fiery contempt for the fashionable nostrums of contemporary art was expressed in foulest language – he is remembered more for his rancour and vituperation than any trenchant canvas that he painted.

Should I gossip about Patrick Procktor, distantly adorable, whose powerful early promise evaporated in frivolity, was fogged by drugs and drowned in alcohol? I was once asked to write a book on him, but I refused – too close, I thought, after a boozy lunch at Odin's and clambering over the railings at the back of his house (a short cut) to smoke a joint, I cannot hurt this man, I cannot tell the necessary truth.

What have I to add to the mythology of Derek Jarman, a scatterbrain, his creative instinct powerful but utterly undisciplined, flamboyantly queer? I knew him a little in his early days, for we had friends and acquaintances in common – Keith Milow, with whom he was in love (insofar as his short-lived fancies merit that description), John Vere Brown, Nikos Stangos, Heathcote Williams, Patrick Procktor, Mario Dubsky, Peter Langan and Joe McCrindle, whom I had persuaded to buy a taut small landscape. I thought Derek intriguing as a painter, technically more than competent, but quite unformed by the Slade School at which he had been a student between 1963 and 1967 and of which he left a disturbing account in his memoir *Dancing Ledge** – ' . . . the Renaissance had at last succumbed to the air-conditioned nightmare of Pop.' I am inclined to argue that this is one of the most revealing records of art and life in England at the end of the twentieth century. There was a long hiatus in our friendship; Derek had drifted from painting into cinema, theatre and high camp, but when, in the late Eighties, he settled in Prospect Cottage, Dungeness, more than a little mad, he was sometimes welcoming, at others anxious to preserve his deliberate loneliness. Of the old band only Joe McCrindle and John Vere Brown

---

* Derek Jarman, *Dancing Ledge*, Quartet, 1984.

survived, the others utterly forgotten. Joe and I trudged the shingle beach with him, hunching into the wind – there is nothing else to do at Dungeness; John took stark and subtle photographs of the cottage, the beginnings of its arid garden, its interior, the *objets trouvés* and of Derek himself, the very first to draw attention to the place that was, as an installation, his last mature work of art. He died in February 1994.

Tess Jaray, for whose paintings and pavements I twice expressed admiration long ago in the Eighties, wrote me a wry note in 2010 when I reviewed, with almost as much respect as I have for Anita Brookner's observations on art, her exquisite slim volume of essays on painting.* She thanked me for the phrase 'with much I disagree . . . ' for in this I had, it seems, ensured that she would not lose quite *all* her friends. I was reminded of the letter sent to the *Evening Standard* in 1994 by the 'art world', demanding my dismissal, for Tess, though not a signatory (she is incapable of any such spite), was closely associated with many of that self-appointed clique and its continued esteem is necessary to her professional wellbeing. I could see her point: my condemnation of a con-temporary artist approved by the art world can easily be dismissed with 'Well, he would say that, wouldn't he?' but my praise causes a flutter of misgiving in the dovecot and might well prove toxic. I almost believe that in the present climate of Jesuitical orthodoxy my esteem is a thousand times more menacing than my obloquy, and am tempted to sing subversive praise of Chris Ofili and Anish Kapoor in hope of ridiculous reputations withered.

This absurd art world is oblivious of Michael Leonard, almost popular for his portrait of the Queen with a corgi. This most scrupulous observer of the nude, academic in the best ancestral sense of form in light and shadow, painted slowly and accurately, is perhaps the last surviving figurative painter whose imagery is not shallow and whose handling of paint is not slick – Freud came

* Tess Jaray, *Painting: Mysteries and Confessions*, Lenz, 2010.

nowhere near in such judgement. His painted athletes have a meditative air as though, in their activity, they are heirs to the Greek and Roman past of our cultural beginnings and perform a rite that reaches back millennia to athletic feats in old Aegean cities. Michael conjures the ghosts of Alexander, Hector and Achilles, not with Olympic triumphalism, but with the drudgery of the discipline that comes before and after it. His portrait drawings are elegant conceits mischievously removing his sitters to the historic period of which they remind him and then drawn as though by Van Dyck, or Rembrandt or Bronzino or whoever is most fitting; that done, he adds a further layer of meaning with the convincing illusion of broken glass, paper torn or crumpled, and the ingrained dust of ages; with these he implies that both image and sitter have been discarded, as though forlorn, forgotten and worthless – wealthy sitters perhaps do not see the point. Me he drew as a genial contemporary of Robespierre after a good day with the guillotine. All the disdain of an art world irremediably dedicated to the Serota tendency cannot diminish such an accomplished artist.

I have said much less of the friendship of my dogs than they deserve, and almost nothing of my cars. Both are a mystery to me. My intense need for the companionship of dogs, and particularly of bitches, I may perhaps attribute to some profound primeval dependence, but for cars, however, there is no such explanation. My interest was first stirred by the sight of a bare Rolls-Royce chassis being driven to a coachbuilder by a goggled driver muffled against the wind and rain, sans screen, sans roof, sans doors. This oddly heroic image of courage in adversity was the sort of thing that Biggles might have done, Biggles the literary model of derring-do for most boys of my generation.

Cars disappeared from the streets throughout World War II, but within months of its end in 1945 they emerged from their garages and the streets of Kensington became an exhibition site of wonders from the Twenties and Thirties, not only of the familiar grandees, Rolls-Royce, Bentley and Lagonda, but of such now long forgotten marques as Autovias and Packards, Salmsons, Railtons and Broughs, Hudsons, Cords and Auburns. I fell into the traps of longing, lust and love, drew them, redesigned them and, at sixteen, invented the hatchback. I still look at cars, but now that art has deserted them and surrendered their design to the computer, they are of little interest. Show me a Thirties Rover, however, and its absurd attempt at streamlining, and I will coo over it as over a friendly mongrel pup; show me a Lagonda V-12 of the Thirties and I will stand in awe as though of a Saluki of long pedigree.

I have had two whippets and an Alsatian of proper pedigree, mongrels and crossbreeds aplenty, dogs found and dogs from rescue homes. I have an affinity with dogs; I so easily attract the interest of other people's dogs that I could play Pied Piper and be off with them; and I know that, were I to up sticks and go to live in Spain, or Greece or Turkey, I would be overwhelmed by them and rendered penniless. Since the day on which World War II in Europe was declared to be at an end, I have had dogs; their companionship has kept me sane, their care has lent me daily discipline, and I cannot imagine my life stripped of their constant and unquestioning affection. That their lives are too short is my only complaint of them, and that their going is not made easier by its frequency. As I write, I know that my old Alsatian is dying and will soon be gone, but I am content to tolerate the consequence of her relaxing sphincters, to wake and put her to the garden in the middle of the night, to sponge the thick fur of her hind legs when the urine dribbles, for there is still light in her eyes and joy in her tail, still an appetite for food, and only when these things fade shall I see to it that what must be done, is done. There is, in the garden, a stone sarcophagus, made by Nicholas Moreton, a sculptor better known for variations on the human figure; it is engraved with one word - DOMINICANES - a monkish pun of which the meaning in this case is The Dogs of God, for if I do not believe in God for myself, I half believe in Him for them.

CHAPTER 16

Death

The old should cultivate the friendship of the young, if for no other reason than that the immortality of ordinary mortals – those for whom there can be no obituaries in national newspapers – lasts no longer than the lives of friends. As a child whose mother seemed only to have older friends, I am the bearer of received memories that reach far back, well into the nineteenth century; she took me to Paderewski's last London recital when I was perhaps eight, he nearing eighty and very very slow, but as a young man in 1890 he had sat to Burne-Jones, and Burne-Jones was born in 1833. My life has been much enriched by many such reaches and inherited awarenesses, but for most of my generation there will be, in the memories of our successors, no recollections of the who and what and how we were; thus, if we are old when we die and our friends are of our age and few, grief and mourning are bound to be short-lived before we and they are all swept away by the waters of oblivion.

The young, however, are carelessly unthinking and unkind. With age no part of their experience they know little of the wisdom of the old and nothing of their inevitable miseries, deprivations and frustrations, nothing of the lust and longing that lurk beneath the wrinkles, sagging skin and thinning hair. Were they to know of it, surely they could only be repelled by the old man of whom, despite the trips and stumbles, despite his uncertainties on stairs (he breathes as breathlessly in their descent as in their climbing), there is, in his mind if not in his mirror, enough of what years ago he was to make him think that he is still a sexually driven animal – a thought mightily provoked by a young man's languor, or his strut, by hair peeping from his chest, or the smooth lack of it, by the way in the underground he lounges in the fuck-me pose of the Barberini Faun, or reaches for support as though he were the Apollo Belvedere. But what is the point of such a thought? What would happen were an old man to let his fingers reach? Humiliation.

In recent years I have had such a young friend. With the visual arts a common interest we were brought together by his importuning – he grasped my forearm in Piccadilly, outside the Royal Academy. I was first taken by his boldness, then by his charm, and then by his imagined resemblance to Salai, the boy through whose curly hair Leonardo da Vinci used to run his fingers, a pickpocket, a thief, a street-boy prostitute. He wished to broaden his experience, expand his knowledge, sit at my feet; he wished to write, to be another pseudo-philosopher of art as unintelligible as the French Foucault, Lyotard and Derrida; and only I could help. I fell into the role of Higgins in *Pygmalion*, a man of Shavian discipline, and at first thought not at all of sexual possibilities, but then the recollection of kisses, licks and bites when I was his age became insidious and increasingly I realised how much I wanted him, wanted what Chesterfield called the ridiculous position, wanted his arse and the reciprocal clinging of the young.

One evening, after I had introduced him to Charles Saatchi, he plonked a kiss upon my mouth, but by then I knew him to be thoroughly heterosexual and deemed the kissing treacherous. Never once had I touched him or reached toward the fine brown skin so often glimpsed between his skimpy top and trousers, but he knew well enough what I felt. I felt as Zeus felt for young Ganymede, but in looks I knew I was Methuselah. 'Pay for my drugs,' he said, 'and you can watch me fuck my girl.' I toyed with the idea, but remembered my stepfather's old friend, Sir Ian Horobin, jailed for watching big boys buggering smaller while he masturbated, and considered the indignity of the spectator not worth the candle. He tried a better offer. 'Pay for my drugs and you can fuck me while I fuck her.' This mercenary response destroyed the very nature of our friendship.

As Methuselah I inhabit an increasingly discomforting world of irrecoverable words, names forgotten, faces unrecognised in the blur of prosopagnosia, and the unconscious confusion of banana for umbrella and night storage heater for the microwave. My spine crumbles, my hips creak, and like most men of my age I have had the dreaded slippery finger of the urologist probing my prostate gland, with the accompanying threats of impotence and incontinence, the twin calamities that most men fear more than any other – though the onset of dementia terrifies me more. I have lost count of my days in hospital in recent years dealing with ischaemic heart disease, vasovagal syncope, uncontrollable drops in blood pressure already very low, the insertion of stents and pace-makers, the surgery of two mastectomies and efforts to remedy a corkscrewing spine, my trunk an old bag of scars and stitches, yet not one of these and their consequences, not even the possibility of sudden death, has seemed as wretched a malfunction as a leaking bladder and the abrupt reduction of one's penis to, as Eric Gill put it, a mere 'organ of drainage'. Drugs keep both in abeyance.

Who, young, girl or boy, would willingly conjugate with so patched and tattered an old man? Yet old men lust after the young, not once a week or once a day or hourly, but in response, if one is out and about, to almost constant stimulus. It is the young skin that does it; the conventions of beauty are a bonus, and all the old triggers of hair and eyes and lips are there, but when the skin of the young is flawless, it is what most makes the fingers reach, as though aching to caress. All the cosmetics of Paris and New York, all the nips and tucks, seams and gussets of plastic surgery, all the perfumes of the Arabian civet cat, all these together are no match for a skin poised in late adolescence or early adulthood. Inside his own skin, rough and wrinkled, pallid with approaching death, the old man feels the same sensual sensations as the young, but he may not touch. It is a terrible predicament. We laugh with sympathy at an old dog's sudden jauntiness when he sniffs a bitch in heat, but old men we mock, and despise as trull or catamite any submissive object of desire.

Death

And that is age, old age – an age of indecision, confusion and increasing disability, an age of shrunken shanks and shuffling pace, of grasp too feeble on the lid of marmalade, of eyes that sooner or later will not see and ears that will not hear, of padded underpants (not yet) and of a heart that from time to time palpitates like the single-cylinder diesel engine of a Turkish fishing boat. I embraced a girl the other day and quite without thought allowed my hand to stray a little lower than it should – 'He put his hand on my bum,' she cried, and shied away, not putting hers on mine. Our friends laughed. I blushed – the one thing that without hesitation I can still do as well as a teenage boy. Old men *are* sexual animals, but we make fools of ourselves when we lose our sense of the ridiculous. And in a sexual sense that is precisely what we are – ridiculous.

*   *   *

An eerie business, writing a will, dispassionate and coldly rational. It takes a man outside himself, detaches him from his possessions and makes him judge and jury of his friends, reward and revenge standing at his elbow ready to nudge his pen. It makes him make a judgement on himself, his life, his work, his character, not unlike writing an autobiography.

To make a proper will a man must think of himself as dead and gone, his house occupied by other men, his garden the demesne of developers who do not care for trees and ponds, his books as the stock of second-hand shops whose owners neither know nor care how thoughtfully he formed his library, his pictures as the possessions of the blind. Who of his friends will take his loving dogs? Who of his friends will see to his physical departure?

I have made several wills, the first as a young soldier, all of them the precautionary wills of those who do not think of death as immediately relevant. Even on the night before my ribcage was sawn open and my heart re-plumbed I was prepared to make a joke and bequeathed my eyes to Sarah Kent, the gushing art critic of *Time Out*, who is not blind but cannot see. Now, years later and of an age when almost every obituary page tells me of the deaths of old acquaintances, I no longer joke. Miss Kent is out of my will and my eyes and any other bits and pieces that could be useful are bequeathed to total strangers.

If no one wants them, then my cadaver is willed to any teaching hospital that has a use for bodies as material for aspiring anatomists. I quite like the idea of such absolute surrender to tactile intimacy, the hands that once played the violin reduced to bones and tendons, the brain that for so long thrilled in wonder at masterpieces of art and architecture, poked, prodded and perhaps preserved, like some old sheep or shark, in a jar of clear formaldehyde. As for the irreverent things that medical students are reputed to do with penises – so what? I too had my moments of adolescent ribaldry in the communal baths after playing rugger in my youth. And when the anatomists have done with me what George Stubbs and Leonardo did with the horse and criminal, what then? Ideally, what is left of me should be buried in the garden with the bones of the dozen dogs already there, nourishing the roots of yet another tree.

As for dying, I do not for one moment believe that death is 'the most beautiful adventure' or 'an awfully big adventure', or, indeed, an adventure of any kind; nor can I see it as an art. These are the romantic sentiments of poets and the brave. Death, in my experience, is a girl of twelve or so in the back of a crashed Peugeot 404, her skull cracked open like a box with a hinged lid. Death is the old man who had a heart attack in Kensington High Street a few months ago. Death is Lilian, an old friend, a sometime ballet dancer fallen on hard times, in a geriatric ward, her ascetic beauty hung about with tubes and drips, her spare body, even in its frailty, resisting the inevitable end; trained to endure, it instinctively resisted her intellectual command to let her go. Death is my mother, once of a beauty that stopped men in their stride, thirteen years a-dying, outliving all her friends, so that any who knew her at her death knew nothing of the former body and the former wit, but could recall only her senility; after those dreadful thirteen years even I struggle to leap the boundaries of memory to recover what I know to be another and a better truth.

'Men must endure their going hence,' said mad Lear in a sane moment. Endure; what a terrible prospect. Endure the crumbling memory. Endure the trembling hand of the octogenarian unsteady with the fork, unsteadier still with the lavatory paper. Endure the rheumy eyes that see hues differently, endure the creeping deafness that first denies conversation and then the music that might have made the loss of conversation tolerable. Endure the slackening sphincters and the stinks. What torment for the fastidious, lasting for years perhaps before the brain is addled and one is numbed to it. Imagine the slow erosion of pleasures, not of the flesh, though deprivation there induces madness in some men, but of the mind – no opera, no Schubert songs, no violin concertos, no theatre, no galleries, no books. Imagine not managing an oyster, the salt sea of it dripping from one's chin, the exquisite flesh of it running down one's shirt.

'A merciful release,' we say of death, and so it is when dying takes so long. Can we separate death from dying? The one is the inevitable consequence of the other but they seem two very different things, the dying often merciless, a prolonged torment as ingenious, excruciating and pitilessly cruel as any devised by Torquemada in the service of religion, death a sudden relaxation not only of the body, but the will. What virtue is there in such suffering? What virtue is there in the accompanying squalor? 'Who sweeps a room as for thy laws makes that and the action fine,' was all very well for George Herbert comfortably putting the seventeenth-century servant in her place, but does it really apply to bedpans and pisspots in modern hospitals where nurses vent their impatience on miserable males until they are gibbering with anguish and embarrassment? Death is not the great leveller – dying is. Dying reduces a man to leaking, dribbling and snivelling, to the helplessness of a baby, to impotent distress, to the long slow misery of being alive when he would rather be dead. That is levelling indeed.

I ask who of my friends will see to my physical departure? I think I know what natural death is like, having crept back from it; it too is a creeping thing, a slipping in and out of consciousness, the senses dwindling, waning, flagging and the will to resist falling away – and that is how I want to go, but swiftly. And if I cannot, if my body refuses when my brain commands, then I want some help. 'Do not go gentle into that good night . . . rage, rage against the dying of the light,' advised Dylan Thomas at thirty-eight, and at that age I too would probably have advocated rage, but most of us on reaching our allotted span would rather go gently, quietly, swiftly, cleanly, and some of us may need a push. I can think of no more loving act of friendship than that push. To me it seems a very cruel society that insists on my not determining the day and the manner of my going if death eludes me when I long for it.

Index

Index

Index

Index